68-   26769   (1/15/09)

DAILY LIFE IN EARLY CANADA

RAYMOND DOUVILLE
AND JACQUES CASANOVA

DAILY LIFE
IN EARLY CANADA

Translated by Carola Congreve

THE MACMILLAN COMPANY
New York

Library of Congress Catalog Card Number: 68-26169

FIRST AMERICAN EDITION 1968
Translated from the French *La Vie Quotidienne en Nouvelle France,*
© Hachette, Paris, 1964

INTRODUCTION

Until 1760 France reigned over nearly the whole of North America. This supremacy had begun when François I had protested strongly against the decision of the Borgia Pope Alexander VI to divide the world between Spain and Portugal: 'I should very much like to know,' remarked the King of France, 'what clause in the will of Adam excludes me from my share in the world.' On his behalf Verrazzano had already twice explored the coast of North America and had outlined the map of Gallia Nova, New France. François I arranged another expedition in 1533. It was a propitious moment, for he had lately signed the Peace of Cambrai with Charles V.

The navigator Jacques Cartier, who came from St Malo, offered his services and was accepted. He put to sea under orders 'to make his way to certain islands and countries where, it is said, a great deal of gold is to be found'.

After a crossing of less than a month he reached Newfoundland and its fishing-grounds, already regularly frequented by European fishermen. Cartier sailed bravely into the immense Gulf of the St Lawrence, where he was struck by the beauty of its wooded shores, and from whence he penetrated to the heart of the New World by the most accessible route. Some of his seamen navigated with an assured hand, since they had already made the crossing.

Cartier did not discover the 'proper' Canada. But during his second voyage in 1535, he penetrated far into the country. François I had given him orders to take possession of it in the Royal name, and to raise there crosses carrying the emblem with the lilies of France.

The crosses at Gaspé, Quebec and Three Rivers, from Mont-Royal to Montreal (Hochelaga as it was then) were the official landmarks of French discovery, and symbols of the foundation of New France. They manifested the Royal wish to possess that portion of the new continent.

But, alas, Jacques Cartier came face to face with a hostile force. Not of native inhabitants, for these were more or less friendly in their welcome, nor did he have to contend with a lack of natural

5

resources in the country, but the terrible Canadian winter. Long, hard, bitter, and most of all endless, it imprisoned the ships in the river ice, and reduced the men's food to salt tack. The party was struck down with scurvy and its numbers seriously diminished. Cartier wished to return to France in the spring—the rigours of winter had taken toll of his enthusiasm.

This seaman from St Malo undertook his second voyage to look for precious metals. He felt as he dug in the sand on the beach that he had found gold and diamonds. This new wealth would give Canada the kind of attraction which Mexico already possessed, and François I would be as powerful as Charles V. Cartier, full of enthusiasm, speedily returned to France. The royal alchemists banished his illusions, the diamonds were only pyrite, the gold mere mica. The disappointment was too bitter. Disillusioned, the navigator returned to his property at St Malo.

Cartier's retreat was the signal for the neglect of New France by those in authority. For sixty years only the fishermen who continued to fish its cod banks ever spoke of it. And then the explorer Samuel de Champlain arrived on the scene, and at the beginning of the seventeenth century laid the foundation for the French colonization of America.

CONTENTS

ILLUSTRATIONS

CHAPTER ONE

CHAMPLAIN DREAMS OF AMERICA BECOMING FRENCH

When Champlain set out on his first voyage to the West in April, 1603, he knew little of the land towards which he sailed. Burning with the desire—the obsession of the age—to find a route to the Indies shorter than the way through the Magellan Straits, he came upon the post of Tadoussac, at the confluence of the St Lawrence and Saguenay rivers. Tadoussac was a meeting-place for trappers. Indian tribes of the Algonquin race rested there during the summer months. Champlain, however, was more interested in exploring the new country than he was in the fur trade, and sought to establish friendly relations with the natives he encountered on his way up the St Lawrence.

These natives, known as 'Indians' ever since Columbus, who had thought when he saw them that he had reached the Indies, formed two separate groups: Algonquins and Iroquois. The latter were less numerous, but the more intelligent and energetic; they swore everlasting hatred of the Frenchman, vowing to destroy him, thus ranging themselves along with the English and Dutch communities in New England.

On his third voyage in 1608, Champlain once again ascended the Saguenay, exploring the banks of the St Lawrence as far as the Island of Orleans and the St Charles river. He was fascinated by the place and decided to found the first permanent post: Quebec.

Now the French were on the great trade route which was to determine the country's development. Soon 'l'Abitation'[1] went up comprising food shops, a magazine and dwellings. It rose up like a little fort, defended moreover by three cannon.

Like Cartier, Champlain suffered from the winter. Scurvy, the relentless scourge, took away sixteen of his companions. Spring came and with it renewed confidence, and with Algonquin Indians

1 Champlain's own spelling.

as guides he made his way past Lake St Pierre, which lies alongside Lake Richelieu, and on to discover yet another wonderful lake of great length which is called after him. The Algonquins who led him to it were themselves particularly interested in seeking out a meeting with their hereditary enemy the Iroquois.

In 1609 Champlain returned home once more to France in order to convince Sully and Henry IV, the French King, of the importance of Canada. The King consented to make him Governor of the new colony. One doubt troubled the explorer. He had been astonished by the cruelty of his allies during their engagements with the Iroquois. Clearly these tribes must be civilized. Only by their conversion to Christianity through the Church, could this be achieved.

During his stay in Canada, which was interrupted by many journeys to France, Champlain applied himself on three fronts: colonization, exploration and evangelization. The first from the outset was very much circumscribed, since only Louis Hébert, and later his son-in-law Gouillard, were to reclaim and cultivate the land. Exploration brought Champlain to Hochelaga (Montreal) 'where grasslands abound, there is no shortage of fish and there are any amount of animals to serve as game'. Here he built a small fort which he called 'Place Royale'. Lastly, when he was in Paris in 1612, Champlain recruited four Recollect Fathers who were put in charge of the work of conversion to Christianity.

From 1613 to 1616, Port Royal in Acadia was devastated by pirates from Virginia, and when his own expedition against the Iroquois, backed by strong Tsonnontouan tribes, failed, Champlain realized that it was time to stop looking for the uncertain road to the West and establish himself firmly and finally from Acadia to Ontario.

What was the point in pursuing a chimera when the wealth of Canada lay in her soil, her forests and her lakes? The labour of establishing New France was to be long and wearing. Champlain at last, after superhuman endeavour which brought him to a premature grave, managed to make his view convincing.

His unflinching devotion, at a time when misery and famine were rife in most parts of France, should from the first have caused a significant emigration. But, apart from the French people's stay-at-home reputation, powerful companies who possessed a monopoly of business in this far-off country set out to stifle as far as possible any movement in such a direction. The Company of Merchants, although Champlain himself had interests in it, turned a deaf ear to entreaties. It wanted 'neither to populate the country nor turn savages into clerks, nor yet to allow business to be transacted with settlers at the post'. It sought in every way to obstruct the attempts of the first colonist, Louis Hébert.

Confronted with this sort of avarice Champlain disassociated himself from the group and turned to the Chamber of Commerce in Paris, to whom he addressed a concise and truthful account of the situation which compelled attention. New France would yield up her unlimited riches if only the resources she had to offer could be co-ordinated efficiently: furs, fisheries, crops, stock-rearing and timber from her forests. In order to bring this about, it would be enough to send a few families every year (many of whom, he thought, would be ready enough to emigrate), a small military force and some missionaries.

This was a judicious programme from every view, and one which the Commissioner Talon and Pierre Boucher in their turn were to try to impose. The Chamber of Commerce accepted it in every line. It informed the Company of Merchants that it should help to send out at least ten families a year in return for its privileges. The Society pretended to agree. But in fact not a single colonist was to cross the Atlantic. The ships left empty and returned laden with furs. The merchants persisted in their determination to carry on their extremely profitable trade unaided. They did not want witnesses to their transactions with the Indians. When in 1627 the Company of the One Hundred Associates was formed, it elected to admit within fifteen years at least 4,000 colonists to be chosen by the authorities. But twenty years later the population stood at barely 500 and this included missionaries, members of religious orders, administrative officials and soldiery. A census ordered by Talon the Intendant in 1666 enumerated only 528 families with a total of 3,215 whites: 2,034 males and 1,181 females, the great majority born in the country, namely in the only three places inhabited at this time: Quebec and its immediate surroundings, the village of Three Rivers and the fort of Ville-Marie. From 1666 to 1700 the population increased a little more rapidly, rising from 3,200 to nearly 10,000, but here again statistics showed that the great part of the population was indigenous. Because of the

13

exceptional fertility of the women, the colony developed in this way more or less in isolation until the cession of Canada to England in 1760. At this time the population was estimated at 60,000 settlers, excluding troops. Within this same period the immense emigration from England to her colony of New England reached 1,000,000.

The first stages of settlement were accomplished in two very different ways although an identical result was achieved; emigration by whole families and marriages of immigrants and soldiers with the 'King's Daughters'.

Because of the prestige with which Champlain had endowed the country, during the first years whole families, carried along by a few adventurous and realistic leaders, made up their minds to emigrate. They set forth, sometimes singly, sometimes in groups of relatives or in groups belonging to the same village. They nearly always established themselves in the same neighbourhood, put down roots there, then launched out one after another as colonization proceeded. The unhoped-for success of this halting attempt throws up into ever-increasing contrast the lamentable apathy of the authorities at a time when, with the excuse of not wishing to depopulate France, they turned deaf ears to the urgent appeal of various governors, far-sighted Intendants, and missionaries. These singular families, by their courage and tenacity, not only succeeded in maintaining the prestige of France in the colony through unhappy and desperate years, but they also formed, thanks to their remarkable sense of kinship, the grass roots of the Canadian French-speaking nation which exists today.

CHAPTER TWO

THE FRENCH POPULATION ESTABLISHES ITSELF

THE FOUNDER-FAMILIES

Louis Hébert was the first man to try to think in terms of settling whole families. His success in this field was very limited but he serves nevertheless as a pattern of persistence in colonization. Son of the apothecary to Marie de Medici, he reluctantly entered his father's profession. Then in 1604, when he was barely thirty, he accompanied the bold adventurers led by Pierre de Gast, Sieur of Monts, who went out to colonize Acadia. 'Hébert takes pleasure in husbandry,' observed Poutrincourt. Champlain had noticed this, too, and found no difficulty in persuading him to settle down in Quebec with his family. The prospective colonist sold his furniture, settled up his affairs and left for Honfleur, the point of embarkation, with his wife, three children and his brother-in-law. A last attempt was made to prevent his departure. The captain of the ship, together with representatives of the newly-formed Company of Canada, refused to allow him to embark unless he would put himself under contract in their service. The conditions were draconian: Hébert might reclaim land, labour, and sow, but the products of his harvests would go to the Company; in exchange it would pay him 300 *livres de Tours*. What was more, the colonist must in no circumstances whatsoever trade in furs with the Indians; if he did so his entire property would be forfeit. Hébert despairingly gave in. He signed the agreement and embarked on April 11, 1617. After two months of a difficult voyage the *Saint-Etienne* dropped anchor at Tadoussac. By August the first Canadian family had arrived in Quebec. Further difficulties arose. Instead of the promised fifteen acres, Hébert received only seven. What is more the Sieurs de Caen persecuted him endlessly, fearing that he might interfere in their dubious transactions with the Indians.

But Hébert had no commercial instinct. Though disillusioned

by human dishonesty and meanness he was not discouraged; with the help of some Indians he immediately started building a cabin to house his family for the coming winter. He cleared some land and soon possessed a small patch of ground whence he dispensed his ideas on medicine to other Whites living in the neighbourhood who, following his example, had also begun to cultivate the land —land of a fertility which Champlain had already extolled in order to attract more colonists. 'I travelled about and saw well-cultivated land already sown and laden with good grain, gardens full of every sort of plant; cabbages, turnips, lettuce, purslane, sorrel, parsley, as well as other vegetables as good and as forward as any in France.' Already he could envisage a host of French colonists settled in Quebec and in its outskirts. He thought the example of Hébert would persuade them. But Champlain's dream, alas! was to be of short duration. In 1627 the courageous man fell from a scaffolding and then died from lack of care in the hard winter weather. Two years later came the English occupation. Some thirty Frenchmen who could not or did not wish to return to France were forced to stick it out. Members of the Hébert family who remained behind included his widow, Marie Rollet, their son Guillaume and their daughter Anne, who in 1621 had married Guillaume Couillard. There was also a surgeon, Adrien Duchesne, who came from Dieppe, and some interpreters who, in order to escape the occupation, had retreated into the woods where they lived like Indians. In 1632 the Treaty of St Germain-en-Laye gave Canada back to France. And now another colonizing explorer, one Robert Giffard, revived a long-cherished dream of settling down to life in this new country which he himself had already visited.

The colonizing activities of Giffard and his compatriots from Mortagne-sur-Perche were very much more fruitful than those of Louis Hébert. The little group formed the true foundation-stone of a new people. Giffard had practised for years as both doctor and chemist in the ships which traded with New France. The historian Sagard notes that in 1627 he built himself a cabin in which he lived with a servant while he waited for the sailors of the ship to complete the loading of furs plundered from the Indians: 'From fifteen to twenty thousand *livres'* worth of beaver pelts, not to mention the other species.' The young surgeon's mind was centred from now on upon the idea of settlement in this country, and the foundation here of a permanent colony with people from his own

16

1. Quebec c. 1700 (Sketch by Franquelin)

2 a. Jacques Cartier haranguing his people, after Vallard's map, 1546
One of the first drawings concerning Canada

b. Champlain's drawing of the Habitation of Quebec

A/Storehouse
B/Pigeon-house
C/Building for storing arms and housing workmen
D/Workmen's quarters
E/Sun-dial
F/Building containing forge and artisans' quarters
G/Outside galleries
H/Champlain's private quarters
I/Main door with draw-bridge
L/Walk (10 feet wide) all round the building
M/Ditch surrounding the building
N/Platforms for artillery
O/Champlain's garden
P/Kitchen
Q/Terrace in front of the building on the river bank
R/The St Lawrence river

poor soil. He knew that from time immemorial his compatriots had, at seed-time and harvest, moved *en masse* to the rich province of Beauce. The land in New France resembled this province and possessed unlimited resources. Giffard came back to Quebec in the following year, made his way along the banks of the St Lawrence and chose his site. He was forced to return to France during the English occupation, but he was able to point out on the contract the exact location of the site he had chosen.

Giffard tried to convince his compatriots of the fact that, even if the Company of New France was determined to preserve its monopoly in skins, there were other openings for trading. To demonstrate this he signed a contract in which he associated himself with Pierre Le Bouyer, Sieur of Saint-Gervais, adviser to the King and his counsellor in the bailiwick of Perche. Each contributed a sum of 1,800 *livres*, 'which would be used for merchandise, for food and wages for the men sent out on the first voyage to America, that is to say to Canada or New France, where the said Giffard would take the said men and would change the said merchandise and manpower into other merchandise and manufactured goods which he would then send to France, which goods the said Le Bouyer would receive and sell to the common benefit of all'. The contract was to remain valid for a period of ten years. If Giffard happened to sell the goods in New France he would be responsible for reporting the fact to his associate, and the sum thus accrued would be used to send 'other men, victuals and other objects vital to the continuance of the said commerce'.

Giffard's project therefore laid as much emphasis on trade as it did on colonization. In his mind both objects were complementary. He hoped, through his views, to convince the members of the One Hundred Associates that if they granted him a stretch of land in New France for his colonists to settle, not only would they be respecting the agreement they had made, but they would at the same time preserve their monopoly in the fur trade.

Giffard returned to Mortagne with the precious piece of paper which designated his rights to property and colonization. The first to join him were artisans of essential trades; the master mason Jean Guyon and the master carpenter Zacharie Cloutier who, besides their wives, had five and six young children respectively.

A labourer, Gaspard Boucher, and his wife sold the farm at Mortagne, which they had purchased only the year before, keeping the furniture and other domestic objects which 'might be of use elsewhere' for themselves or their five children. Marin Boucher followed the example of his brother and also agreed to emigrate with his family.

They left Mortagne itself at the beginning of April, 1634. The families crammed themselves into heavy wagons laden with provisions, furniture, implements, tools and family souvenirs, and by way of Rouen reached Dieppe where they were to embark. Here they were joined by Jean Juchereau Sieur de Maure, his wife Marie Langlois and their four children, the youngest of whom was barely a year old. A few unmarried men who thought they had nothing to lose by attempting such a venture completed the party. After a long though uneventful crossing the ship set down its little cargo of resolute men, brave women and wondering children off the rock of Quebec. In all forty-three people, including six complete families, deliberately surrendered themselves to their destiny, which (though they did not know it) was to found a country unbelievably more vast than the one they had left behind.

When grants of land had been distributed each man set himself to his task. First, in accordance with the agreement, all hands laboured to build a manor-house for the *Seigneur* Giffard. And then a few humble dwellings were hastily knocked together to house the families of the colonists before winter set in. At the same time the first forest clearings were made. Everyone joined in the work. 'They are their own horses, their own oxen, lifting and hauling timber, trees, rocks.' The Jesuit missionaries were amazed.

A nation continues to hope as long as crops grow and mothers give birth. The little settlement increased. Every year other families, attracted by the example of relations or friends, emigrated in their turn, leaving, regretfully or otherwise, their little towns of Mortagne or Tourouvre and the adjoining villages. Giffard welcomed them eagerly, and within less than ten years he was able to count among the immigrants members of every profession and trade: a carpenter, notary mason, stonecutter, surgeon, tailor, weaver, musician, wheelwright, hatter, magistrate, butcher, tanner, cooper, gardener, draper, chandler, joiner, charcoal burner, miller, cutler and gunsmith.

The sons of Robert Giffard did not perpetuate his name, but the registers serve to do so. His worth is obvious from the works he undertook and from his unwavering example to his compatriots, the fifty or so heads of the families he brought out from his native land between 1634 and 1663. These were the men who founded the parishes around Quebec, with their attractive names: Beaupré, Charlesbourg, Boischâtel, Cap Tourmente, Courville, L'Ange-Gardien, Château-Richer, Beauport. The whole of this region owed its rapid and intense development to the colonists from the district of Perche. The census taken in 1666 shows that nearly half the entire population of New France at this period was settled in this region: 1,439 settlers from 240 families, out of a total of 3,418. The shores of Beaupré alone, so much praised by Talon as well as La Hontan, attracted 87 families, numbering 678 souls, greater than the population of Quebec itself, which was 555 including missionaries. These were the immigrants who formed the basic stock of today's population in French Canada. Thus, Jean Guyon and his wife, Mathurine Robin, together with their six children married and stayed on to live in the new colony. In 1920 one of their descendants was sufficiently interested to make a count of the nine generations which succeeded them. Among the thousands of individuals of so many different names directly descended from Jean Guyon and Mathurine Robin were a cardinal, seventeen archbishops and bishops, nearly 500 priests and hundreds of monks and nuns. In 1650 Claude Bouchard left his native parish of St Cosme-de-Vair. In 1950 more than 100,000 of his Canadian descendants celebrated the tri-centenary of this event. There are hundreds of examples of this kind, like that of the three Gagnon brothers, Mathurin, Jean and Pierre, who had come originally from Tourouvre, and of their sister Marguerite and their cousin Robert, all of whom left many descendants in the country they had chosen and to which they had been led by Robert Giffard.

In 1636 a little collection of forty-five people disembarked. They were outstandingly enthusiastic and energetic and, according to the words of Sulte the historian, they formed a 'clan' composed of the Le Gardeur and Le Neuf families, themselves related, whose chieftains were members of the small nobility in Normandy; wrangling, autocratic, energetic and gifted with a good business sense. For a long time they had stifled and mouldered in their crumbling manorhouses. They heard talk of New France, this young country where enterprising men might make their fortunes. Its priceless furs were becoming ever more sought after in Europe.

So many had grown rich, why not they? They took serious stock of the situation and realizing they had nothing to lose by emigrating they made up their mind to set forth. Some of them had small children. No matter, they would soon acclimatize themselves.

These families arrived in Quebec on June 11th, and were received by Father Le Jeune as a gift from Heaven. Only a short time before he had written to his Abbot in Paris: 'Our people have increased in number far beyond our expectations. The most reputable people have now struck root in our forests in order that they may live in freedom.' When he greeted the Norman group, whose leaders had announced their aristocratic names, the Jesuit bubbled over with enthusiasm. 'These are marvellous gentlemen,' he wrote. But these marvellous gentlemen were first and last men of business and they had no religious vocation. They had not come to colonize. First and foremost they were there to get rich and would use any means to do so.

The outstanding figures in the group were the two Le Gardeur brothers, Pierre, Sieur of Repentigny, and Charles, Sieur de Tilly, together with their widowed mother, Pierre's wife and three children; two Le Neuf brothers, Michel Sieur de Hérisson and Jacques Sieur de La Poterie, who had married Marguerite Le Gardeur, sister to the two Le Gardeur brothers; the Le Neufs' mother, Jeanne Le Marchand and their sister Marie, aged twenty-four, were also in the party. This little group was guided and advised by Jean-Paul Godefroy, a constant visitor to Canada, whose father, a notary and entrepreneur from Paris, had been a founder member of the One Hundred Associates. Godefroy was an adventurous spirit who at an early age had signed on as a seaman in Champlain's fleet. He had carefully watched those companies which had made a success of the fur-trade and he knew where they were strong and where their weaknesses lay. He was undoubtedly responsible for the arrival of the group, and he became an integral part of it through his marriage to the daughter of Pierre Le Gardeur de Repentigny.

These families gave the new land something still more important; they brought to it their new and vigorous blood. They formed a class which took its place among the lofty and insecure aristocracy of the governing body which provided the administration for the country and the colony. These 'provincial noblemen', the Le Gardeur and Le Neuf families, were willing to exchange their familiar existence for a venturesome and free life, and they never regretted it. They were to found the stock of some of the finest families of the new nation. Descendants of Pierre Le Gardeur de Repentigny, who had four children, and of Charles Le Gardeur de Tilly, who had fifteen, provided men who followed outstandingly brilliant military careers and filled posts in public administration in successive generations. The chances of war took them far and wide, as in 1784, when we find a Louis de Repentigny installed as Governor of Senegal. This Louis was descended in direct line from Pierre and he inherited his adventurous nature. One of Pierre's daughters, Catherine, who had been born in Normandy and had married Charles d'Ailleboust, Sieur de Musseaux, gave birth to fourteen children who were the ancestors of the families of Argenteuil, de Périgny, de Manthets, Daneau de Muy, among others. Of the fifteen children of the Sieur de Tilly, eleven were married, most of them to Canadian officers or the daughters of Canadian officers. Some acquired lands and titles and some went on to become heroes on the fields of battle. In 1800 Etienne, Simon de Tilly, a native of Quebec, served with Napoleon's armies.

The descendants of Le Neuf are possibly less remarkable since their own children were less numerous. Michel was a widower when he first landed, bringing with him an only daughter, Anne, who married an unknown colonist Antoine Desrosiers, originally from Forez. Because he was a fine worker and an intelligent man, Desrosiers soon became one of the leading citizens of the borough of Three Rivers. When he died he was fiscal procurator for the seigneurie of Champlain. Of the eight children of this marriage seven of them have founded long lines which are today a genealogist's dream. Jacques de Neuf de la Poterie had two daughters, Catherine and Marie, and one son, Michel. The latter was known as the Sieur de Beaubassin and was one of the founders of Acadia. Catherine and Marie are ancestors of the families of la Ronde and Robineau de Portneuf.

These examples demonstrate once again that New France was not built upon famous names, nor upon one generation of noble quarterings, but rather upon the productiveness of groups of people and upon individuals of great character. Pierre Boucher was the finest example of this.

Two Boucher families had accompanied Robert Giffard when the Mortagne group had emigrated; Pierre, son of Gaspard Boucher and Nicole Lemère, was then twelve years old. His whole career was conspicuous for his total devotion to the service of the new colony. With his widespread social work, his Christian principles, his integrity, he was the most praiseworthy figure of his time. There was no shadow or stain upon this generous and creative life. Even while he was crossing the sea to Quebec his future was becoming clear. His good humour, his lively wit, and early signs of his ambition were noticed by two Jesuits, Charles Lalemant and Jacques Duteux. Father Lalemant, who had known the country for ten years, also knew that the missionaries required young men of his calibre to assist them in their work among the Indian tribes. Pierre Boucher was to leave at once to take part in this work. For four years he shared the lives of the missionaries and made himself familiar with the native dialects. Then he was taken into service by the Governor of Montmagny. He fought in every battle against the Iroquois and distinguished himself by his astuteness and level-headedness. When the little town of Three Rivers was besieged and was appealing for a captain to lead it, the Governor at once thought of Boucher, and sent him there despite his tender age. With only forty-six men he attacked and drove off the enemy. Soon afterwards at the age of thirty he was made Governor of the town he had so brilliantly saved.

His duties as soldier and administrator were at an end. These parts might now be played by others. He himself wished to resign from public life and devote himself wholly to developing a seigneurie with carefully-chosen leaseholders. The Commissioner, Talon, awarded him the seigneurie of Boucherville, 300 kilometres from Quebec and totally 'savage'.

Although on his return from duty Boucher was once more appointed Governor of Three Rivers, was raised to the nobility and later even called upon by reason of his great experience to fight the ever aggressive and dangerous Iroquois, he had made up his mind by now to retire to his seigneurie which was to become, as he had always dreamed it would, the very pattern for a seigneurie, with model colonists. He based its foundation upon the seigneurie of Robert Giffard, that fellow citizen to whom he owed his existence in this new land. In order to strengthen his resolve he drew up with infinite pains a document setting forth the highest of moral purposes. It was entitled: 'Reasons which bind me to the establishment of my Seigneurie in the Iles-Percées which I have named Boucherville.' Here is an extract: 'Second reason: in order to live a more cloistered life freed from the cares of a world which serves only to busy us with its trivialities and thus to sever us more finally from God, and also to enable me to work out my own salvation and that of my family.'

Pierre Boucher was to see his dream of 'a new world in a New France' fulfilled. What is more, he himself was to help to accomplish it by bringing up fifteen children, some of whom would ally themselves with the most successful families in the country, others with military and noble families. One of his sons became a priest, one of his daughters a nun, one of his sons-in-law a governor. According to the custom of the time his sons took new names, many of them inspired by the names of districts in the Perche. They founded, among others, the following families: de la Bruère, Boucherville, Montarville, Montbrun, Niverville, Montizambert, Grandpré, La Perrière.

The seigneurie was organized to be a model of its kind and faithful to the conception formulated by Pierre Boucher in his statement of 1662. Land was conceded 'by degrees' and each colonist had his dwelling within the confines of the village to ensure protection from exterior dangers. The colonists were carefully chosen from among those pioneers who had proved themselves elsewhere, and from among regular soldiers of the Carignan regiment, 'in order that all may be instructed in the husbandry of the land'. Before he could assume ownership of the piece of land allotted to him and embark upon its cultivation, each was obliged as an appointed or potential settler to serve a trial period of from three to four years. The spirit within the group was such that on April 4, 1673, all thirty-seven of them were summoned to the seigneurial manorhouse, where they were formally and legally registered as freeholders, in exchange for purely nominal seigneurial rents: one *sou* for every acre granted, two live capons for each acre of cultivated land, and six pennies for *cens* or quit-rent, all payable at the feast of Saint-Rémi.[1] The first dignitaries of the seigneurie were chosen by Boucher from among those fitted for the post by reason of their superior education: Réné Rémy, a teacher of young people, was to be seigneurial judge, Thomas Frérot, Sieur de la Chenaye, notary and scrivener, Joseph Huet, otherwise known as Dulude, fiscal procurator. Jean de Lafond, Sieur de la Fontaine, and a former sergeant in the Carignan regiment, was appointed

[1] October 1st.

captain of the village. The latter could 'neither read nor write', but the seigneur had many a time had visible proof of his courage and loyalty. Civil organization of the seigneurie was thus completed. Religious rules were laid down at the seigneurial manorhouse even before the installation of a priest, for whom Boucher had set aside a piece of land within the seigneurie. The authorities were astounded by Boucher's results. The Governor, Denonville, wrote to the Court in 1686 that all the well-being of the colony was due to Boucher's efforts alone; the one man who had never spared himself to achieve it. Never was praise more justly bestowed. Ten years later Champigny was to write: 'the seigneurie of Boucherville is one of the richest and most magnificent territories in the colony'. The engineer, Gédéon de Catalogne, who was ordered by the King to inspect each seigneurie in 1712, remarked that the people of Boucherville were more content than those of any other township under the government of Montreal.

Pierre Boucher died in 1717 at the ripe old age of ninety-five. His mind remained clear until the last, and he used his latter years to record his last wishes—memoirs touching in their simplicity, in which he remembers each one of his children separately, and gives them good advice according to their different temperaments. He begins: 'I leave you little wealth, but such as it is was well earned. I endeavoured to leave you more. You all know how by spending wisely I left no stone unturned to this end. But God disposes and He did not will that I be given more. I bequeath to you my friends, many of them persons of rank and distinction. I leave you no enemies since I do not believe I know of any. I did all I could to lead a blameless life—try to do as much. Endeavour to help people and hinder no-one lest you displease God.' These thoughts, together with their practice, exemplified the spiritual ideal of the missionaries and of the founders of the colony. For generations the priests of the parish would by tradition read the last wishes of the founder of Boucherville as their sermon on each New Year's Day.

This pioneer of the French colony in the New World lived for twenty years under Louis XIII, for sixty-three under Louis XIV, and for two years under Louis XV, during which time he knew the first thirteen Governors and the first seven Intendants of New France.

EMIGRATION OF THE WIVES-TO-BE

Another source of population was to prove just as effective, although it seemed more hazardous and unusual. Unmarried volunteer officers and soldiers of these first years in Canada, mostly from the Carignan regiment, were very willing to live in New France when they came to be released from the Service, provided they could find themselves wives. But there were very few white women in Canada. Of course there were native women, but they were few and for the most part jealously reserved for the chiefs of their tribes. Moreover, despite legend to the contrary, they had nothing attractive about them once they had turned twenty, and they were lazy and dirty to a repulsive degree. Only a few of those whom the nuns and missionaries had managed to instruct and civilize a little found husbands among the Whites instead of returning to their villages. Accordingly the immigration of girls and widows was begun, at first on a voluntary basis and then encouraged by the religious and civil authorities. The immigrants were assured that when they arrived they would find husbands suited to their own station in life. Almost 1,000 came to Canada in this way between 1636 and 1673. Those who were out for scandal were bound to look askance upon the reputations of these maidens who threw themselves blindly into marriage. The scandalmongers did not fail. In 1639 *Mercure François* wrote disdainfully that 'every year a fairly large number of girls is removed to populate these desert lands'. Tallemant des Réaux and Bussy-Rabutin took this sort of thinking as inspiration for their *grivoises*[1] *songs*. These fashionable authors confused New France with the islands in America[2] to which women of ill-fame and prostitutes were forcibly deported. Later La Hontan repeated, practically to the point of plagiarism, the cynical assertions of *Mercure,* and these assertions form the most false and innaccurate part of his works: for La Hontan knew these immigrants personally, and was welcomed into their homes after they had become merchants' wives, middle-class wives, or had married officers or soldiers and colonists.

In fact only girls, orphans mostly and some widows, hand-picked and of spotless reputation, were sent to New France. Those chroniclers of the time who are most to be trusted, Marie de

[1] Bawdy in character.   [2] Islands of St Christopher and Martinique.

l'Incarnation, the Intendant Talon, Pierre Boucher, and all the Jesuits who had helped to compile *Relations* are agreed on this, and their word is worth ten at least of La Hontan's. The fact that these girls chose exile in an unknown country, agreeing to marriage with men of whom they knew nothing, was perhaps enough to place their reputations under a cloud. But if they did accept this risk it was because they realized something of the dreary future awaiting those of their schoolfriends who had married in France. From school age upwards the young French girl was buried in a convent. 'Soon the marriage bells will ring for her,' writes Georges Mongrédien[1] 'often soon after she reaches adolescence. One might suppose that this would mark the moment when a girl comes at last to experience some kind of personal life. By no means. Hers is the smallest part in the decisive act which is to settle her whole future. The middle classes and the officer class saw marriage as something which concerns parents alone. It is the linking together of sacks of gold, minutely calculated merchandise, where the size of dowry occasionally balances out the gift of a title—a girl must not listen to the dictates of her heart—she must not show her longings. If she refuses to submit to her parents' brusque authority no alternative is left to her but return to the dismal convent. What is more she is about to learn a new obedience: the tryanny of a husband who preaches obedience to her while assuming for himself the greatest possible amount of freedom ... There are so many Agnès[2] thus ill-wed! How easy to understand Molière's liberal campaign throughout his life in support of love marriages, the freedom of choice for a girl and of her rights in love.' Orphans from every walk of life, young widows with no security, working women and farm workers, devoid of a future in their own country, they all hoped to find one in this uncharted land. They did indeed resemble Molière's girls of spirit, and in accepting adventure, also hoped to hold the 'right to choose' instead of life in the 'sad convent'. A new horizon spread before them. They did not realize it when they embarked, but their real destiny was to go and found a new nation.

This emigration of women was accomplished in two stages. From

---

[1] In *La Vie Quotidienne sous Louis XIV*.

[2] Agnès: a character out of Molière's *l'École des Femmes* (1662) who, brought up in a completely unsophisticated way of life, becomes the centre of amorous intrigue.

1634 to 1662 and from 1662 to 1673. All through the first period young women and widows from fifteen to twenty-five years of age sailed either alone or in family groups of three or four. Most of these came from the west of France, and accompanied relatives from their province or family friends. Others, currently servants in the households of middle-class families, agreed to follow their employers, who in turn would be repaid either in money or by work should the girls marry or prefer to return to France. These girls were all orphans. Often they were children of poor families who would not or could not emigrate themselves. Some of those who came from the Ile de France, and particularly those from Paris, had been educated in the workhouse. 'They are the children of legal marriages, some are orphans, others are from families who have fallen on hard times.' Those who were accepted had to prove some basic suitability. 'They must be amenable, hard-working, skilled and intensely religious.' Within the group only one undesirable girl of doubtful morals was discovered and she was at once returned to France at the expense of the ship's owner. Gustave Lanctot wrote with some justification when he described the little colony as becoming more and more concerned with the well-being of the immigrants, both male and female. 'The arrival of the girls who come here to get married is quite an event,' he remarks, 'when they first tread on new soil, charmingly dressed in close-fitting coats of camlet over farandine skirts, with their taffeta hoods, lawn kerchiefs in their hands, lofty officials and Jesuits, middle-class people, artisans and colonists hasten smilingly to welcome them, these daughters of France who bring sunshine to a new country while they wait for a morrow which will bring them new homes in which they will later become the mothers of many children.'

What of the future of these volunteer immigrants? Some, a very few, married in Quebec and returned to France with their husbands. Marguerite Banse, who had arrived with her brother Guillaume, married in 1642, one Jean Bossier. Fifteen years later, no one knew why, the couple went back to their native land. A young Parisian widow, Marie Joly, who had arrived with her cousin, René Maheu, went through a contract of marriage in Quebec with Antoine Damiens of Rouen, and from there they left to settle in La Rochelle. Another couple, Claude Poulin of Rouen and Jeanne Mercier, who had come over with Robert Giffard and his companions, married in Quebec in 1639. Poulin brought back his wife to his native town where they lived for a few years and from there they went back to end their days in New France. They later had several children and, in 1687, died within three days of each other.

Can it be that homesickness had something to do with these cases of indecisiveness? The ordinary people of the country left behind them nothing to tell us about how they adjusted themselves to the new life. Nevertheless a reference in the *Annales de l'Hôtel-Dieu* in Quebec may reveal something of their frame of mind. Of two Régnard-Duplessis sisters who had become nuns, one had been born in France the other in Canada. The latter wrote: 'My elder sister remains in France because of her memories, her feelings and her heart. Thoughts of her loyal and enduring friendships beyond the seas bring her pleasure.' The Frenchwoman speaking of the feelings of the Canadian-born sister wrote: 'She is completely French by inclination.' These are the observations of nuns bowed to a discipline which was hard and at the same time simple and sincere. Most of the immigrants who remained in secular life were integrated into Canadian life less than ten years after they married, and very few of them evinced any longings for home. They had no time for longings. The climate, the perpetual presence of danger and privation enveloped them in an atmosphere which at once swamped their personalities and fashioned their future.

Marie Marguerie, a native of Rouen, arrived in New France in 1639. She had come out at the wish of her brother François, an explorer and companion to Champlain who had become an interpreter of Indian dialects. François was staying in the town of Three Rivers where she came to join him. Here she met Jacques Hertel, who had been born in Fécamp and was therefore a Norman, as she was, and what was more 'one of the foremost and most important inhabitants of the neighbourhood'. The marriage took place in 1641. Three children were born of whom one, François, was to become one of the most brilliant of Canadian heroes, the equal of Le Moyne in courage and gallantry. François Hertel had one quality which Le Moyne did not possess; he was educated; a valuable asset which he owed to his mother who had been one of those girls who had sailed alone to New France and had been criticized by the editor of *Mercure François*. Marie Marguerie's life did not end here. On August 10, 1651, Jacques Hertel died suddenly. He was buried in a side chapel of the parish church which he had had built at his own expense in recognition of prayers answered; in this case the granting of his prayer for the resistance put up by Three Rivers to Indian attack. Marie Marguerie was scarcely twenty-five years old, and young women who had proved their courage and skill in the new country were of more value than those who had only just reached its shores. What is more she was much sought after by the bachelors of the colony. High-ranking officers within the entourage of the Governor and the Intendant paid her court. She was unwilling to decide upon her choice, not unreasonably since she was now alone in New France with her three children. Five years earlier her brother François had been drowned crossing the St Lawrence off Three Rivers. She could have gone back to France; various officials there had proposed marriage to her. But she preferred to remain, for her children belonged here. Two years after Jacques Hertel's death, she married Quentin Moral from St Quentin, still only a humble colonist after a career as a soldier, but later to become King's Lieutenant and afterwards a judge in the civil and criminal Court. She never regretted her choice. Four children were later born of a marriage which was to last thirty-four years. Marie Marguerie would never again leave her home in New France. Quentin Moral died in 1686 at Three Rivers, Marie Marguerie died in her turn on November 24, 1700, and on the day of her funeral the Recollect priest of the parish of Three Rivers, Luc Filastre, sang her praises: 'Today, November 26, 1700, Marie Marguerie, widow of the late St Quentin was buried. She died fortified by the rites of the Church and with every sign of extraordinary devotion, having lived for more than fifty years in the service of all in this town, their constant helpmate in time of need, showing incomparable charity and zeal, she worked for the Church performing the duties of the sacristy, and caring for the Church appointments incomparably well. She was buried, according to her wish, next to the body of M. Hertel, her first husband.'

This story of adjustment is not unique. It is merely a typical example taken at random.

Barbe Poisson's is the story of a more active life. In 1648 when she was fifteen years old she married a colonist from Montreal, Léonard Lucault, who was killed by Iroquois three years later, leaving her with two children. In 1652 she married Gabriel Celle, otherwise known as Duclos, a judge in civil and criminal law in the Court of Montreal. This trading post was the object of the first Indian attacks. Courage was an everyday commodity and everyone knew his own turn would come. Barbe Poisson's came one day in February 1661, with a surprise attack by a force of 150 Iroquois. The colonists were working without special heed to danger, since the enemy did not usually appear so early in the year. But this year had been particularly mild. The Indians were about to overwhelm the fortress and Barbe realized the danger. She immediately took action as described by Dollier de Casson: 'Since there were no men around she herself took up an armful of firearms and despite the bands of Iroquois swarming everywhere up to her house from all sides she ran forward to meet our Frenchmen who were being pursued, and as she got up to Monsieur Le Moyne, who was almost borne to the ground and overcome, she handed him arms which miraculously strengthened the French and thrust back the enemy.' At the time, Barbe Poisson was barely twenty-seven years of age. The country of many perils had become her own, and she could never more desert it.

Here is a typical example of the way in which undreamed-of wealth could be acquired by emigration: Madeleine Couteau of Saint Jean-d'Angely, widow of Etienne de Saint-Père, had two daughters, Jeanne and Catherine. She was in a state of near-poverty when she heard that certain acquaintances, among them members of the Guillet family, had embarked at La Rochelle on their way to New France, which they found so much to their liking that they made up their minds to settle there. She followed their example and took her two daughters with her. Jeanne was twenty and Catherine thirteen. The widow married first on October 12, 1647, to her second husband. He, like her, was a Saintongeois as one Emery Caltaut. He brought her to Cape La Madeleine where he owned land and where two brothers Pierre and Mathurin Guillet also lived. Caltaut was killed in 1653 by Iroquois. Some months later his widow married Claude Houssart, a native of Plessis-Grimoire in Anjou. She had no children by her Canadian husbands, but her two daughters simultaneously married the two Guillet brothers. Catherine de Saint Pierre's husband, Mathurin, was killed by Iroquois in 1653. She then married Nicolas Rivard who came from Tourouvre in the Perche. The latter's brother, Robert Rivard, was to marry in his turn in the year 1664, Madeleine, daughter of

Pierre Guillet and Jeanne Saint-Père, and thus became Madeleine Couteau's grand-daughter. In short, when Madeleine Couteau died on September 9, 1691, aged eighty-five and after forty-four years of life in Canada, she had given to New France through her two daughters twenty-one grandchildren and sixty-five great grandchildren. As was customary at this time these families subdivided and changed their original names, and from them descended the families of Lavigne, Laglanderie, Lacoursière, Lanouette, Préville, Beaucour, Dufresne, Loranger, Feuilleverte, Montendre, Bellefeuille, Maisonville, Saint-Marc, Cinq-Mars, Lajeunesse and others, not to mention the stock of the Rivards and the Guillets and the colonists who married the daughters of Nicolas Rivard and Pierre Guillet; the families of Rouillard, Moreau, Macé, Baril, Deshaies, Champoux, Dutaut, Lafond and Marchand. This then was the heritage which a young widow of La Saintonge, who one fine day had decided to emigrate to New France with her two daughters, bequeathed to her adopted country.

Thanks to official records and family histories, it is possible to follow the destinies of most of these immigrants. Such optimistic and satisfactory reports came from secular as well as from religious authorities that from 1662 Colbert thought it might be possible to increase the emigration of women and decided to this end to devise some sort of system. It was not altogether a new idea. England was using it at the present time to fill her American colonies. Even in France it was customary for girls without any money and for orphans from the workhouse to be sought in marriage by people of rank as well as by the middle classes and artisans who were comfortably off. They were 'in demand' because it went without saying that they had been brought up in the sort of discipline which would fit them to be good housekeepers. Generally they were married in the orphanage chapel and the administration presented them with a varied trousseau instead of dowry.

Colbert knew of this custom and it gave him some ideas on the organization of the selection and emigration of girls designed for marriage in New France. He arranged for each girl to be given a dowry taken from the King's Privy purse, which each affianced girl would receive upon the day she put her signature to the marriage contract. The dowry usually consisted of fifty *livres*. For girls who were well-born and who were later to become the wives of worthy but impecunious officers, 'the King's gift' ranged in value from 100 to 500 *livres*. From this custom the name 'King's daughters' was given to these young emigrants. Other essential expenses were added to this statutory sum. The first disbursement was fixed at 100 *livres;* ten *livres* were undesignated or for their recruitment, the 'levée', as it was called, thirty *livres* for clothes and sixty towards the crossing. Apart from ordinary clothing a small money-box, a hood, a taffeta kerchief, shoe ribbons, one hundred sewing needles, a comb, some white thread, a pair of stockings, a pair of gloves, a pair of scissors, two knives, a thousand pins, a bonnet, four braids, and two *livres* in silver coin were all provided. From the King's Council of New France came 'a few clothes suited to the climate, and certain items chosen from the King's stores. After this the Intendant gave to each emigrant fifty Canadian *livres*' worth of provisions suited to her household needs'.

Almost 1,000 girls provided for in this way went out to New France during the ten years when this form of emigration was at its height. Not all of them came from Paris, since the authorities in the colony stipulated that the 'girls must be in robust health and accustomed to farm work'. We need not concern ourselves over-much with statistics compiled by learned archivists, but one of the more qualified of these has left us the following list, showing the place of origin of 852 of these girls:

ILE-DE-FRANCE 314	BRIE 5
NORMANDY 153	BERRY 5
AUNIS 86	AUVERGNE 5
CHAMPAGNE 43	LIMOUSIN 4
POITOU 38	ANGOUMOIS 3
ANJOU 22	PROVENCE 3
BEAUCE 22	SAVOIE 3
MAINE 19	FRANCHE-COMTÉ 2
ORLÉANAIS 19	GASCOGNE 2

From the ports of Dieppe and La Rochelle there sailed each year the convoys of ships which, in Robert de Roquebrune's appropriate words, held the future of a new nation. When the French frigates were sighted at the approach to the Gulf the Governor spread throughout the colony news that women were about to

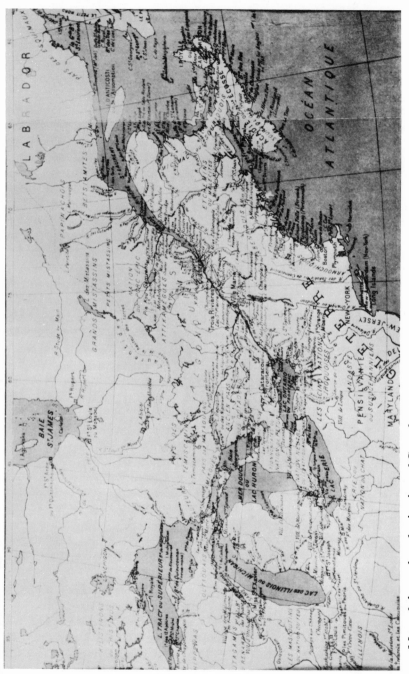

3. Map of the early colonization of Canada

4 a. A Canadian's winter equipment   (After La Patherie)

b. A portage in the region of Mich
makinac (Jefferys, Coll. Imperial C

c. Arrival of Radisson at an Indian camp in 1660 (Jefferys, Coll. Imperial Oil)

disembark. The priest announced it during the sermon in the Dominican Mass. Seigneurs made it known in the grants of land. Bachelors flocked to the capital. For a long time a legend was rife which told of avid colonists, at the sight of a sail, throwing themselves into bark canoes at breakneck speed, and racing to board the ship in order to seize the healthiest or the most comely of these girls, according to their several tastes. The perfect inspiration for a romantic novel, but very far from fact. The trains of immigrants were put under the authority of a monitress delegated by royal warrant, who had been ordered to place the King's protégées upon arrival in the care of the local nuns.

On a day fixed long in advance, a solemn ceremony took place in the great drawing-room of the Governor's chateau, in the presence of the Governor, the Intendant, senior officers and ladies of Society. Madame Bourdon, who concerned herself particularly in the work of protecting these 'King's Daughters' and other immigrants, was nearly always accorded the honour of making the official presentations. She knew the name and ancestry of every girl, which meant that she was able to keep a discreet eye on their activities from the moment they arrived. She assigned to each immigrant a place to stay, Quebec, Three Rivers or Montreal.

In the weeks that followed the mutual agreement, the execution and signing of the marriage contract took place at the notary's. It was always a moving ceremony at which friends and relations gathered. Then, formally betrothed, the young couple returned to the convent, the almshouse or to the family which had agreed to house them until the religious consecration of the marriage. The engaged couple saw each other a little oftener and got to know each other better. It sometimes happened that one or other of them, occasionally both, regretted their first unduly romantic choice, made in an excess of emotion or nervousness, or for some other reason. Then both would return to the notary where by mutual consent the agreement would be annulled, following a sacred formula: '. . . Whereas there is no longer affection between them and having in mind that this might lead to lack of concord, the parties declare the agreement to be null and void and as if it had never been and without future and that thus the said parties agree to part without further claims on either side.' Immediately after an act of this sort had been drawn up to annul a marriage contract between Jean Bellet and Madeleine Beaudouin, the notary

Séverin Ameau married the girl himself, and their married life lasted almost half a century. Madeleine Beaudouin had come from Courcival in Maine and had emigrated with her two brothers, Jean and René. The first of these fell victim to the Iroquois and the second became the inseparable companion of the explorer Nicolas Perrot whose sister-in-law he married.

Marie Fayet, who arrived in Quebec in 1661, came of a middle-class family from the parish of Saint-Sauveur in Paris. She agreed to marry the colonist Jean Durand who owned territory in Cap Rouge, a suburb of Quebec. The contract was signed on October 3rd and then revoked on the following January 12th. Marie then agreed to marry Charles Pouliot, but on reflection changed her mind. Again the contract was revoked. She took no definite decision until July 24, 1662, when she married Nicolas Huot, by whom she was to bear eleven children. Her first intended, Jean Durand, not unnaturally of the opinion that Parisian women were very capricious and fickle, preferred to marry a Huron orphan, Catherine Annennontak, who had been brought up by the Ursulines. Another example is that of Anne Guitton whose contract of marriage with Jean Mouflet, otherwise Champagne, was annulled on August 17, 1669, three days after it had been drawn up. Jean Mouflet, on the same day and before the same witnesses François Trotain, Sieur de Saint-Surin, and Jean-Baptiste Gosset, married Anne Dodain before the same notary, Romain Becquet. If we read these stories carefully we learn that between the annulment of the contract with Anne Guitton and the signing of the legal act with Anne Dodain, a religious ceremony had been enacted with the latter. Jean Mouflet and Anne Dodain remained united for the rest of their lives and faced their future in Lachine where they settled down and where later eight children were born to them. During the great massacre in 1689 they were taken prisoner by the Iroquois.

These breakdowns did not often occur, and were invariably settled in a friendly manner. Very few marriages were lightly undertaken on the spur of the moment. The parties preferred to think hard and to ponder on their future. Even in these days it is surprising to read of how successful these unions, upon which depended the future of a whole nation, could prove. Inevitably some dramas arose, often because of the selfishness of narrow-minded people. Sometimes, because of prolonged indecision or sheer bad luck, one of these 'King's Daughters' would take a long time to find a spouse. She would then take a job in domestic service until the ideal husband came along. Anne Lejonc, a widow, was engaged to work for Michel Le Neuf for one year. A few months after this agreement, a settler, Jean Desmarais, also widowed, wished to marry her. The wedding was arranged for January 15, 1656. But she was a good housekeeper, and her employer did not want to part with her and so made difficulties. He even insinuated that Desmarais was already married in France. Enquiries showed this to be untrue, but Le Neuf put her clothes and personal belongings under lock and key, forbidding anyone on any pretext whatever to return them to her. This was an exceptional case. More usually the authorities regarded these marriages with favour. Anne Bouyer, born in La Rochelle, was servant to the Governor, Pierre Boucher, when she was wooed by Pierre Pinot, otherwise known as La Perle. The Governor sent for the notary and stood as witness to the couple at a ceremony attended by every prominent person in the neighbourhood.

All these girls had one quality in common—their courage. Constant daily courage. Very few of them failed in the tasks they had to face. And yet it is sometimes tempting to wonder how some of them could have managed to survive the bitter climate and the sort of conditions in which they had to live. A number of them, either by inclination or else because they were less adventurous, preferred to marry settlers from their own provinces, or if possible, from their own villages. But these were a minority. Most of them were more than ready for adventure, and the women helped each other through difficult times. Those who had come from neighbouring regions of France tried to marry settlers living in the same area. The census taken in 1681 makes it plain, for example, that of the fifteen colonists settled in the seigneurie of Lanougère, thirteen married 'King's Daughters' who had come from Maine and Poitou. Michel Feulion, who originated from Saint-Pierre-Le-Vieux in Poitou, even married a fellow citizen, Louise Bercier. The two Gautier sisters, Catherine and Anne, married Jean Picart and Pierre Cartier who owned neighbouring farms. Only one of these girls came from Paris. She was Françoise Hobbé, who married the seigneurial notary, Michel Roy. Since she was an educated girl and had been very well brought up, she agreed to become teacher-companion to her friends' children, and she remained to them an unfailing example of intelligence and fortitude.

In this way family life based upon mutual understanding and helpfulness was built up in the new territories. Three immigrants from the recruitment of 1668, Jeanne-Marie Gaultier, Madeleine Philippe and Marguerite Robineau, all went through a form of marriage on the same day, before the same notary, and in the presence of the same witnesses, to Gilles Masson, Pierre Tousignan and Michel Gorron, all colonists. Immediately afterwards they left for the almost virgin seigneurie of Saint-Charles-des-Roches, where their spouses had begun to reclaim small pieces of land. In the early days they had only a temporary hut to shelter them. But children were born, and then after a few years the settlers set out to conquer new territory on the other side of the St Lawrence river. The young wives bravely followed and took up their pioneering lives once more. When a birth was imminent they helped to deliver the child and a neighbour hurried to baptize it.

Certain statistics have been taken to indicate that those who came from Paris had more trouble in settling down to the tough Canadian life than did girls who had come from the provinces. It is a fact that three or four of the Parisian girls were sent back to France: 'The air of the country is not at all beneficial to their health.' Others, who had married officers, returned to France when their husbands were recalled. But the majority were successful in their adjustment. When Madeleine de Verchères wrote her account of the defence of the Verchères fort she spoke in disdainful tones of 'Mlle Marguerite Antiome, the wife of the Sieur de Fontaine, who, being extremely nervous, like all the women in this country who have come from Paris, begged to be taken to another fort'. This anecdote was written with goodwill and it is accurate but at the same time unfair. Marguerite Anthiaume had an instinctive fear of Indians, which was by no means strange, since her husband had been murdered by them and she had had to protect her seven little orphans. Parisian she undoubtedly was. Her father, Michel Anthiaume, had been Constable to the Chief Justice at the Hotel de Ville in Paris, and lived in the parish of Saint-Nicolas des Champs. Marguerite was one of the 'King's Daughters' who married an officer. On January 12, 1676, she married a Dauphinois, André Jarret de Beauregard, who died suddenly in 1690, leaving her with seven children, all infants. When the fort of Verchères was surrounded by Iroquois, this Parisian girl feared for her children's lives, although her second husband Pierre Fontaine, himself an officer, was there to protect them.

What of the future of girls born into the small nobility who had for various reasons emigrated to Canada? Perrine Picoté de Bellestre was the daughter of a Councillor, the King's physician in Paris. She yearned for convent life and agreed, on the advice of Mademoiselle Mance, to go to the Hôtel-Dieu in Ville-Marie. But her vocation lay elsewhere. In 1664 she married Michel Godefroy de Lintot, the first white child ever to have been born at Three Rivers. She had eleven children; the sons were to perpetuate the names of Tonnancourt and Normanville; the daughters were to marry Hertels, Jutras, Le Moynes, all families who, after three centuries, still flourish. Catherine Gauchet de Belleville, who had been Perrine's companion on the crossing, married one of Montreal's notable citizens on November 26, 1665. He was Lieutenant-General Jean-Baptiste Migeon de Branssat. She became a widow in 1693 and retired to the Hôtel-Dieu, where she died in 1723, having spent fifteen years in a convent. One of her daughters became an Ursuline nun in Quebec. Her name was perpetuated through the Juchereau de Saint-Denis family.

Another of these girls who had been labelled as 'women of ill-fame' by La Hontan, was Aimée Chatel, the daughter of an apostolic notary from Troyes, who made the voyage with Madeleine Bourgeoys. She was also sought after in marriage but was unable to make up her mind, and finally agreed to contract 'for life' with Marie-Barbe of Boullogne, the widow of the Governor of Aillеboust, who she accompanied to the Hôtel-Dieu in Quebec. She died there in 1695. Madeleine Mulloys de la Borde is another very typical example. She was an orphan and had come from Blois. Like her companion Perrine Picoté de Bellestre, she thought she had a vocation to be a nun. But she returned to the secular world where she met and married a fellow countryman, Etienne Pézard, Sieur de la Touche, who had just been appointed Governor of Ville-Marie. Soon afterwards M. de la Touche obtained Champlain's seigneurie, and retired there with his wife. They were to make it the model seigneurie of New France.

The survival of so many of these susceptible immigrants from the French provinces, and their perseverance and energy, was almost miraculous. Their arrival, their marriage, their dispersal throughout the countryside was repeated anew each year for fifteen years. From now on the new population gathered impetus as it moved towards its future; ninety per cent of marriages produced children. These children were tirelessly praised for their vigour and vitality. Mother Marie de l'Incarnation was enthusiastic: 'It is surprising how very many exceptionally good-looking children are born every year.' The Intendant Hocquart was to meet them later in adolescence: 'The Canadians are tall, well-made and strikingly handsome.' Since, according to Father Le Jeune, 'women have a new pregnancy almost every year', births in some years attained a figure of six or seven hundred in a population of scarcely six thousand. In view of the high morals obtaining, it is not difficult to agree with Lanctot that New France had been populated with 'choice immigrants who by their quality, hard work and devotion deserve to carry into history as symbol of distinction and honour the unique title of "King's Daughters".'

CHAPTER THREE

ADJUSTING TO THE COUNTRY

THE CANADIAN WINTER

The climate of Canada has long been held to be on a par with that of Siberia. It is a country of everlasting snows and intolerable cold, or so we are led to believe. Voltaire, himself susceptible to cold and rheumatism, expressed his views on the subject: 'The most horrible country of the North!' he exclaimed, never having seen it, 'for eight months of the year it is covered in snow and ice, inhabited by barbarians, bears and beavers . . . fifteen hundred leagues of it, three-quarters of which is frozen desert . . .' The terrible cold which decimated Jacques Cartier's expedition after he had been compelled to spend the whole of the winter of 1535 to 1536 in Quebec did not help to improve the reputation of the Canadian winter. This explorer from St Malo described the episode in detail from a scientific point of view in his *Brief Récit et Succinte Relation*. Rabelais' satirical anecdote in *Quart Livre* did not help either, since knowledgeable readers not unreasonably believed it to have been inspired by the reading of Cartier's essays. According to these, the cold in Canada was so intense that words froze on the lips of the sailors and remained suspended in mid-air. When the spring sunshine came the words thawed, and then sailors returning to the same spot might hear, from the captain's bridge, words which had been uttered the previous winter. Voltaire had evidently read and marked this little story, which was not calculated to render him indulgent towards a dry and crystalline cold. Those who had made the passage never ceased to deplore the climate. Bougainville, for instance, complained bitterly about the winter in Canada; its rigours, and more particularly, its length: 'It is an extraordinarily cold country where snows abound and where winter generally lasts through six months of the year.' In 1757, Doreil, the Commissioner for War, in a letter to the Secretary of State responsible for the Colonies, was moved by the plight of the soldiers in the garrison in Quebec and commiserated with them for having to put up with 'excessive expenditure of energy', unbelievable fatigue and all the other disagreeable things which they found in Canada, 'a country so hard and so entirely bare of resources'.

The first Europeans to tread the soil of this new country were more charitable, and more understanding than these critical visitors. They were surprised to find that the winter in Canada was both harder and longer than in Europe and that there was a remarkable difference between the climates of the old world and the new, even in the same degree of latitude. The explorers were completely thrown off balance by the unexpected cold, which paralysed the movement of their ships for almost six months of the year.

The Canadian winter is unlike any other. Modern geographers like Pierre Deffontaines have commented upon this fact: 'French Canada is noted for its bitter winters, possibly the most severe in the entire world.' Since he became 'tamed' by it, to cite an anonymous editor of one of the *Relations des Jésuites,* then clearly it was just possible to exist through its course. This conclusion is more than confirmed by impressions, to be cited later, of people who themselves knew the Canadian climate and had survived the harsh conditions which were part of Canadian life. These observations we owe to Frenchmen who had patiently and intelligently succeeded in defeating the climate and at the same time adjusting themselves to its severity and its vagaries.

The climate in Canada really consists of two seasons, winter and summer, both almost equal in length and with diametrically opposed extremes of temperature. The short spell usually known as spring is only the end of the winter and lasts but a few weeks. In the same way autumn is but an extension of summer, and sometimes one may hardly notice its existence. Winter approaches swiftly at the beginning of November and establishes itself firmly. It will last until the end of April.

Most forms of life within this planet can tolerate winter, and their adjustment to the cold is one of the strangest of physiological phenomena. Some, like the bear and the marmot, spend long months curled up in their lairs in total unconsciousness. Others change the colour of their coats. Hares, which are brown all summer, in winter become white as snow.

When all animal life has nearly come to a standstill, either through migration or in sleep, the winter has set in. Man is the only being who has so much difficulty in adjusting himself to the cold. The Indian inhabitants of the previous century in Canada had only partially succeeded in doing so. And the first Europeans, Jacques Cartier's mariners for example, were quite overcome by the inexorable foe. A century later in 1635, the companions of Laviolette who founded Three Rivers were to succumb in the same way during their first winter. This 'earth sickness', as scurvy was called, is a triumph of cold over human beings.

The winter climate is made more difficult for man to bear since it is almost invariably preceded, with no marked period of transition, by several torrid summer months with occasionally tropical temperatures. The findings of modern geographers are illuminating here—especially since one must bear in mind that the winter climate of three centuries ago was much more severe than it is today, for at that time the country was still largely clothed in forest.

These statistics, although varying greatly from year to year, provide, nevertheless, a fair idea of the variation between summer and winter temperatures. Raoul Blanchard the geographer observed that within a period of fifty years in the lower reaches of the St Lawrence, there was an average winter temperature of $-12°C$, and a summer one of $+18°C$; that is to say a difference of $30°C$. The extreme temperatures in Quebec recorded by Blanchard were a winter one of $-37°C$, and a summer one of $+39°C$, which represents an almost unbelievable contrast of $76°C$. In some winters the thermometer falls to 50 degrees Centigrade below zero in regions most distant from any source of humidity, even though these regions lie along the same latitude as the South of France. Thus, the neighbouring towns of Windsor in Canada, and of Detroit in the USA are on latitude 40°, which also passes just south of Rome; yet in February their average temperature is as low as $-5°C$.

Periods of intense cold are usually followed by heavy blizzards which last for three or four days. Snow is more cruel, more treacherous than cold, rendering all activity impossible. It can reach a depth of nine or even twelve feet, engulfing houses, blocking roads, rendering any activity impossible. Sometimes neighbours living a quarter of a mile apart are unable to meet for several weeks on end.

At the beginning of April, certain signs like the lengthening days and the increasingly warm rays of the sun filtering through seem to indicate that winter is about to relax its grip. Then the ice in the rivers breaks up. Rushing waters, a symbol of returning life, bring drifting ice-floes in their wake, which disintegrate in thunderous resurrection. The forces of nature are in the process of a sudden vast explosion. Three weeks later the face of the land has undergone a fundamental change. Warm rains and a sun with broiling rays have awakened the roots of trees and plants. On certain nights in May it is as though one can hear the buds breaking and the grass growing in the fields. Mankind, beasts and plant life have all woken from the torpor of a nightmare.

Although winter became progressively kinder through its contact with mankind, it still needed to demonstrate its superior strength. It seemed to remain in control and every year brought disaster in its wake. The tragic story of Jacques Cartier's sailors was merely one tale among thousands like it. The captain carefully set down the details of the story of the protracted martyrdom of his men, and how they gradually became dominated by the cold. One recalls how the little ships were imprisoned in the ice at the mouth of a narrow little river close to Quebec. 'In December, 1535', writes Cartier, 'we were warned that a sickness had struck down the said people of Stadaconé so violently that there were already fifty dead. Then disease of the most foul kind, completely unknown, struck us likewise: some deteriorated physically, their legs swelled and became enormous, their muscles shrivelling and blackening like coal; in some cases the men were spattered all over with purplish drops of blood. Then the said malady made its way up their legs, their thighs and shoulders, and from thence to their arms and necks. In every case the mouth became so infected, the gums so rotten, that the flesh at the roots of the teeth contracted and nearly all the teeth fell out. And so stricken with the malady were our sailors that by mid-February, of the hundred and ten men we had been, only two remained in good health.'

Father Anne de Noue, at one time page at the court of Henri IV and later a Jesuit missionary, was attached to the post of Three Rivers. In January, 1646, he set out with two soldiers and a Huron Indian to the mission at Fort Richelieu less than seventy-five kilometres away. A blizzard blew up and smothered the soldiers so

that they were unable to proceed. The *poudrerie*[1] numbed their
eyelids. Father de Noue set off alone to fetch help. He wandered
on to the white expanse of Lake St Pierre. Three days later he
was found on his knees in the snow; a statue carved out of ice.
Death by piercing cold is said to be rapid and comparatively
gentle: the blood in the arteries congeals, and induces heart failure,
then the joints stiffen and the flesh becomes rigid. Hundreds of
coureurs de bois[2] died in this silent manner. In the spring their
flesh, preserved by freezing, became choice food for carnivores.

Despite these inevitable tragedies the Canadian winter is in
fact full of splendour and magnificence. Those who decried it had
experienced only two or three inclement winters and had not been
able to accustom themselves to the vagaries of the climate. But
serious chroniclers of the time, among them some writing in the
first period of colonization, were stimulated by the spirit of the
new country with all its contrasts. And these extolled its benefits
and salubriousness.

Father Paul Le Jeune was in and around Quebec in the winter
of 1631. It was so cold that the ink froze while he drafted his
colourful *Brieve Relation*. Yet he could find only praise for the
qualities of the winter: 'It has been beautiful and fine and prolonged,' he wrote from his smoky little cabin. 'It has been beautiful
because it has been white with snow, and without mud and rain.
I do not think it has rained more than three times in the last five
months although it has snowed often. It has been fine because the
cold has been severe. It is held to be one of the worst cold spells
for many years. Everything has been covered with four or five feet
of snow, in some places there have been more than ten. In front
of our house there is a mountain of it, it drifts in the wind while
we toil to cut a little path in it up to our door. It rises to a white
rampart taller by a few feet than the roof of the house. The cold
is sometimes so intense that we can hear the trees cracking in the
woods, and it is like the noise of gunfire.'

Father Vimont wrote in the same vein about those young and
sensitive girls who, apprehensive of a single flake of snow in France,
here were undeterred by veritable mountains of it: 'A rime of

[1] *Poudrerie:* Highly fragmented snow which is a feature of blizzards in
countries of extreme cold and dryness.
[2] Colonists who preferred the freedom of the forests to the security of settled
agriculture.

frost would have chilled them in their well-protected houses, now a bad and prolonged winter armed from head to toe in snow and ice gives them scarcely a sensation of discomfort save possibly for an increase in appetite. Your damp and clinging cold is irksome; ours is piercing but still and calm and in my opinion is more agreeable, if harsher.'

Ruette d'Auteuil never tired of praising the winter in Canada. He admitted its harshness, but the settlers of the country bore it well, especially those who had been born there. He lays stress on the use of snow from an economic point-of-view; it helped in forestry and every sort of communication, since with the rivers and streams frozen over it was no longer necessary to construct bridges and embankments; an ox or horse could easily pull a load which in summer would require four animals to draw it. Having risen so enthusiastically to its defence, Ruette d'Auteuil even points out the way in which frost destroys weeds.

Winters were not always marked by extreme temperatures. There were severe ones, but there were also temperate ones; 'beautiful winters' as they have been called. It was possible from certain indications to forecast these, and the Indians were hardly ever wrong on this score. Generally speaking people put their faith in native opinion and so prepared themselves adequately. A note in *Journal des Jésuites* tells us that on December 25, 1646, the weather was so mild that it was not necessary to heat the church for midnight Mass. Marie de l'Incarnation wrote in January, 1670, that winter was excessively long and hard that year and that there had been nothing like it for more than thirty years. The following year, she notes that winter of this year did not begin until the middle of January, and was over by the middle of March. Montcalm in a letter of 1756 observed that the winter had been very mild; 'there has been only a little snow and hardly any cold weather.'

Nevertheless, generally speaking the Canadian winter is long and hard. How did the settlers in the country survive it, particularly those in poor and isolated districts? By no means was it received with enthusiasm, but nor was it viewed as a calamity, although every year it brought some tragedy with it. One became accustomed to it, making the best of things since there were practical means available by which one might come to terms with it: a house, wood, furs, game.

One of the greatest achievements of the first colonists, missionaries, *coureurs de bois* and explorers was the way in which they overcame the cold; what is more they made friends with it and learned control over it. With its help they were to found in less than one century an entire new nation. Because the white man tried to understand and tolerate it, the Canadian winter in its turn inspired him to seek out the best means of housing, to dress and feed himself, and, while the long winter months held him captive, the time to reflect upon his new destiny.

HOUSING

Particularly at the outset of colonization the Canadian had two foes to contend with: winter and the Iroquois. Winter was predictable and could be prepared for in good time. But Iroquois knew no special season. Housing, therefore, had to take account of both these factors.

At the three posts—Quebec, Three Rivers and Montreal, which Champlain wisely held to be strategic points, a central homestead to shelter the first comers was built at the very beginning. In Quebec this took the form of the 'habitation', plans for which were drawn up by Champlain himself: three sets of lodgings each eighteen feet long and fifteen wide were surrounded by a gallery on the level of the second storey. On the roof of one of the lodgings was a sundial and a great mast flying the standard of France. Another housed a store and dove-cote. A covered walk ten feet wide surrounded the homestead, which was protected by a moat fifteen feet wide and six deep, and spanned by a drawbridge. Cannon were mounted on platforms at the corners to defend the post. Commander Laviolette built a more or less identical, if less comprehensive fort at Three Rivers. The missionaries who accompanied him built him a temporary cabin constructed out of a few tree trunks cemented at the joins by a mixture of grass and earth. It covered an area of about twenty square yards in all including the chapel and the dwelling-house. The first wintering in these huts was disastrous. There were many deaths from scurvy. On December 1, 1635, the homestead at Three Rivers was burnt to the ground and almost immediately rebuilding began on two sets of lodgings, a magazine and a platform mounted with cannon. At Ville-Marie, established as an advance post against the Iroquois, the first steps towards civilization were taken with the construction of a fort, enclosed by pointed stakes and measuring a hundred yards along its sides. Enclosed within this stockade were a rudimentary chapel built of birchwood, lodgings for the Governor, missionaries, the women who had come to help the missionaries, and the colonists. There were also a magazine, a barracks and other buildings. In the following year bastions were added to the settlement to give better protection against the enemy.

At first there were temporary homesteads; lodgings were provisional. But soon the colonists grew bolder. They could not remain perpetually under the Governor's personal protection. They wanted at least a degree of independence, and this led to the gradual construction of modest houses for individual pioneer families. To begin with these were built of wood to the standards imposed by the climate. Because of the danger of avalanches it was necessary to pitch the roofs or to build hipped-roofs, well sloped and reinforced with rafters. The house which Pierre Guillet and Elie Bourbaux, themselves carpenters by trade, built for the colonist Michel Peltier measured 26 feet by 16. Despite the slenderness of the structure, the specification stipulated 'strong ties to the quoins, to bring the joists of the building well together, to raise the chimney in the shape of a dome, surrounding the house with cedarwood stakes, and covering it with two layers of boarding and one of thatch, constructing a browed roof to the north-east side in order to avoid any build-up of snow'. The barn, which included the stables, was as important and essential a building as the house itself. Since it had to contain enough fodder to keep the animals through the six or seven winter months it was a building of imposing size. The barn which was built for Michel Peltier measured 66 feet by 23, and was also constructed with a sloping roof in order to hold back the weight of snow. The ties here had to be even stronger, and it was necessary to place 'two pointed pins from ground to summit, and to rivet each joist to the ridge-plate and wall-plate'. The beams were to be placed eight or twelve inches apart, and made firm with rivets and spikes. It was necessary to exercise particular care in the construction of the building which contained the stables. All farm animals, horses, cattle, cows, pigs, fowl and sheep, had to be cooped up in this building throughout the winter months, therefore the walls had to be thick, and carefully insulated to keep out the cold, and the building must at the same time be well-ventilated so as to prevent epidemics, especially during February and March when the female stock was producing young.

Generally speaking wooden houses stood up reasonably well to the effects of cold, but there was a constant risk of fire even when the hearth, very often the only method of heating, was constructed of stone and conformed to certain elementary demands. The greatest danger lay in the towns, and after a series of tragedies the authorities were forced to lay down specifications for the materials to be employed, particularly for roofing. An order issued by the Intendant Dupuy in 1727 stipulated that 'townsmen who have collected laths for the purpose of roofing their houses must remove them and leave them for the use of those building in the country. Lath coverings may not be used in towns.' The order also stipulated that the houses of citizens must have a firewall at each corner and that the roof must be tiled.

In order to guard against the danger of fire in the countryside, houses were at first built in the normal way and laid on stone foundations mostly in districts where a great deal of rock was to be found. But it was soon clear that the sort of stone house which was constructed in France did not suit the climatic conditions of Canada. Stone is a conductor of cold; the mortar which binds it crumbles when affected by ice. Moreover the foundations of such houses lay directly upon the ground and when the springtime thaw came they were loosened. Carpenters and masons then attempted to use a wooden framework which would move with the settlement of the earth caused by the thaw, together with a mortar made from a mixture of ingredients flexible enough to withstand both the outside cold and any heat generated within the building. But this was insufficient to protect these houses from the damp cold rising out of the ground. The next idea was the use of a sort of stone foot wider than the base of the brickwork, hollowed out to allow air to circulate. The house itself was then raised upon this platform. In winter the foundations were covered with straw and rammed-down earth. This operation made it necessary to invent new words which are no longer to be found in the dictionary of the *Académie*—a pity since they are derived from the purest of roots. The stone base upon which the foundations of the house were laid was called the *solage*. The construction made from earth and straw which surrounded the *solage* and protected it against the cold was known as the *renchaussage*.

Another step then became essential—to line the interior of the house throughout with wooden laths upon which was laid plaster or roughcast made with a clay base. It appears that this is the process referred to in ancient deeds as a house *à la gasparde,* a term which, however, has not survived and whose etymology is uncertain.

The manorhouses, schools and stone houses of the eighteenth century, whose construction has stood fast for centuries so that numerous examples still remain extant after more than two hundred years, were built according to the same techniques, which descended from father to son amongst carpenters and masons. The plans for a house of normal dimensions, that is of from 50 to 60 feet long, and 20 to 23 wide, provided for foundations of 4 feet in depth and $3\frac{1}{2}$ wide; the wall to measure 2 feet 8 inches deep and $10\frac{1}{2}$ feet high from the ground floor. The rafters and quoins supporting the sloping roof were of pine or cedarwood.

Even though all houses of this type, which became a classic form of Canadian architecture, seem from the outside to be very similar, yet modern ethnographers are able to distinguish two different types of construction; one representative of houses in the region around Quebec, and another from around Montreal. R. L. Séguin offers the following explanation: usually houses in the Quebec region are rectangular, of medium height, their walls broken by shuttered windows, their roofs by dormers. The walls are whitewashed and roughcast. They have all the features of the style of building in Normandy. Indians were less inclined to raid the country around Quebec than elsewhere, therefore the settlers there felt themselves to be more secure. Their homesteads were more welcoming, less impregnable. Around Montreal, things were different, for this was the advance post on the way to the East. The Indians waged merciless guerilla warfare. The population was perpetually on its guard. Every house in the Montreal district was forced to make itself into a little domestic fortress, 'Square, massive, flanked by heavy chimneys, it was built out of great stones from the fields, and these were wedged with solid mortar. Slits were let into the walls, and concealed behind thick shutters. It was through a loophole of this kind that the settler shot at the Agnier Indians when they were out collecting scalps. Montreal houses were chiefly inspired by Breton architecture, introverted, solitary, forever watching.'

Regional differences were less marked indoors. The way in which the houses were laid out was more or less the same in all, since they had to answer identical needs. Firstly and most essentially they were built to house large families. The historian J.-Edmond Roy describes them: 'On entering the house there is a room which serves both as kitchen and bedroom. The first thing that strikes one is the huge chimneypiece, with its open fire and flagstone hearth: there are hooks for pots and pans, firedogs, a shovel, the great cauldron and stockpots, stewpans and dripping pans, the piedishes, a gridiron, a demi-john, a whole army of utensils, for the Canadian housewife has always made sure of sufficient stock in her kitchen. On a ledge hangs a set of flatirons, a tin lamp and some candlesticks. At the further end of the room stands the bed belonging to the master and mistress of the household: the bed is "furnished by the community of property" to quote the solemn words in the deeds of notaries. It is a great edifice hung with a canopy of almost 6 feet high, and fitted with a palliasse covered in ticking, a featherbed, woollen blankets and sheets, pillowcases and a bolster covered in red calico, the whole covered with a counterpane . . . The children's beds—*beaudets* or cradles, lie in the shadow of this enormous piece of furniture. The rest of the furniture is of the most fundamental kind: five or six wooden chairs with rush seats, a spinning-wheel with its spindle, a loom for weaving canvas, a trough, a table, two or three coffers, a wardrobe and, next to the door, the water-carrier. It is a proper home where men, women and children foregather together with house and farm implements. It is here that food for both family and beasts is prepared, where clothes are warmed, and where working tools are placed to thaw out.'

One of the permanent features of the Canadian house was that it was constructed in such a way as to resist all strong winds and squalls, as well as snow and rain. It was a solid spacious homestead built by reliable workmen from carefully-chosen materials.

CLOTHING

The early French colonists did not persist, as did the proud pioneers of New England, in wearing the native dress of their own country. They very soon adopted the sort of clothing which the climate and their mode of life dictated. Nowhere in *Relations des Jésuites,* nor elsewhere in chronicles of the time do we find any mention of traditional provincial or of regional French costume; not even for holiday occasions. The Sieur de Maisonneuve, who founded Montreal, having mislaid during the voyage some of his official apparel of 'lace and fine linen' was very pleased 'to be well-rid of all those vain ornaments'. And his clothing became that of the humblest dwellers, 'a grey serge cape, in the style of this country'. Even if Lambert Closse, an officer who arrived in 1674 wearing 'a hat of otterskin tied with a silver cord, capes, *petites-oies,*[1] and flame-coloured silk stockings', and if Dollard des Ormeaux, a soldier, wore the simple outfit known as the 'rhin-grave', or knee-breeches so much in vogue in many European countries, yet it does not seem as if these imported fashions were retained for very long. The colonist soon learnt to dress to some extent like the Indians or else to manufacture his own working garments, which meant he was able to avoid as much as possible the monopoly of materials so jealously guarded by the French merchants. One of the first of the *coureurs des bois,* Thomas Gode-froy, simply wore his mooseskin coat and his *mitasses* (a sort of gaiter made from material or hide). An inventory of his belongings taken at his death showed that in his modest homestead he possessed: '$5\frac{1}{2}$ ells of yellowed cowl material, 16 ells of damasked silk, 2 ells or thereabouts of silk', yet the brave Norman explorer had never made use of these imported materials.

Many people continued, nevertheless, to buy fine materials from the French drapers who had stores almost everywhere in the colony. Members of the Governor's and the Intendant's entourage still aped the fashions of the Court and faithfully imitated its whims and caprices. 'On reception days', writes Peter Kalm, 'the women of Quebec dress in such finery that one is led to believe that their relatives hold the highest offices of State.' An ordinary officer of the Sarre regiment, Meritens de Pradals, who had journeyed throughout the inhabited part of Canada, was said to be scan-dalized by the sight of such luxury in the colony: 'Luxury holds sway to a surprising extent,' he wrote to his brother. 'You never set eyes on a girl but she is dressed in damask velvet or some other silken material. Clothes are made of silk or of some beautiful Indian cotton. The peasant girls never venture out without their

---

[1] Yards and yards of ribbon used to decorate men's clothes.

lovely capes of Brussels camelot. Other people's capes are made of silk.' This was perhaps a slightly ingenuous and superficial commentary, but it was nevertheless the honest impression of an officer who had recently landed and who was able to compare life in Canada with that of the France he had left behind.

A notary, Barbel, was sufficiently indiscreet and unprofessional to furnish detailed descriptions of both the official and private wardrobe of one of the Governors of New France, the Marquis de Vaudreuil, who died at Château Saint-Louis in Quebec in 1726. Apart from ceremonial attire, the Marquis's wardrobe held twenty-two shirts of Rouen linen, decorated with batiste, twenty-three cravats of muslin, as well as others of broderie Anglaise, coifs of fine linen, caps and socks of knitted linen, dressing-gowns of taffeta, figured satin cloaks, gloves of mooseskin and beaver, etc. Nothing in this list seems to have been of typically Canadian origin. Official personages and those in their entourage invariably wore imported underclothes.

Among the working people rare mention is made of these imported materials. From 1660 onwards there were deerskin and mooseskin gloves, lined with fur, belts of catfish skin, jerkins made from the skins of bear and caribou. Gradually the peasants became used to domestic products, and the vagaries of the climate required the use of a whole gamut of different clothes. An itinerant French officer mentions not without a certain note of scorn that the country people were nearly always badly dressed and that they made their own working clothes. In fact they could not afford vanity in their dress. Despite the efforts of the Intendant of the time, Talon, the fact is that sheep-rearing seems to have been difficult and uncertain of success by reason of the proximity of the forest in which carnivorous animals swarmed. Wool remained scarce and it was necessary to use other products such as linen or hemp. But clothes made from hemp or linen have no warmth. They had to be lined with leather or some sort of common fur. Wool was reserved for undergarments for 'the body' as it was usually called, as well as for stockings. The agricultural worker wore woollen underclothes both summer and winter, for wool rapidly absorbs sweat and protects against sudden chilling.

Women with families spent nearly all their time making clothes and winter coverings, especially if they had several children. A wife was not able to think of her husband only, for her children

51

needed special care, even if they were kept indoors during the coldest spells. Since houses were not heated at night, the beds had to have warm coverings, and these were usually of fur. Housewives in search of novelty soon found a way of making *catalognes*— costumes resembling those worn in the Basque country—they collected their old clothes and cut them up into fine strips or into squares, putting them together to form a multi-coloured patchwork quilt. The less worn pieces were made into scarves or used to tie up the hair. Obviously the settlers wore clothes very different from those worn by the elegant and the soldiers. When an inventory was made of the wardrobe of Marguerite Le Gardeur, married to the Chevalier de la Grois, who had lived for a time in one of the rural parishes, it was found that Madame owned 'a costume of gold damask, one of satin, one of silk gauze from the East, a dressing-gown and a black skirt made of satin, two dozen embroidered nightgowns, and a satin scarf'.

Nicolas Rochon froze to death during the winter of 1727, and was discovered when the thaw came. 'On the said body was a cape of *cinchinas* [*sic*], a coat of white material, a waistcoat of *carise* (on the front of which was a piece of blue and red printed calico), a scapular, *malamas* [*sic*] gaiters, white hose, buskins, a belt of calico, a cotton handkerchief, a small empty purse, a tin cup, a knife, a pipe of peace with two small casket keys attached to the buttonhole of the said coat. The hair was plaited with black ribbon.'

The way in which the hair was dressed was also influenced to a great extent by the regional climate. In the first years of the colony's existence, the *tapabor*—a form of sou'wester—was worn; made of felt for winter and of straw in summer, this large-brimmed headdress kept the sun from the head, and when the brim was lowered it protected from the sun and wind. It was a headdress which had been imported, and it was very soon replaced by the cap, which was easy to make and was suited to every temperature and requirement. The gentry and the middle classes generally wore beaver hats, made from genuine beaver fur, or sometimes the 'half-beaver' made up from the fur of some other forest animal. But no one lost caste by wearing a cap, since it was a fashionable article in every class of society. It sounds a lowly form of headdress and by no means exclusive to New France, yet the Canadian cap was original because it was of interest as much for the quality and variety of the fur from which it was made as for its amusing colours when made from wool, or because of both these factors combined. Everyone tried to make his cap more original and such individual peculiarities worked towards exclusiveness. Still more so when the name of 'tuque' was devised; a term apparently derived from an old French expression 'touche', meaning a wooded hummock; a word used by Rabelais: *Les unes touches de bois haulte, belle et plaisante*. For the Canadian cap took the form of an elongated cone displaying at its tip a tassel of fur or wool, multicoloured and beautifully made.

To judge only from most inventories made after death, women seem to have been content with less complicated and striking head-dresses than men. They wore only coifs or ordinary bonnets; these ordinary caps or bonnets were 'white satin caps embroidered in imitation silver, hoods of crepe decorated with veiling, quilted bonnets of black taffeta lined with white linen, the so-called "coiffures de Bazin" '. But these inventories were drawn up by men, conscientious notaries possibly, but ill-acquainted with the extensive vocabulary of feminine dress. Peter Kalm, an educated man, supplies us with a more exact and accurate description. He observes that society women gave their coiffures 'an excessive amount of attention'. Scriveners did not take account of the fact that the *'fontange'*, the bow of ribbons which gave to seventeenth-century France so extraordinary and eccentric a range of headdress, also gave the maximum amount of trouble to Canadian ladies of fashion, though this detail did not escape the steely eye of La Hontan.

Although there was no typical costume for the Canadian under French rule, engravings and sketches of the time illustrate him wearing a woollen cap with a tassel on his head and his body encircled with a loose belt, his feet shod in native boots. This 'national costume', as it was called, of the Canadian settler owes its popularity to the fact that it became the rallying sign of patriots during the rebellion of 1837–1838 when the French-speaking Canadians revolted against the ostracism of the English. They were right in adopting it, since it owed its origins to the most deep-rooted tradition of the first settlers of New France.

FOOD AND COOKING HABITS

The high incidence of scurvy during the first wintering can directly be ascribed to an insufficiency of food. Men paid with their lives for lack of forethought in providing for the long winter, which they could not possibly survive on their diet of dried peas and biscuits. Sailors even scorned the frozen fish which kept the Indians in good health. The Canadian winter demands a rich and sufficient diet. The colonist soon realized that the provision of adequate heating and clothing for the long winter months was not enough; he must also accumulate food, as did the native animals. The right food for this sort of climate is meat and its by-products. The colonist soon grew accustomed to this theory, and from it a Canadian cuisine evolved, sometimes despised in certain milieux for its lack of refinement, but nevertheless finding favour with one observer frequently adverse in his views of the customs of this new nation.

In the spring of 1684 La Hontan made his way along the coast of Beaupré, visiting farms and interviewing the population to see how it lived, and what remained most clearly in his mind was the excellence of the tables and the warmth of the hospitality he received. He accepted invitations to dine and stay the night, and La Hontan noticed how comfortably off these people seemed and how well they lived, so much so that he wrote: 'I could wish that our impoverished aristocracy lived so well.'

The first colonists found very different sources of food from those in their own country. Different and far more plentiful. There were numerous animals. The meat of moose was wholly excellent and quite replaced the former beef and lamb. Caribou was also eaten, and American moose, usually known as venison; porcupine, hares in quantity and beaver too, sought after as much for its meat as for its fur. There were masses of birds; bustards and duck, especially, as well as pigeons, partridge, snipe and teal, which were enough to content the most demanding gourmet. Fish of fine quality was also to be found in abundance, and the St Lawrence provided a pleasing mixture of sea as well as freshwater fish; of salmon and haddock, sturgeon, bass, shad and shoals of other equally delicious commoner species, which teemed in the lakes and rivers. The commonest of these was the eel, which was very

54

often eaten—smoked or salted; a fashionable dish which provided a sizeable industry.

With all this abundance of game and fish, nevertheless there were periods of scarcity, especially during the first years of colonization. This was because certain basic products such as bread, milk and salt were lacking. Canadians have always eaten a great deal of bread, particularly wholemeal bread. 'A workman will eat two loaves a week, each six or seven pounds in weight,' wrote the author of the *Relation* of 1636. Radot, Intendant at the time, observed that 'the colonist eats two pounds of bread a day and six ounces of bacon'. If there was a bad corn harvest the settlers had to fall back on bread made from barley or rye.

Gradually with the extension of the ever-increasing reclamation of land, the colonists were able to sow and harvest enough basic products such as corn, oats, barley, peas, lentils, beans and asparagus. Other vegetables appeared in the course of time, or were imported. Cabbages were harvested from around 1675. We find no mention of celery, shallots, onions, or carrots until after the beginning of the eighteenth century. Pumpkins, which were after all indigenous products, did not appear as food until about the same time. Cucumbers and melon were perhaps the most sought after of any dessert even in high society. Peter Kalm goes out of his way to observe: 'Cucumber cut in slices, and eaten with salt is a delicious dish. It is sometimes served plain; each diner secures one of these refreshing *cucumis*, peels it, cuts it into slices and eats it with salt, quite plain as one does a radish. Melons are plentiful here. They are always served with sugar, never with wine or brandy.' Peasants working in the fields far from any water supply found another use for cucumber—it assuaged thirst. The potato, or the 'root' as it was known with disdain, was ignored by the Canadians throughout the French administration. It was made use of only when other crops were in short supply. 'This root,' remarked Champlain, 'tastes of artichoke.' Even the missionaries in the parts of the country inhabited by Indians refused to look at it except in times of extreme need. The Mother Superior of the Hôtel-Dieu in Quebec, Marie Duplessis de Saint-Hélène, wrote to a friend in France on October 17, 1737, that Canada had just borne so terrible a famine that the settlers had been reduced to eating 'the buds of trees, potatoes and other foods never intended to be used as food for human beings'.

The national food of the indigenous population was maize, known as Indian corn by the first white people, because Christopher Columbus had thought when he first tasted it that he had reached the Indies. The Indians cultivated it freely and the French soon adopted it as a basic food, since it was easy to grow, had a high nutritive content for butcher animals, and was easy to use in traditional recipes. It was eaten roasted over the coals, mixed with game or fish and mashed. Mashed Indian corn, frozen and kept through the winter, gave pea-soup or the vegetable or meat broth a distinctive taste. When Indian corn was completely ripe and slightly dried it was ground in a mortar or between two stones. Its flour was not suitable for making bread, but it was possible to make from it a sort of pancake which could be kept longer than bread made from wheat or rye. It was also eaten in the form of *sagamité*, a soup made from the flour mixed with dried fish and peas.

There were many varieties of fruit growing wild, of many species, deliciously flavoured and producing an important source of revenue for the country people. Fruit was eaten raw or in the form of jam or jelly. The commonest fruits were strawberries, raspberries, wild plums, blackberries, cranberries, currants, wild cherries and bilberries, fruit particularly relished by bears. *Les Relations des Jésuites* in 1633 and 1634 spoke of apples: 'The savages eat apples which grow wild and are sweeter than those in France, and which are to be found in the St Lawrence islands.' As early as 1608, the year when Quebec was founded, Champlain planted some apple trees from Normandy which had been sent by M. de Monts, and which survived the Canadian climate so well that twenty-five years later they were still yielding fully.

The most fashionable food, and one dating from the inception of the colony, was the pie or 'pièce tourtière' as it was called, together with salt bacon and eel, either smoked or salt. These foods were popular for economic reasons. The pie could be used to make an almost endless variety of dishes. Salt bacon and smoked eel had the advantage of being able to survive the hottest weather.

In France the *tourtière* pie-dish was a kitchen utensil for cooking pigeon and other birds. The contents of the dish were known as 'pièce tourtière' and during the first years in New France these distinctive words were used. The *Journal des Jésuites* notes that in 1646 the seigneur of Beauport, M. Giffard, sent to the Holy Fathers 'two raised pies'. Over the years the word 'tourtière' came to mean a pâté of fowl or game cooked and seasoned according to a special household recipe in the family stewpan, for into it went not merely turtle-doves but every kind of edible bird: partridge, 'white birds', snipe, teal, plover, bustard, duck. Every housewife possessed her own secret recipe, jealously preserved from generation to generation. It was in this way that some venturesome housewives began to prepare 'pièces tourtières' not only with birds but with the meat of both wild and domestic animals. Such recipes held additional appeal since they provided more filling and sustaining meals. Something like the 'tourtière' became very popular in the coastal regions; this was a dish called 'sipaille'—a word taken from the English 'sea-pie'. Into a casserole, separated by thin layers of pastry, went every kind of seafood: haddock, cod, shad, bass, salmon, sturgeon. The preparation was then well-seasoned with herbs and simmered in a covered dish over a slow fire for several hours. Eventually 'sipaille' came to mean a dish similarly prepared but in which the ingredients consisted of meat, herbs and vegetables. This was a dish which enjoyed a great deal of popularity in community life, and in large families, since it was both economical and nourishing.

Salt bacon, which could be kept for months, demanded meticulous preparation in order to enable it to withstand the many variations in temperature. If even one hogshead of this precious food were to go bad, a situation near to famine might arise within the household during the winter months. The same degree of care which went into the preparation of the actual meat and the saltpetre was used to see that the willow wood was of the required quality. Salt bacon was very convenient for farmers who had to have their meals in the fields during the hot months. The *coureurs des bois* and the missionaries enjoyed it that much more since it was so great an improvement on the loathsome Indian food.

An officer who had come originally from the Languedoc, one Jean-Baptiste d'Aleyrac, writing down his impressions of Canada for his family in the year 1755, observed that the preparations made by the Canadians for the winter reminded him of the behaviour of ants. 'They provide themselves with everything', he wrote, 'for the winter, while summer is still with us. They kill everything they require for the period from the end of November until the end of April, when the snow has gone and the thaw has come. They stock up with meat as if they would eat it at a single meal, and they put it in a storehouse where it freezes and is thus preserved. When they want to eat it they thaw it over a stove, and then prepare it as if it came straight from the butcher; for by this time the meat is still as fresh and good as when it was killed. Milk freezes in the winter to a degree where it is possible to carry it about in a solid state in sacks for sale in the town.' D'Aleyrac noticed too that the Canadians ate well and were big meat-eaters. 'There is not a single person with a wife and two or three children who in winter does not kill an ox and a cow, as well as two pigs, sheep, chickens, geese, turkeys, not to mention the game and fish which they hunt for in quantities throughout the winter.'

Despite this abundance of food, much was still imported. Especially sweetmeats, fruit and, above all, drink. Fruits such as lemons, oranges, olives and figs were imported. The *Journal des Jésuites*, to which we must return in order to find these small and homely details, informs us that in 1664 the Fathers received as a present 'a branch of plums from Tours'. Olive oil, walnuts and fish; quantities of spice; pepper, cloves, nutmeg, cinnamon, vinegar and salt; sugar, especially brown sugar, as well as molasses, were imported. Maple sugar produced in the country did not come into fashion and was not used until the English administration.

To describe fully the drinks of the country would require an entire chapter: brandy, rum, Spanish wines, madeira, malaga, anisette and other refined liquors were imported. Spirits were served a great deal at social gatherings in the towns, and at the taverns and inns were sold at an exorbitant price, especially to newly-arrived officers and soldiers. Expensive refined spirits of this kind did not suit the ordinary people, and the cost of importing them went some way to weaken the country's economy. From the start of colonization the people had dreamed of making 'poor man's champagne': beer, *cerevisia*[1]—the so-called bouillon', and cider, which would remind immigrants of the modest drinks of the old country. 'There is in this country', wrote Pierre Boucher in 1664, 'a beverage which is called "bouillon"; it is drunk universally and in almost every household.' This was a mash of wheat or maize, fermented, diluted with water and allowed to mature in cask. As with beer, the Sovereign Council forbade its sale to the natives; but this law was ignored by those who manufactured the bouillon. Brandy or 'fire-water' which was given to the Indians in order to

[1] A sort of barley beer.

extort their furs from them at rock-bottom prices, was usually a horrible mixture of domestic beer with fermented wheat and barley and certain types of boiled roots. The settlers continued to make their 'bouillon', and the only inn-keeper in Quebec at the time, although he answered to the name of Jacques Boisdon—not inaptly—had a particularly large clientele of itinerant soldiery which preferred imported and refined drinks. Later, especially after the royal route between Quebec and Montreal was opened, inns grew up at the staging points. But there also, particularly in winter, the traveller preferred 'warming drinks'. An order issued by Dupuy the Intendant in 1726 stipulated that every innkeeper must hang from the door of his establishment for the purposes of identification, 'a branch of green pine needles or of some evergreen which will keep its leaves through the winter'.

A description of the habits of the townspeople has been left us by Peter Kalm. Meals were, as they are to this day in Canada, breakfast, dinner and supper. Breakfast which was normally at eight o'clock was a fairly light meal; 'some are content with no more than a piece of bread soaked in brandy, others begin with a glass of brandy and this is followed by a slice of toast or a cup of chocolate. Many of the ladies drink coffee. Dinner, which is around mid-day, and supper which is between seven and eight o'clock in the evening consist of more or less the same kind of food. A great variety of dishes are served both in upper-class as well as middle-class houses, when they entertain,' Kalm goes on. 'Bread, baked in an oval shape is made from wheatflour. Each person's plate is laid with a napkin, a spoon and a fork. Sometimes knives are laid but more often they are omitted, for each lady and gentleman brings his or her own knife. The meal begins with soup, together with a large helping of bread, and this is followed by every kind of fresh meat, boiled and roasted, by game, fowls, fricasséed or stewed in casseroles, all served with various sorts of salad. At dinner the drink is usually claret, diluted with water. Spruce beer is also fashionable. The ladies drink water, or occasionally wine. After dinner there is dessert, which comprises a variety of fruit, walnuts from France or Canada, either fresh or preserved, almonds, grapes, hazelnuts, various species of berry which ripen in the summer, such as currants and cranberries crystallized in molasses, sweet jams made of strawberries, raspberries, blackberries, and other briar fruits.

Cheese also appears with the dessert, as well as milk which is taken at the end of the meal with sugar.'

In the countryside, especially when there was a lot of hard work to be done on the farm, the peasants needed four full meals a day. They rose at dawn and before they sat down to table at eight in the morning they had already done three or four hours' work. Therefore breakfast was, together with the evening meal, the most solid meal of the day. It usually consisted of pancakes made from wheatflour, and a bowl of creamy milk in which a lump of bread was dipped. Milk nearly always replaced tea and coffee—an enormous amount of it was drunk. In some families it was poured into a great earthenware crock in the middle of the table. In it were thrown crusts of bread and everyone helped himself in the same way as he did with soup. The other meals were eaten at mid-day, at four o'clock and at eight o'clock in the evening. The mid-day and four o'clock meals were considerably lighter in character, they were eaten hurriedly between the carting of loads of hay or grain, and in working hours when the horses and cattle themselves required rest.

During the Seven Years' War, a new and unheard-of dish appeared, to which the Canadians took instant loathing—horse-meat. The settler in the countryside possessed other resources and kept secure hiding places for the prey he caught out hunting. But the townsman was forced to content himself with what he could get and he cursed the Intendant and his entourage for having already carried off all the oxen and sheep.

The Canadians strictly observed the long periods of fasting which were imposed upon them by the Church. Not only did they abstain from eating meat and the by-products of milk every Friday and Saturday, but these foods were also forbidden during the forty-nine days of Lenten fast, which included the forty days of Lent, followed by the nine days' vigil for the religious feast-days. There were even more days of abstinence: during the seventeenth century, for example, there were one hundred and forty-three, that is to say ten less than in the preceding century. Generally speaking 'Lenten behaviour' was laid down by rules in the *Catéchisme* by Mgr de Saint-Vallier, which had spread into nearly every family. This Canadian bible decreed that on prescribed days one could eat neither meat nor milk products, eat one meal only each day, nearly always at mid-day, and a light collation when required. So if meat and milk products were forbidden, what was left? Bread, fish and vegetables. Slices of bread were parsimoniously weighed in order not to exceed the prescribed weight. The peasants had never particularly enjoyed eating fish. Some of them resorted to eating beaver or muskrat meat, which were allowed by the Church since these animals were amphibious.

Such was the religious discipline of these people that 'to miss one's Lenten duties' was always considered a serious sin. Menus for days of abstinence were laid down: Kalm observed that 'the peasants make a great meal of onions which together with a slice of bread comprises their dinner menu on Fridays and Saturdays and fast days'. The *coureurs des bois* did not respect the rules as rigorously as did the peasants: 'Many of our oarsmen ate meat today—Friday', a missionary drew attention to it as if by confessing on their behalf he could absolve them. These people with their hard lives needed a substantial amount of food; everyone knew this well, and generally speaking small lapses were ignored. But, both in town and country penalties for those who deliberately transgressed the rules of the Church, and so caused scandal, were severe. Thus, when a citizen of the Ile d'Orléans, one Louis Gaboury, was denounced by a neighbour for having ignored the rules of Lent, the seigneurial tribunal condemned him 'to forfeit a cow and one year's profit from the aforesaid cow' to the man who had denounced him; furthermore he was condemned to be tied to the public stake for three hours, and then to the front of the parish chapel 'kneeling, hands tied, bareheaded, to ask God's forgiveness, as well as that of the King and the Justice, for having eaten meat during Lent without asking leave from the Church to do so, and in addition a fine of twenty *livres* is to be paid to promote pious works in the parish'. The colonists of New England scornfully referred to the Canadians as 'bacon and pea-soup eaters'. But no one could persuade them to change their daily menu. With her various sorts of meat-pie, her salt bacon, game and fish, the Canadian housewife was able to produce with an amazing skill an astonishing variety of dishes, full of flavour, which would invariably appear on feast-days or on occasions when travellers from 'the country up North' returned after a fruitful voyage.

CHAPTER FOUR

THE ARMY AND THE ADMINISTRATION

THE ADMINISTRATION

Champlain was accorded the title of Governor of New France in the year 1627. He received the privilege from Richelieu in accordance with the charter of the Company of One Hundred Associates. Thenceforward, however, all his successors were to be nominated officially by Royal Commission, and invested with military, administrative and civil powers. Since the central government in Quebec was remote, special Governors were appointed for Three Rivers and Montreal at the inception of these two towns. The title of 'Governor' was bestowed with the special purpose of impressing the Indians, although real powers were limited by royal decree 'to those conferred upon the commanders of fortified places and castles, and only on questions pertaining to the control of weapons'. As time went on these special Governors, chosen from among the military, built up their own little courts, imitating the Governor-General himself, who would have liked to copy the French Court.

In 1635, when the colony boasted scarcely 600 settlers, the first Government with any democratic pretensions was set up. The Company of One Hundred Associates had just given place to a Canadian society which took the significant name of the 'Community of Habitants of New France'. The principal aim of this society was to manage and legislate for the fur trade on the spot. But the Community had at heart the welfare of those families who had decided to adopt the new country as their own.

This new form of government was administered by the Governor-General, the Superior of the Jesuit Seminary in Quebec, the Governor of Montreal Island, and three syndicate members elected to speak and act on behalf of the citizens of the three towns in existence at this time. In 1663, after various experiments, the colony recognized a form of administration which would from now on remain unchanged—a Governor-General, an Intendant, a Council made up of the most important citizens in the colony. The organization of religious life itself had just been put on a proper footing by the appointment of Mgr de Laval.[1]

The administration set up in 1663 was inspired to some degree by that of 1645 which had won itself a good reputation—but it was not of the same quality, for this time the people were no longer represented by an electoral vote. Members of the Sovereign Council were nominated jointly by the Governor and the Bishop, and this entailed a certain amount of conflict. The Bishop was then replaced by the Intendant, whereupon further difficulties arose. Finally, in 1675 the King reserved for himself the right of nomination and appreciably reduced the functions of the Council, thereby increasing the Intendant's powers without augmenting those of the Governor. Deprived in this way of some of its prerogatives, the Council, a body which portrayed an image of autocracy, was no longer Sovereign. Even so, the King was not satisfied, and in 1703 he deprived the Council of its title of 'Conseil Souverain', and substituted the term 'Conseil Supérieur', bringing the Intendant back into it as member.

It was Colbert who succeeded in convincing Versailles that the Intendant was the real inspiration of all activity and progress within the colony, and from then on the principal administrative powers were gradually increasingly delegated to this great deputy; justice, finance, the police. The people themselves accepted with apparent resignation the fact that they no longer enjoyed any direct representation in the administration of the colony. As Lanctot correctly observed, if a particular law or ruling was especially unacceptable, they did not even show their displeasure—they simply ignored it: 'The irresistible force of inertia.'

Inevitably misunderstandings arose between the Intendant and the Governor whose prerogatives were limited to organization of the military, but who sought nevertheless to interfere in civil administration. The Intendant was nearly always given the benefit of the doubt against the Governor, and sometimes against the Bishop, because he was nearer to the spirit of the people and he listened to and understood their demands. The Intendant, to a greater extent than the Governor, had the confidence of the

[1] The first Bishop of Canada.

Secretary of State responsible for the colonies, and for much of the time, of the King himself.

Furthermore, the Governor and the Intendant did not come from the same social milieu. While the first was chosen for his military qualities, or his social background, the second was nearly always recruited from the middle classes, and had either a political or a legal background. In any case successive Intendants, with the exception of the last one, Bigot, did not generally misuse the power which went with responsibilities. Their behaviour may be summed up in two words: integrity and devotion to duty. They were conscientious servants of the State. When the Intendant Talon wrote to Colbert after years of service, full of enthusiasm about the programme he himself had drawn up, he was not boasting; he was speaking the truth. 'I have for some time now denied myself the pleasures of life: indeed I may say I have preferred my task in Canada to any other, and I can assure you that I sacrifice everything to my work and that it is my one and only pleasure to attempt to honour you through my duties.'

Until around 1730 the Governor lived permanently in Quebec. Subsequently he set up his headquarters in Montreal for the first four or five months of each year. It was here that he received the chiefs of Indian tribes and commanders of remote outposts, and verified the lists of trading permits which he had to approve. The Governor's progress was one of the great events of the year. As on other occasions the King's representative in New France travelled with the same ceremony as the great Monarch himself. Franquet, the engineer, was in the entourage of the Governor Dusquesne when he made the journey from Quebec to Montreal during the winter of 1753, and he described his voyage in his *Mémoires:* Twenty officers were included in the Governor's suite, as well as his personal servants, chefs, and a large company of soldiers. Since the favoured route had to be in good repair, the procession was led by the chief surveyor. Behind him followed a dozen or more chaises and sleighs, and it was his job to instruct the local inhabitants to clear snow-drifts, and to prepare the way for the carriages of the representative of the King, and his entourage. The return journey was made by barge and the people of those seigneuries which the Governor had indicated his intention of visiting, received orders to leave their work in the fields, and to foregather dressed in their best clothing in the courtyard of the seigneur's manor-house, which, cursing, they obeyed. The spirit of independence and liberty was already sufficiently entrenched in their attitude to life for them to suspect that the King's representative was exceeding his powers in forcing them to come and admire him when they could easily dispense with his patronage. Furthermore they were aware that most of the privileges they did enjoy were obtained from the Intendant and not from the Governor.

The colonists had not forgotten that Talon's first public gesture on his arrival had been to visit their families, and that during a famine the Intendant de Meulles had 'procured bread for a thousand unfortunates who without his help would have died of hunger'.

The efforts which Intendants made in order to understand and to treat fairly these fiercely independent people mitigated the burden of ordinances which were seldom appreciated by the people for whose welfare and safety they were devised.

Two separate bodies of the army contributed to the defence of Canada: the colonial militia, and the regiments which were sent out from France. The militia had been engaged, either individually or in small improvised groups, first for defence against the Indians, then against the English. Their lack of experience was compensated for by their courage and instinctive sense of self-preservation, until the next generation was able to adopt native methods of warfare. The French troops known as 'troops of the Marine detachment' were directly under the Secretary of State for War but their equipment and their pay were provided for by the Naval budget, after a disagreement between Louvais and Colbert as to the urgency of the need for such troops being sent to Canada.

The militia dated back to the arrival of the first immigrants. Raised exclusively from the settlers in the country and those engaged without experience of military strategy, its principal aim was to deal with the enemy attacks by any means temporarily available. The immigrants had been promised soldiers to accompany them and protect them against the Indians. This promise was only in part fulfilled. The colonists therefore not only had to double as soldiers but also to manufacture their own essential weapons. Quebec, which was a kind of natural fortress, was less exposed than both Three Rivers and Montreal.

Ville-Marie (Montreal) was the town most threatened. The first thing M. de Maisonneuve, the first Governor, did on his arrival in 1642 was to set his men to build a fort. The Governor based his construction on the scientific methods being used at the time in Europe, and he believed that a building entirely surrounded by water must be invulnerable. But he soon realized how much he had misjudged native habits. The Indians hid themselves in small groups sometimes for hours on end, behind trees, or lurking in the bushes, noiselessly creeping from one tree to another, silently, like snakes. They lay in wait for some isolated colonist to appear. An arrow sprang from no apparent source, and the wretched man fell dead to the ground before he could cry out. This was a period of long and painful martyrdom. From 1642 to 1659 almost 500 people came to Ville Marie. By the year 1660, despite the birth of more inhabitants, there were barely 300 left, and only fifty heads of families. Here is a typical example of almost routine tragedy: one August morning in 1660, the Sulpician Abbot M. Jacques Lemaître returned from Mass and set off with about fifteen colonists, to make his way to a farm, St Gabriel, a solid stone construction. It was a beautiful day, ideal for cutting the corn. In the customary way some of them set to work while others remained on watch. M. Lemaître, although realizing from certain indications that Iroquois were near, hesitated to inform his companions. Musket in hand he went forward alone, silently searching the surrounding bushes. He was alarmed, and with reason: suddenly twenty Iroquois rushed out of a nearby coppice shouting war-cries and brandishing tomahawks. M. Lemaître acted swiftly; allowing his companions to escape, or at least to have time to recover their senses and to take up arms, he fell upon the Indians who had paused momentarily out of respect for his cloth: he was cut down almost at once but his colonist companions were able to retreat meanwhile in good order to the farm. One of them was riddled with arrows before he reached the door. Another was taken prisoner. To demonstrate their contempt for the people in the fort, the band of Indians carried out their war dance around the farm walls, flourishing spikes stuck with the heads of the Sulpician Abbot and the murdered colonist. One of the Redskins put on the priest's cassock, using his shirt as a surplice.

These atrocities could largely have been avoided had the defence of the colony been conducted with a little more intelligence. Maisonneuve still placed faith in the possible aid which France might send. By the time he realized that no help was forthcoming, he had only fifty men left with him in any condition to fight. His ordinance of 1663 was twenty years too late. 'Paul de Chomedey, Governor of Montreal Island and of its dependent territories: on advice we have received from various sources to the effect that Iroquois are intending to take this settlement by surprise, and in view of the fact that the aid which His Majesty promised has not yet arrived, in consideration that this island belongs to the Blessed Virgin, we have thought it our duty to pray and exhort all who are anxious to serve to form themselves into forces of seven men each, and after electing a leader by majority vote, to seek enrolment in our garrison, and thus to fulfil the orders received by us to defend our country.' Maisonneuve had watched the finest elements in the colony dwindle away, and this was why he decided to issue his ordinance. Shortly afterwards a secret instruction from the Court recalled him to France.

While these unhappy developments were taking place in Montreal, the situation was no better around Three Rivers. The town was fortunate in having Pierre Boucher as commander; an intelligent man and one who understood the mentality of the Indians, for he had lived among their tribes. Governor d'Ailleboust realized in 1651 that only by holding this post could the colony be saved, and he issued strict orders to Boucher as commander to instruct the population in marksmanship. Furthermore each settler was to go from house to house at regular intervals in order to ascertain that no one had disposed of his arms without permission. Every citizen was responsible for seeing that those who went to work kept constant watch and were at all times armed with loaded muskets. When the stockade and the redoubt had been completed the Commander was to divide the village into three or four detachments if there were sufficient men available; these detachments were to take it in turns to remain on guard each night in the little fort overlooking the fields. A permanent sentry was to be posted so that there could be no risk of surprise by the enemy from outside; the Commander must do everything in his power to complete the construction of the stockade as quickly as possible, and must record the number of working days put in by each individual as his share in the task. Failure to obey these rules and any act of insubordination to be severely punished.

These orders record the first serious attempt on the part of the settlers to organize the defence of their country. Pierre Boucher was no more a career soldier than were his companions. But he was aware that the settlers must be taught to be self-reliant. His first care was to effect radical changes within the town. A reconstructed plan showing the grants of land as they were at that date indicates that these extended over almost the whole area of the lower part of the modern town. Boucher attempted to concentrate the homesteads and to enclose the population within an area of 120 by 200 yards, encircled with a structure of solid stockades continually watched over by a group of sentries raised by order of the Governor. Every individual received as his share a stretch of land of hardly more than fifty square yards instead of the forty acres which he had formerly possessed and which he had begun to reclaim. It was specifically laid down that each had to build a house for himself, and to work upon the construction of 'an enclosure of strong spikes'. Thanks to his inborn sense of leadership as well as to his influence upon his fellow citizens, Boucher succeeded in holding back the enemy, at least for the time being. In the words of the Governor, Lauzon, when he accorded Boucher the accolade: 'Had it not been for you, the country would have been lost.'

Despite such relative success, the safety of the colony remained largely in the balance. Nevertheless the miracle of seemingly impossible survival gradually came to pass and inspired the minds of orphan children whose fathers had fallen victim to the Iroquois. These young men took implacable revenge. The original settlers had been colonists first and soldiers afterwards. Their sons were to be soldiers first. They themselves had come to share the subtle and automatic instincts displayed by the Indians in self-defence, and they were soon to win the admiration of the authorities, who entrusted them with the future safety of the colony.

The hardiness of this younger generation was past belief, and the authorities relied upon it. As children they had survived the worst possible winters. As adolescents they had run wild in the woods, had paddled canoes, lived among the natives whose habits and cunning they had come to understand, and whose language they spoke. By the time they were fifteen they were perfect athletes.

68

Until then no one had looked after them in any way except perhaps to try to prohibit them from hunting, their sole means of survival. The Governor, Denonville, who had observed them carefully, summed them up. 'The Canadians are difficult to govern. They love liberty and have a loathing of authority.' This remark, intended as censure, was more like praise, and the Governor soon realized it and revised his views.

In the autumn of 1685 came the shattering news that the English installed in Hudson Bay had just carried off four thousand pounds' weight of beaver pelts, and were now engaged in dressing them in preparation for the transport of these precious commodities to London. To steal beaver from the Canadians was like taking bread from their mouths. It was also a humiliation. An expedition was planned; it was a long and dangerous journey of more than 1,800 kilometres, which must be made overland, for France would not risk ships on such a foolhardy expedition which she thought to be foredoomed. 'Only the Canadians could put up with the discomfort of such a dangerous expedition,' declared one of the directors of the *Compagnie du Nord* to Denonville. The soldiers were reluctant since the detachment was commanded by the Chevalier de Troyes of whose former exploits they knew nothing. Besides, soldiers born in New France did not accept command under a Frenchman no matter who he was. But one of their number, d'Iberville, was appointed second in command, and when d'Iberville agreed to go off to war his fellow citizens followed him without question. The expedition set off in February, 1686, not to return until they had beaten the foe—by which time these 'men of steel' would have journeyed almost 4,000 kilometres in six months.

Denonville marvelled at so much courage and tenacity. He advised the Court to form an army which should be completely colonial and made up from *coureurs de bois* and from these young men so eager for adventure who knew the country so thoroughly. Where the Governor went wrong was in waiting, before taking action, for the approval of Versailles. This never reached him.

Meanwhile, the Governor Frontenac had gone swiftly into action. He too was convinced that there was only one way to defeat the Indians, and this was to use their own methods against them. And these methods were understood only by Canadians born in the country. It was in this vein that he wrote to Pontchartrain: 'War in Canada is not conducted as it is in other countries. Each

officer takes up his tree. It is impossible to fight in formation.' To
'take up a tree' meant to ambush in Indian fashion. Without
awaiting the Court's permission, for time was short, Frontenac made
his Canadian officers responsible for deploying their men in whatever way they judged best. He knew perfectly well that he could
trust these young but experienced fighters, who had lived, either
voluntarily or as prisoners, the same lives as the Indians, and who
had carefully observed their fighting habits.

In 1689 there took place an appalling massacre of the people of
Lachine, a village standing at the very gates of the city of Montreal.
Within a few hours, every man, woman and child had been killed
or taken prisoner, every house burnt down by fire. Everyone knew
that this was the work of the Iroquois, but it was soon apparent
that they had been organized and armed by Dongan, the Governor
of New England, an Irish Catholic, whose hatred of the French
was notorious. At an urgent council of war summoned by
Frontenac it was d'Iberville who summed up in a few words the
determination of all present: 'I see no reason why we should not
give as good as we have received.' These words were marching
orders, and the subsequent campaign conducted against the villages
of New England was one of the most savage in the whole of
American history; in skilful methods, in bravery, in swiftness of
action, as well as in sheer horror, it exceeded anything that de
Frontenac could possibly have envisaged.

The strategy for the occasion was meticulously planned in the
Governor's office: three commanders were chosen, one from each
of the three Governments, and these in turn chose their men
from their own native towns. d'Ailleboust of Manthet, who had
been born in Montreal, was twenty-seven, and had already acquit-
ted himself well in earlier campaigns which had taken him as far
as Lake Superior with du Lhut. His task was to take Corlaer.
Robineau de Bécancour, aged thirty, had been born in Quebec.
Since his youth he had fought in Acadia. He wished to occupy
Casco Bay near Boston, since he had already explored this region.
François Hertel, the eldest and most experienced of the group, was
forty-eight, a native of Three Rivers. When he was only sixteen
he had been captured by the Iroquois and came to understand
their language and customs to perfection. His task was to take
Salmon Falls. His force was the largest of the three, consisting of
fifty men from Three Rivers and twenty-five Abenaki Indians.

These three armed forces, numbering barely 250 men in all, marched out to conquer New England. They set off in the depths of winter to cover 500 kilometres in a trackless region. But distance meant nothing to these Canadians. Wearing snowshoes they raced through the snow, their baggage trains carrying a few necessary provisions to be used only in cases of extreme emergency. They marched for a week on the icy windswept waste which was the great Lake Champlain. They slept in the snow, ignoring the cold and the *poudrerie*, maintaining life on a diet of frozen hare, biscuits and suet. Their Indian auxiliaries instructed them en route in some of the stratagems of defence which they had not yet learned.

Each group reached its objective and events moved swiftly. The force from Montreal, commanded by d'Ailleboust de Manthet, second in command to d'Iberville, and his brother Sainte-Helène, arrived at Corlaer, a fortified village, under cover of darkness. Eighty houses were looted and burned. Those who tried to resist were massacred by the Indians, who had no understanding of war without bloodshed, but the bulk of the people surrendered without any resistance. François Hertel reached Salmon Falls, which was better defended than Corlaer, and divided up his men into three parties. The besieged town soon realized that it had no alternative but to surrender. Hearing of this capitulation, 200 citizens of the neighbouring village of Pescadouet advanced to attack the enemy, but Hertel deployed his men at the entry to the bridge, and surrounded the assailants. Leaving the Abenakis who were with him to guard the prisoners, he made his way rapidly to Casco Bay and found Robineau de Bécancour already there together with his small force of men from Quebec. The English offered no resistance. In order to avenge these three defeats, Admiral Phipps was sent out by Dongan a few months later to lay siege to Quebec. Frontenac, however, knew that he was safe: 'I will reply to your Admiral through the mouths of my cannon,' he said to Phipp's envoy who had summoned him to deliver up the town. Whereupon Phipps raised anchor.

'They have done the most astonishing things,' Frontenac wrote after this episode in his official report, referring to the colonial militia who had, after all, like the hero of 'l'Aiglon' fought for nothing more than glory. It was true, for they had received neither money nor food, nor compensation for the uniforms they

71

had fought in, nor for their provisions. They had gone off to fight in the way they went off to work in the fields, with their own weapons, their uniforms sewn by their wives in the regulation colours of each government. This country which they were defending and which they sought to protect and preserve, was theirs to live and die in, and they were ready to make any sacrifice to keep it so. They made only one proviso; that they fight in their own way and without intimidation from anyone.

Nevertheless it was not long before the experience and hardiness of such valuable recruits came to be exploited. In 1712 the Intendant, Bégon, and the Governor, Rigaud de Vaudreuil, expressed their intention of reducing the number of horses in the countryside in order to force the settlers to wear snowshoes. They explained quite unabashedly: 'Knowing full well that it is essential to encourage them in this method of getting about which will always ensure their superiority over the English. . . . It is in the interests of those in charge of the colony that the settlers be strong and healthy.'

It was now obvious that the Canadian militia was indispensable, and it was treated as such. The Governor Dusquesne, went further than de Vaudreuil or Bégon. He compelled the Canadians to enlist. Conscription is never an agreeable measure, even if those upon whom it is imposed may be brought to accept it when their country is in peril. Dusquesne had seen that the newly disembarked regiments were under strength, and he was determined to force the settlers into compulsory service to repair the gap, thereby showing how completely this newly-appointed Governor lacked any degree of understanding of his people.

The captain of militia, who had to take orders from the recruiting officer, was in fact the head of the parish, in cases where the seigneur was not himself a soldier. He was the chosen representative of the authorities and was appointed to the post by the militiamen of his parish, after a carefully organized election. It was usually the Governor who approved the choice and who granted the commission. The captain of the militia acted as a link between the authorities and the parishioners, receiving and communicating orders, decrees and judgments and supervising their execution. If he considered an order to be too severe or draconian then he alone was privileged to present the people's grievances to his superiors.

Training for the career of officer was carried on in this sort of environment during boyhood. When, in 1684, the Governor of La Barre remarked that Charles Le Moyne had 'fought in more actions against the Iroquois than has any other officer in Canada', he was commemorating forty years of soldierly exploits begun at the age of fifteen, interrupted only by a spell on the staff of Marshal d'Humiéres on the battlefields of Europe. The sons of Le Moyne, who were numerous, lived in this atmosphere of daily warfare and were all to follow in their father's footsteps. By the age of thirteen d'Iberville had already sailed the whole way up the St Lawrence from Montreal to Gaspé and the island of Anticosti—and this river is harder to navigate than the Atlantic itself. François Hertel was the same age when he fought a guerilla action alongside colonists who were temporarily acting as soldiers. He was taken prisoner by the Iroquois who adopted him. From them he learnt their language and customs. His career was both remarkable and one of the most glorious imaginable.

The Governor, Denonville, sent some of these Canadians to France, to allow them to learn something of 'the rules of warfare'. His successors followed his example. When they returned to their country these soldiers were able to put into practice the techniques they had learned, combining them with their own military skills. They very soon supplanted the French officers in command of the force of marines, whose stay in Canada was unlikely to offer them much chance of promotion since they were engaged in a 'peculiar form of war'. These Frenchmen felt themselves to be inferior to the Canadian officers and their men who accomplished such miracles with whatever equipment they had been able to muster. The exploits of d'Iberville left them spellbound. This small dynamic character never waited to act on Court or Governor's orders. He was always so many thousands of kilometres distant from headquarters that he had usually carried its orders out before he even received them. His sole aim was the defence of his country, and he, more completely than anyone, knew what measures he must take to achieve it.

Canadian officers, now under official discipline, regretted the good old days when they had been free to take action on their own initiative, as for example under the Governor Frontenac who had given them 'carte blanche', or again under d'Iberville who had led them to adventure. Neither course was now open to them. In

1722 the Governor de Vaudreuil drew up a list of officers serving in Canada, and added his comments on their record of service as well as upon the qualities and defects of each. More than half of these officers were Canadian by birth, and de Vaudreuil seemed to take pleasure in emphasizing their nationality as if by so doing he was investing them with some kind of honour. For he knew them well. He had fought with them when he had been Commander-in-Chief of the Army.

When, for example, he was considering the potentialities of the Sieur de Sabrevoix, he wrote: 'He has seen better days and has a sharp eye for personal advantage, and I would not myself appoint him to a post which involved dealing in trading activities. Apart from this he has a record of good service and good discipline.' This man might be mercenary but at least he was a gallant officer. M. de Vaudreuil was at pains to point out the fact.

The son of the great hero François Hertel was the subject of very special mention: 'The Sieur Hertel de la Fresnière who is fifty years old has served very well and is fit to serve again in spite of being badly wounded in the wars against the Iroquois. He is sensible, astute and prudent, is pious and potentially useful, for he can interpret several native tongues.'

The Governor in this way gave his considered opinion on every officer from those on the staff down to ensigns. He wished to keep them under his care and above all to treat them with the utmost fairness. He did not usually waste his sympathy on French officers. The Sieur Tiersan, who was thirty years of age, was fit for duty, 'but his character leaves much to be desired by reason of his bad habits and behaviour; it is to be hoped for his own sake that he will improve'. Thus at least a shred of hope was left to this old reprobate.

When they were discharged from military service, officers who were unable to obtain administrative posts were forced to fight another engagement which they rarely won—the struggle for a reasonable pension. In this they hardly fared differently from those serving in France, although in Canada they were lucky enough if they so desired to earn a seigneurie where they could establish soldiers from their own companies.

Others worked to obtain 'leave to traffic in furs' which would bring them, if not a fortune, at least an honest living or simply an opportunity for adventure.

74

Whilst these officers of the early years of the colony grew old in peace and poverty, their sons continued to carry swords and muskets on every front in America, alongside their faithful Indian companions. They moved through the Ohio Valley and the Alleghany mountains, setting up military posts. Most of them accompanied Céloron de Blainville, and Charles Le Moyne de Longueil who, at the instance of the Governor of Louisiana, were to carry the war against the Chicaca Indians into the adjoining region. When Blainville received this order he and his men were patrolling the lands around Lake Michigan. Without hesitation he left to join forces with de Longueil, who had set out from Montreal with his own force and a few French officers. Most of the force were Canadians: Sabrevois, Le Gardeur de Saint-Pierre, Ligneris, Coulon de Villiers, Drouet de Richerville, Hertel de la Fresnière, Robineau de Portneuf. It was a disagreeable march over 3,000 kilometres undertaken in appalling conditions. The Canadian winter gave way suddenly to the torrid heat and virulent humidity of the Mississippi basin. Barely 500 men had been sent out to impose reason upon several thousand clever and cruel Indians well versed in cunning. The expedition was on the verge of failure when Céloron, in a final effort, made an attack in 'Canadian fashion'. These tactics served temporarily to save the inhabitants of Louisiana.

The French soldier was an incongruous even an intrusive figure among all these colonials who were trying by some means or other to adapt to a new mode of life. Forced to submit to discipline, they soon realized that whereas in European countries the enemy's actions could be judged in advance since they followed unshakeable traditions, matters were very different in Canada where the enemy was often invisible and quite unpredictable. The Marquis de Tracy received orders to send troops into the country of the Agniers, of whom he had never even heard but the country was bigger than the whole area of France. From morning till night a cadet who had come perhaps from a sunlit country like Gascony was now forced to wage war with ordinary equipment in a region whose climate was even more cold and freakish than that of Siberia.

The first organized troops which France sent to the colony were those of the Carignan–Salières regiment in 1665: 'The King is sending the Sieur de Tracy with four infantry companies and the Sieur de Courcelles with a thousand good men of the Carignan regiment, wrote Colbert to the Intendant Talon in the spring of that year.

These 'good men' of Colbert's arrived, however, in a fairly halting condition. They had come from Germany where they had been helping the Emperor in a fierce war against the Turks. No sooner were the gaps in their ranks filled than a number of soldiers refused to embark. They had heard they were going into a country lost in snows in order to fight savages. To crown their misfortunes the crossing was difficult and an epidemic ran rife through the ships.

The soldiers were not to enjoy the hospitality of Quebec for very long. The last of them arrived in September. As winter approached, the Governor ordered those who were fit enough to the River Richelieu, the advance post in Iroquois country. Under the command of experienced Canadians, whose authority was however unacceptable to the soldiers, they were put to constructing forts. The first and most important of these was Fort Richelieu, which faced the confluence of the St Lawrence. Then seventy-five kilometres upstream were Fort St Louis, Saint-Jean and finally Fort St Anne from which the whole surface of Lake Champlain could be seen. By July, 1666, the works were completed. The military authorities decided unexpectedly to carry the war into a territory more than 500 kilometres away, into the very heart of Agnier country. It was a foolish decision, condemning troops who had no understanding of the Canadian winter to certain disaster. Each man carried his military pack, fifteen *kilos* to be hauled through the forest; for the first time in his life his feet were shod with snowshoes. The climate of January took these men unawares. Scorning the advice of both their Canadian and native companions, they underwent tortures of cold. Painlessly, for frost numbs without pain, first their ears then nose and fingers took on a bluish pallor and finally dropped off. One after another the soldiers fell out from exhaustion. Some of them were brought back to life by massage with snow. The rest died and were abandoned in the woods without burial, prey to wolves and foxes. The *Journal des Jésuites* records that more than sixty soldiers died in this way.

Such was the baptism of fire for soldiers of the Carignan regiment, gaining their first experience of war in New France. They realized that their greatest enemy was not the Indian but the winter. And some of them did not care for the Canadian winter; so they returned to France. Most of them, however, returning from the war to a more or less civilized country on the banks of the St Lawrence, chose to stay in this new colony where the King promised them special privileges by way of reward for their heroic campaign against the Indians. The officers could be awarded seigneuries, and the soldiers grants of land in regions of their own choice.

They realized with satisfaction that when they were in garrison at the posts they would benefit from special treatment. As Kalm observed: 'There is no country in the world where soldiers are given so many advantages. Every soldier has his own small garden outside the fortifications which he can cultivate as he wishes and plant what he likes. In peacetime the soldiers have few duties, and since the lakes are alive with fish and the woods swarm with birds and animals, those who are alert and hard-working, can live very well and eat with discrimination. Every soldier receives a new cape every two years and a waistcoat, cap, hat, trousers, cravat, two pairs of socks, and two pairs of shoes every year. They are paid five *sous* daily and sometimes this rises to thirty *sous* if the King calls on them for some particular task. If a soldier falls ill, either he is taken to the hospital or else the King provides a bed, food, medicaments, nurses and servants. Leave for one or two days is easily obtained when circumstances allow, and this without loss of rations or pay, provided a comrade will agree to take guard duty while the soldier is absent. Soldiers respect and honour the Governor and their officers, and while officers and soldiers often converse together like good friends, without undue ceremony, their familiarity remains within the bounds of decorum.'

When they were not campaigning or garrisoning at a post, soldiers were usually billeted on the settlers in the country. Officers were put up by the seigneur and the great families. Other ranks were dispersed here and there among the colonists, who hired them to perform various tasks on the farm, for which they received an average wage of ten *sous* a day and their food. Officers who were exempt from fatigue duties fell into two categories; some were regular soldiers, often of good family, who were pleased to be able to live with people of the same social class as themselves whose houses provided gaiety and hospitality. Sometimes they found they all originated from the same part of France. These officers were undemanding guests, and their hosts were sorry to see them go when their marching orders arrived. The second group, on the other hand, often caused scandals and left distasteful memories behind them in the district. Some of these officers were gentlemen's sons, sent to Canada at the express wish of their parents. Others, and these were in the majority, were also well-born and destined to follow military careers, but now determined to make the fullest possible use of their freedom. They believed they could behave as they liked, and their arrogance and unscrupulous behaviour made them intolerable to those around them. An incident which occurred around the year 1690 well illustrates how this latter group of officers behaved. One of the melancholy heroes of this gossip was an officer, Jacques François de Bourgchemin, who had come from Maine, and was related to the Marquis de Sourches. The Governor, Frontenac, in a letter written in November, 1695, to the Secretary of State for the colonies, made a detailed report of this man's misdemeanours: 'There are three or four officers out here whom I am forced to return to France by reason of their bad behaviour and things they have done, which should have been punished with more severity had they been more fully investigated . . . (The Sr. Roussel, Chauny, the Sr. de la Ragotterie and the Sr. de Bourgchemin.) As for Bourgchemin, his deeds are even more wicked: he has been accused of poisoning his wife, in which he did not succeed, and of being apprehended in an attempt to repeat the deed a second time, and this because of an immoderate passion for a girl, who they say encouraged him in the crime in the hope of marrying him herself, both of them have now fled and we are working to bring them to justice on a charge of contempt. . . .'

The force under Saint-Jean, which arrived in 1687 and which included Bourgchemin, stayed in Champlain's seigneurie. The company of Blaise de Bergères was billeted on the settlers in the neighbouring parish of Batiscan. The charms of the girls in these two parishes seem to have worked swiftly on the newcomers, for the parish registers for the years 1687–1695 record several marriages with the soldiery, officers as well as men. Social differences, however, were generally acknowledged. Soldiers in the ranks married the daughters of humble colonists. In the first months of 1689 alone three soldiers of Bergères' company—François Brusson, otherwise known as Lafleur, Denis Huet, otherwise Laviolette and Robert Cuy, otherwise Saint-Laurent—married the daughters of colonists who had reclaimed land in Canada. The officers themselves had an eye on bigger things; the daughters of seigneurs or of tradespeople who were anxious to preserve or to add some vestige of nobility. The aristocracy and the soldiery were pleased to ally themselves with the middle classes 'whose money regilded their coats of arms and burnished their crests'.

Humble working men and women shunned the taverns and saloons where cards and billiards were played, especially in Quebec, Three Rivers and Montreal where most days ended in orgies, fights, and very often in duels. The historian, Aegidius Fauteux, has related the history of the duel under the French regime in Canada. Swordfights usually took place in the latter part of the afternoon or the early part of the evening, and the rivals were certain to emerge from the same tavern. Sometimes an interesting scene would draw these sophisticated and dashing officers to the foot of the gallows to watch the execution, either in person or in effigy, of one of their brother officers, who had been clumsy enough to administer a lethal wound to his temporary opponent. After which they would return to the inn to drink and to play cards there into the small hours.

The ordinary soldier quickly became used to peasant life. Forced to remove himself from the towns and villages of provincial France, he was able to find with the colonists the sort of life to which he was accustomed. A stay in a peasant family in Canada meant for a conscript, when he was not actively engaged in fighting, material security, relative comfort, and often love. Most of these recruits in any case were the sons of country folk, labourers and artisans of fairly low estate and they reverted gratefully to the homely ways of the life of which they so often dreamed. In New France they easily adopted the routine and chores of those with whom they lodged.

There was great rejoicing when one of these soldiers married the daughter of a farmer. He had already served a tough apprenticeship; he had worked hard, reclaimed land, shared in every sort of work on the farm. The farmer, after watching how he worked and gauging his worth, would then offer him the hand of one of his daughters; and so the soldier became in his turn a colonist. The girl's father would usually have the young couple to share his own house for a year, after which they would move to their own land. The fact that the parents had 'fed, housed and given hospitality' to the engaged couple served as a substitute dowry for the young girl.

There was another kind of soldier who could not or would not adapt himself to life in Canada. Undesirable both in character and habits, he was the terror of the people among whom he lived. His days were spent in playing cards in taverns, in fights, in getting drunk and in planning to desert. On December 5, 1738, a settler in Lorette, near Quebec, one Charles Valin, was murdered, slashed and battered to death with sticks and swords by a gang of soldiers. On another occasion a soldier, Maugrain, accused of indecent assault on a young girl, received twelve strokes of the birch, in the presence of the girl, her mother and two other women. Soldiers were often charged with rape, in spite of the severity of the punishment for this crime, hanging or nine years in the galleys. Deserters who remained unapprehended by justice were irretrievably lost in the woods or taken prisoner by the Indians. Those who were not interested in farm-work followed in the steps of the *coureurs de bois* and the fur-traders.

The Seven Years' War, which ended in the cession of the country to England, served to emphasize the disagreements and pronounced lack of understanding between the metropolitan French and the Canadians. Regiments which had just disembarked bearing glorious names such as La Reine, du Béarn, du Languedoc, de Guyenne, de la Sarre, du Royal-Roussillon, were commanded in succession by Dieskau, Montcalm and Lévis. The colonial army was largely composed of French troops commanded by Canadian-born officers. Above them all stood the Governor-General himself, Rigaud de Vaudreuil, also Canadian by birth and the son of a former governor; both qualifications which entitled him to assume the post of supreme Commander-in-Chief. It seemed that no French general could bear to serve under a colonial, even if he were a governor. The Canadian officers who knew the country well and had won their promotion in its service found it difficult to find much in common with generals they did not know and who treated them with disdain. Montcalm had hardly set foot in Canada before he began to show his contempt for Canadian officers. He had no hesitation in expressing it in an official report: 'Le Mercier is ignorant and weak-minded. Montigny a looter, Marin worthy but foolish.' Every member of his staff seems to have agreed in advance to depreciate and slander the colonials. Brigadier Desandrouins proclaimed his opinion that 'the Canadians have lost all their former fighting spirit'.

This prejudice and arrogance showed not only in their thinking but also in their action. Baron Dieskau, who was German by birth and lineage, had a reputation for leading his soldiers in the German fashion' and he 'continued to irritate the Government of country as well as the Army', according to the *Mémoires* of Pouchot de Maupas. At the same time de Vaudreuil was complaining that Montcalm 'shows too much harshness towards the Canadian troops'. Which was undoubtedly true, since the Minister of the Admiralty went out of his way to warn the General in command to show 'more consideration' on their account. Furthermore he ordered Montcalm to see to it that 'French officers made an effort to expunge the unfortunate impression they had made in the colony, by the fact that they have on more than one occasion treated the soldiers with too much severity'. The pillaging from the civilian population by the troops was another item added to the list of officers' delinquencies, as well as the daily sorties into the country-side organized by the Intendant to ensure ample provision for his sumptuous banquets.

When one understands the sort of conditions in which the Seven Years' War took its course, it is tempting to ask whether, if victory had tipped the scales in France's favour, the Canadian soldiers would not immediately have thrown the French troops out of their country. Certainly Bougainville had this in mind when he commented, not without a hint of melancholy: 'It seems we are different nations, if not enemies.'

CHAPTER FIVE

CIVILIAN LIFE

After no more than half a century the colony had developed its own customs, a way of life of its own, all the characteristics, indeed, of a distinctive population. Quebec, the capital, set the tone exactly. By 1700 it had built up a population of 2,000 settlers, divided into two different sectors, rather alienated from each other, in the higher and lower parts of the town. In the other two centres of Three Rivers and Montreal, known as towns since they were also seats of government, their geographical setting allowed artisans to be both agriculturists and *coureurs de bois,* and to mix freely with those who were influential in the towns. In these places the atmosphere was always more democratic than in the city which Champlain had chosen to be the intellectual hub of the colony: a right that Quebec has never ceded.

Within the capital 'a little select world', as it was described by Charlevoix, already existed. He had observed it closely and concluded that Quebec contained every feature necessary to a pleasant society. This Society revolved for the most part around the residence of the Governor, the Château of Saint-Louis, where lay the heart and soul of the social world to which the historian referred. The Governor was surrounded by a staff whose personages sometimes changed individually, but whose traditions remained unalterable; here the nobility, 'noble at least in name', officers and soldiers gathered 'where moved distinguished personages accustomed to frequenting the Courts of Europe'. The Intendant, Members of the Council, rich tradespeople, or 'those who behave as if they were', seeking the custom of this aristocracy, however impoverished, also lived in the upper part of the town. It was a small world, nearly as restricted and exclusive as that which moved around the residence of the Governor. Sometimes Indian chiefs were invited to the receptions there. They always arrived dressed in full regalia and although at first they would appear a little strained and formal, their naturally versatile intelligence soon led them freely to adapt themselves to French manners. These proud natives felt obliged to ape the customs which they observed. They adopted, for example, the custom of kissing the hand of a lady on first meeting her, although Frenchwomen disliked them instinctively.

More or less excluded, but still geographically speaking in the upper part of the town, the more serious-minded people devoted their lives to prayer and contemplation. The nursing sisters in their Hôtel-Dieu and again later in the general hospital as well, cared for the misfortunes of their fellow men and women with heroic patience.

Another peaceful oasis lay in the little company of Ursuline nuns situated halfway between the Château of Saint-Louis and the Hôtel-Dieu. Every day the daughters of colonists, together with a few little Indian girls, made their way towards it, there to be initiated into the mysteries of religion, the rudiments of the alphabet and the 'hundred and one little niceties of housewifery' which the nuns understood so intimately. Only distinguished visitors were privileged to penetrate into the cloister itself, and this only at certain times of the year.

Travellers, whether native, French or foreign, were welcomed in Quebec with all the deference which their rank demanded. The Swedish naturalist, Peter Kalm, in recognition of his social standing, was received with a truly royal welcome.

It was in these surroundings that Charlevoix lived and found such contentment: 'There is everything here to ensure that almost anyone can pass his time agreeably. This is exactly what happens, and everyone contributes to the enjoyment of life in any way he can.' The historian particularly enjoyed observing the carefree junketing of the social set centred on the Governor's residence. 'They amuse themselves, drive out in barouches or paddle in canoes during the summer, in winter they drive in sleighs or skate upon the frozen lakes. There is plenty of hunting. For a great many of the gentry this is the only way by which they can earn enough to live in comfort. There are no rich people in this country as far as one can see, which is a great pity, since it is pleasant to take advantage of one's wealth, and no one really enjoys hoarding it. There is excellent living provided one can afford to dress well at the same time, for otherwise one economizes on food in order to wear better clothes.' This indolent and improvident way of life was not peculiar to the turn of the seventeenth century. Half a century later a French officer, Méritens de Fradals, who had just landed in Canada and had spent only a short time in Quebec, noticed the same sort of atmosphere: 'Quebec is more full of pageantry than is the Court of France. You see people driving out in their carriages for long spells throughout the day—yet they have not eaten for twenty-four hours and they have no idea what they are going to eat for dinner. But they look very happy in spite of this.' It was undoubtedly a frivolous existence and as useless a one as that led by the ambitious class of officials, so taken up with climbing socially and enjoying themselves to the full that they never contributed to the foundation of the new nation. If the Intendant happened to be a hardworking and conscientious man the Governor might be arrogant or ineffectual. By the same token if the Governor used his powers wisely, then his chief aides would neglect their duties. This situation may be explained by the fact that most of these officials were in posts which were either temporary or else thought to be so by those who occupied them, so that their tenure of office depended entirely on the whim of those in authority.

Travellers visiting Quebec and describing it later, concentrated mainly on the official life on show in the upper town. A long, tortuous and stony way just wide enough to allow the passage of wagons led to the lower part of the town. In order to avoid a lengthy detour a flight of steps was built to make a direct link between the fort of Saint-Louis and the wharves. The steps were found extraordinarily useful. The settlers would drive their cattle and sheep up and down them, until a decree of the Sovereign Council put an end to such misuse. When later the staircase came to be rebuilt, it was 'only of a width necessary to allow the passage of one man at a time' and it was provided with gates at the top and bottom. 'No one is to leave the said gates open or to break them down, on pain of flogging.'

This order is but one example of laws which the authorities were obliged to lay down in order to protect the anomalous population in the lower town, which was made up of merchants, labourers and artisans, who, living haphazardly, had to be protected from their own heedless behaviour. The main ordinances concerned the prevention of fire, public health and the public market. Every house must contain 'latrines and privies'; the owners must clean the front of their houses each day; no person must keep fodder within the house or in any place where it could catch fire; no straw or manure must be thrown into the streets; each house to have exits by way of the attic to allow access to the chimneys or alternatively to have ladders fixed to the roofs, chimneys to be swept every two months. To guard even more completely against the constant danger of fire a tax of thirty *sous* was imposed upon every chimney, half the tax to be paid by the tenant and half by the owner of each house. This sum served to purchase 100 leather buckets. The authorities even succeeded in forbidding people to smoke in the streets of the town. Other rules were directed towards tradespeople: no one was to go round offering fowl, game, eggs, butter or wood for house to house sale without first putting their goods on display until eleven o'clock in the morning on market days. Publicans, butchers, and hucksters must not purchase goods in the market before eight o'clock in the morning in summer and before nine o'clock in the morning in winter, since past experience had proved that the poorer artisans had been exploited by these people who made a clean sweep of all the goods and offered them for resale at exorbitant prices. All weights and measures must be engraved with 'the King's insignia'. These rulings did not in any way hinder the comings and goings of the population. Low-built narrow houses constructed for the most part of black stone taken from the beaches, were piled at the foot of the cliff under Cape Diamant, along roads bearing such picturesque names as la Canotterie, la Canardière, le Sault-au-Matelot, la rue Sous-le-Fort, la côte de la Montagne; here and there as in French towns hung the traders' signboards: Pierre Niel, the shopkeeper in rue Sous-le-Fort, gave his shop the name of *à la ville de La Rochelle*; *au Bien Chaussé* hung outside the shop of the cobbler, André Spénard. The inn-keepers also chose engaging names such as *Le Roi David, Le Lion d'Or, Aux Trois Pigeons, Le Signe de la Croix*.

The lower part of the town displayed the widest possible variety of trades. Since customers were sometimes few and far between a man could not always earn a living from his own trade alone. Although carefully entered in the contracts engaging immigrants, the descriptions of corn-chandler, baker, pastrycook and miller are often misleading and the same person could, if he so wished, practise one or other of these trades without being obliged to complete the

85

prescribed period of apprenticeship to each one. Thus the weaver might also be a tailor and a hatter. The sawyer who had long ago acquired his skill had no hesitation in turning his hand to carpentry. A locksmith could not survive a whole year on his earnings; he might be a maker of edge-tools or an armourer at the same time. Almost every one of these artisans was the owner of a neighbouring patch of ground, a garden and, sometimes, of a few animals.

The Intendant Talon gazed, often with a paternal and attentive eye, from the window of his office perched upon the rock where the upper town stood, and saw the working-class shops down in the lower town. He wanted to improve the condition of young people in the various trades. 'I have created opportunities for work,' he wrote to Colbert. He established workshops for apprentice training. Since ships' carpenters had become rare, he assigned them to train as 'house-carpenters who are capable of every task'. These apprentice workshops and the shipyards which handled works of naval construction contributed in no small measure to maintaining employment among the working classes in the lower town. Children were not forgotten. The school in Quebec was in two separate establishments, one for children who had some facility for learning, the other for those who were 'fitted only to be artisans and who are now learning trades'.

The Quebec artisan was not controlled by trade guilds or corporations, and was free to possess a workshop and a shop and to carry on his trade virtually free of any controls. He was not required to pass an examination, to submit to an apprenticeship, nor to give formal proof of his ability nor obtain certificates. It was sufficient for a man to claim knowledge of a trade in order to be able to practise it anywhere in the country. Life in this respect soon became even easier for him: in 1729 he was able, thanks to the Royal magistrate, Chaumont, after six years or more of practice to be entitled *maître-de-chef-d'œuvre*, and 'to open shop in Paris or in other towns'. Henceforward there were no longer fixed laws for working standards except for those imposed by the employer himself, and his demands were for quality; this explains the infinite beauty, good proportions, solidity and artistic feeling enshrined in work which has come down to the present day. It is more surprising to realize that such works were fashioned by modest colonial artisans who had no contact with their European masters of craftsmanship.

It was a contented little world, if poor. Contented because it was free, because the oldest members had known and lived through misfortunes and privation in the country of their birth; poor because it had to content itself with living from day to day at work on the trade of its choice. Its citizens did a hard day's work without thought for the morrow. Newcomers and strangers to the lower town were apt to pontificate after a quick look round, stigmatizing the Canadian as 'an idle good-for-nothing'. This was a judgment quite at variance with the truth. The true artisan was confused with the idler who spent his day in strolling about the wharves, or with the *coureurs des bois* who were taking time off, or with the country dwellers seeking employment in the shipyards.

The navigational months from June to October were a time of much sudden and picturesque activity. Quebec was the point of arrival for all the French sailing ships which arrived bringing new faces etched with lines of hope, nostalgia, wonder, ambition, bewilderment or resignation. As soon as they had disembarked the newcomers would wander into the twisting streets and come to a standstill on the *Place* of Nôtre-Dame-de-la-Victoire, re-named Nôtre-Dame-des-Victoires in celebration of the two defeats inflicted on the English, which had been ascribed to the intervention of the Madonna. Convoys of native canoes laden with furs manœuvred around the vessels which, awaiting their passage home, lay in the cove of the Cul-de-Sac. In the market-place farmers offered numerous agricultural products that the arid soil of the town could not provide. The exchange of goods was conducted largely by barter, since money on both sides was scarce. This was also a time when sailors mingled with the population, hung around the inns and provoked street fights and brawls. The Indians would look on silently, squatting, at the alien hurly-burly. Then all the bustle would subside into the calm of the long winter, broken only by the Christmas festivities, which sometimes lasted until the end of January.

In Montreal and Three Rivers, the other two headquarters of Government, a warmer and more democratic feeling was found than in Quebec, since there was daily contact betwen artisans, labourers, officials and soldiers. They jostled each other every day in the streets, meeting frequently and often amicably. Here too, the Indians and the *coureurs des bois* were more numerous, bringing with them a never-ending injection of fresh life.

Three Rivers had long been the site of the great Indian fair, as well as the point of departure for travellers on their way to the northern territories. But it had been forced to yield pride of place to Montreal and its trade had suffered much in consequence. Peter Kalm visited Three Rivers in 1749, and was not enthusiastic, characterizing it as 'this little market town which looks like a large village'. He grumbled about the labyrinth of little lanes, swept by blinding eddies of sand blown by the eternal wind. From the years of its foundation onwards the people of Three Rivers had been noted for their casual outlook which, at the first sign of any danger threatening the town, they quickly threw off. One of the *Relations des Jésuites* makes the point that the first colonists 'settled here in haphazard fashion, following their own inclinations and convenience'. Even half a century later it needed a special edict from the Intendant to compel the settlers to construct pavements along the frontage of their houses to cope with the spring thaw and the autumn rainy season. For the streets were in parlous condition and passers-by often sank up to their knees in mud.

Even so, Three Rivers was first and foremost a seat of government in which the principal administrative posts, those of Governor, King's Lieutenant, and Major, were eagerly sought after. Well-known personages would put in for them, often in vain. The Governor's residence, an imposing stone building constructed upon rising ground known as the Platon, dominated the town. Other officials clustered round in more modest houses, rented temporarily. In Church, for example, the Governor took the pew 'the first on the right, next to this is the pew of the King's Lieutenant, and opposite the latter, and to the left is the pew in which sit the officers of the law'.

This centre of administration existing in the middle of a population of several hundred people gave a special character to 'the little unpretentious town, built on sand', which was Three Rivers. Thus the engineer, Franquet, was amazed to be received as if he were one of the great when he visited the house of the Governor, Rigaud de Vaudreuil. 'When I arrived I was presented to Madame his wife, who is incidentally as remarkable for her looks as for her intelligence. She is moreover full of grace and courtesy; after preliminary greetings he showed me the rooms allotted to me, where I tidied myself up and put my clothes in order before rejoining the guests. It was not long before we proceeded into the dining-room. There the table was laid for twenty guests and dinner was served, not I admit just as in Paris, although that is the one place where I have lived most economically, but nonetheless with a profusion of delicacies and food from the most fruitful provinces of France. We drank every sort of wine, always iced; imagine how very pleasant this was in the excessively hot weather of that day. After dinner we played draughts and then drove out to look at the town.'

This town fitted well into its insignificant position. The men who administered it were happy there for they lived in peace and enjoyed the respect of the people. These, long accustomed to being the target of surprise attacks by the Iroquois, seemed timid by nature, and did not much care to venture far outside the stockades. Their natural gateway, the river, opened the way to adventure. The real glory of this town lay in its having been the birthplace of the most daring of the *coureurs de bois*. Radisson, des Groseilliers, Nicolas Perrot, La Vérendrye, Jean Nicolet, François Hertel, Pierre Pépin, all of them explorers, had been brought up in its streets, had strolled and idled there between voyages. This glorious past seemed to the town sufficient, and nobody really cared when the time came for Montreal to steal its thunder. The ambitions of the people of Three Rivers were unassuming enough; but they were also tenacious, and logical. Recalling that the town had given birth to some of the greatest explorers, they launched out into the manufacture of birchbark canoes and showed themselves very competent in this skill. The canoes of Three Rivers, as Franquet, the engineer observed in 1752, are the best ever built. 'As soon as they are completed they are sent off to Montreal, from whence they are destined to sail to the countries up in the North.'

This population, so small but at the same time so carefree and lighthearted, very naturally felt at times the need for entertainment. Hearings at the Court of Justice every Monday provided just the opportunity they craved. The smallest quibbles came up before the judge, who was very often obliged, after carefully listening to conflicting claims, to dismiss both parties without a conclusion being reached. One of the most determined of litigants was Marguerite Hayet, the wife of the adventurer, des Groseilliers. Her husband was able to roam the forests with an easy mind, knowing that domestic affairs lay safely in the hands of his forceful spouse. Marguerite owned some pigs, the despair of her neighbours; and it was nearly always in some attempt to justify the depredations

89

of these beasts that she appeared before the Court. The verbiage she employed in their defence would have entranced Molière himself. On one occasion, being in debt for ten *livres* to the surgeon, Louis Pinard, she offered him two pecks of corn in lieu of payment. It was not enough. She then offered him another thirty *sous*, but in return she demanded a present from the surgeon of 'a jar of ointment for burns'. The dispute waged furiously and was brought before the Court. The case was dismissed by the Judge and both parties were ordered to pay their own costs. On another occasion one Pierre Bertrand demanded three *livres* of Tours from Marguerite Hayet 'for the schooling of her son'. The farmer's wife wished to pay in kind with corn or other foodstuffs, but the professor was a bachelor and was in any case lodged and fed already in a family household. He therefore demanded payment in cash. Marguerite contested this demand and the Judge had to decide the issue.

The carrying out of sentences produced some extraordinary sights. After an enquiry had been held into dealings in alcohol which were being conducted with neighbouring Indians, some of the best-known citizens were found guilty and condemned to thirty days in prison. For the last fortnight of this sentence they were to be 'daily exposed to public spectacle on the back of a wooden horse with placards round their necks bearing the words: "For having dealt in firewater with the Savages".' An exciting scene which idle people would not have missed for anything; the great sitting in pillory! An even more diverting spectacle was staged in 1673. Four men broke into the house of Ameau, the notary, and from it stole wine and brandy. They were immediately arrested, put on trial and condemned 'to be exposed at the doors of the parish Church on a feast day or on Sunday, after the termination of High Mass'. The locksmith who had provided forged keys, one Louis Martin, was to appear bareheaded, his hands bound together, and bearing round his neck keys and bottles, with the following inscription hung about his breast and back: 'Wine-stealer, stealer of brandy and eels, and forger of keys.' Around the necks of the other offenders hung only empty bottles. When these ridiculous rites had been carried out the accused men took their respected places once more among their fellows. Honour was restored to them.

The appearance of the town did not change in any way over the years. Visitors in 1750 found the same atmosphere that had prevailed half a century before. The old stone buildings were still there: the Recollect Chapel, the Convent of the Ursulines, the Governor's house. To these buildings had been added the parish Church, of which the citizens of Three Rivers were justly proud since Gilles Bolvin had embellished it with the most beautiful wooden sculptures to be found anywhere in the colony. Most of the houses, as Kalm remarked, were single-storey wood buildings, fairly well constructed and standing detached from each other, because of the risk of fire. The streets were twisting, the wind swept the sand into them, which made progress very tiring. On stormy days you saw only children, soldiers and Recollect monks moving to and from the monastery and the Church. Everybody else stayed snugly at home.

The peaceful atmosphere of Three Rivers attracted retired soldiers, lazy or disabled rather than aged, who came here to live off their meagre pensions, supplemented by what they could grow in the patch of ground inherited from a father or some benefactor. One of these old soldiers was the subject of an enjoyable anecdote related by the diarist of the Ursulines, who, since their arrival in 1697, had regularly appointed one of their number, probably one of the most inquisitive, to note down any news of importance, rumours of which penetrated to their cloister. Joseph Hertel de la Fresnière, whose house was next door to the Convent, was forty-eight years old in 1750. Already retired, he had been a soldier since childhood, achieved promotion to the rank of officer, and, like all members of the Hertel family was a veteran of several wars. But he was as timid with women as he was brave upon the battlefields. For years he had been associating closely with a woman called Antoinette Bouton, several years younger than himself, who lived with her parents at the intersection of the streets of Nôtre-Dame and of the Château, facing the parish Church. Every evening, the diffident lover would make his way there to play cards with Antoinette. At the stroke of nine, in summer as well as winter, he would rise, give a military salute and depart. One evening around Christmas 1749, Mademoiselle Bouton, in her usual fashion, had just lit the lantern and handed it to Hertel as she opened the door to a flurry of snow. The wind blew out the candle. Antoinette relit it quickly, then, handing him the lantern once more, said suddenly: 'I can't bear to see you go out in such weather!' Hertel at once replied: 'Only you can change that'—'What do you mean?' 'If we lived together I should not have to go out in the evening to play cards.' 'I will consider your proposal.' She did not take long to make up her mind. They were married on January 12, 1750. The previous day the notary, Pillard, had drawn up the marriage contract in the presence of local notabilities: the Chevalier de Saint-Louis, M. de Saint-Ours, Melchior de Jordy, Sieur de Cabanac, François Chastelain, lieutenant in the Army. The daily game of cards was to be played for another twenty years. Joseph Hertel left his wife a widow on November 20, 1768.

Founded with the sole design of bringing the gospel to the natives, the post of Ville-Marie, as Montreal was first known, flourished in this sort of atmosphere for a quarter of a century. Tradition tells of memories of the touching scene when Maisonneuve appeared in 1642. Like Christ he bore a heavy cross for a whole league without stumbling, before he laid it at the summit of the mountain. The walls of the fortifications and of the house rose slowly to the accompaniment of prayers, as if a monastery were being built. One solitary womanly figure moved among the group of men, Jeanne Mance. Her presence there made the noise of axe and hammer a stranger sound than ever in so deserted a spot, 100 kilometres from any signs of civilization. No evil desire, nor dishonourable word could come to the mind of these rough folk while such a sweet and brave maiden moved and spoke among them. This was a new Marie, a Joan of Arc of another age, but stamped with the same quality. Her evenings would be spent in talking at length with M. de Maisonneuve, who also was unmarried. No one dreamed of attaching to this any breath of scandal. From the ordinary human point of view, it is difficult to understand a daily round so mundane and ordinary, yet so extraordinarily pure. But it was exactly this quality which was the key to the success and the supernatural aura of this little township buried so deeply in the forest. 'Labour and charity' seemed to be the insignia of the little colony which Maisonneuve had dreamed of founding in the heart of Indian country in order to help in the work of bringing them to Christianity. The Indians, he felt, would be anxious to live well so that they might benefit from all the blessings civilization had brought them: a chapel to save their souls, a hospital to care for the sick and take in the old, a school to teach young Indians that most beautiful of all languages—French. Self-deception, alas! For these savages were vindictive, cruel, independent, unheeding and thieving. They did not want these palefaces who came to bring them peace. Nearly every day one more colonist failed to answer the roll. He would be found pierced with an arrow, or he would vanish never more to be seen. Within the fortifications people trembled and prayed.

And yet the reclaiming of land, sowing and harvesting had to go on. The colonists went out to the fields protected by armed companions, and at certain pre-arranged times they exchanged their tools for muskets. A few people near the end of their tether refused to venture outside again. A certain Mathurin Joanneau lived for years in a cave and shunned the light of day. This need to live continuously on guard did not help the development of the colony. Every night ways and means of repulsing the enemy were endlessly discussed. A group of youths, bored with the inactivity, decided to make a desperate bid. They learned that a flotilla containing Iroquois was coming down the river Outaouais, laden with furs. They planned to meet it and to fight until death or victory. The year 1660 was famous for the exploit of Dollard des Ormeaux, who became a national hero. He and his sixteen companions sacrificed their lives within their temporary bastion at Long Sault. But so courageously did they fight that the Iroquois lost their nerve and did not dare to attack Ville-Marie. After this, gradually, calm descended. Referring to these troubled times which lasted twenty years, one of the *Relations* noted, not without justification, that they were 'the image of the early Church'.

When the danger passed the town changed its name from Ville-Marie to Montreal, and embarked with gathering momentum upon its era of economic brilliance. While Quebec administered the country, while Three Rivers lay slumbering, Montreal went about its business. To begin with it was only a medium-sized village with a hundred houses sheltering some 800 settlers. But these were active people, carrying on all kinds of commerce, and including representatives of almost every trade. Far from any other township, they lived well.

Three factors served unceasingly to support the increase of trade, the annual influx of Indians for the fair, the assembly and departure of fleets of canoes to the fur-trapping regions, and the presence of the garrison. The fair, the great mart for the skins, was the occasion for high carnival. It took place in June and began with the arrival of a flotilla bringing hundreds of Indians. They moved silently and slowly with their cargo of furs towards their meeting point in the parish of the Pointe-Callières, outside the walls of the town. Each tribe, each group, set itself up in its allotted place to display its finest wares. The Governor of Montreal took his seat in a chair facing the gathering. Then the chiefs of the tribes advanced towards him; one of them lit the pipe of peace and with great ceremony inhaled deeply before passing the pipe to the Governor, who repeated the procedure. The pipe went from mouth to mouth in complete silence and was then laid down upon a fur. After which another chief rose to his feet, stretched out his right hand in salute, and in a loud oratorical voice began a speech which was nearly always a call to peace with the white people. He would then offer the Governor some of his most precious furs. Whereupon the Governor replied while his speech was translated, sentence by sentence, by an interpreter. Then he in his turn would offer gifts.

And so the opening day came to an end. Officially the trading was not supposed to begin until the following day. But from the moment the ceremony ended, the Montreal traders besieged the tribes who usually came with the richest of the furs. Soon the pandemonium was indescribable. Arguments broke out. On one side hoards of furs piled up; particularly beaver, but also wild cat, marten, otter, sable, bear, lynx, fox, deer, moose. On the other side were French merchants offering, either from the market-place or from their own shops, the most varied and alluring of their goods. Firstly there were all the objects whose sale to the Indians was prohibited by law; alcohol, muskets and powder. Then over the counters the oddest assortment of goods were spread out: kettles, tools, saucepans, French clothes, necklaces of china.

By the second day many of the Indians were drunk and the scene became orgiastic, as vividly described by Charlevoix: 'The most awful sights are seen in the squares and streets of Montreal, the inevitable sequel when these barbarians become drunk. Husbands and wives, fathers, mothers with their children, brothers and sisters, take each other by the throat, tear off each other's ears, and bite each other with sharp teeth, like maddened wolves. The nights resound to the most appalling howls, more ferocious than those of the wild beasts in the forest.' When, after several days of this, they returned to normal, the Indians would discover that their wares had vanished. All that remained to them were a few necklaces, a few pots and pans, a few tin plates. Even the muskets traded in exchange for their finest furs had gone. The fair was over and it was now obvious to them that they had been exploited. They swore never to return. But return they did each year, to carry on in the very same fashion, until at last those traders whose livelihood depended upon the fur trade decided to penetrate into the depths of the forest to track the furs to their source.

And so the great convoys of canoes, laden with merchandise and alcohol came into being. While these were being prepared for departure the streets of Montreal were filled with feverish activity, as the wanderers stocked up with supplies from the shops. On the eve of departure the taverns and bars were scenes of celebration —repeated when the travellers returned. After which the town returned to its normal state.

The departure of the explorers also gave rise to tremendous activity. Galinée and Dollier de Casson equipped themselves from Montreal before their departure to the Great Lakes. And so did Jolliet before he went to the Mississippi, and La Salle before he went to Louisiana. They embarked at Lachine, to avoid the dangerous rapids, but their farewells were celebrated in Montreal in the market place, in the inns, along the shadowy and crowded streets.

It is impossible in a few pages to mirror the swiftness of Montreal's development during the course of a hundred and fifty years. Visitors have described it at various stages of its being. Thus in the seventeenth century, 'the Market-place is the meeting-place of the population; it is here that on Tuesdays and Thursdays every week farmers are authorized to sell their wares to the citizens; it is here that the gentry make play with their swords; hence the duel between the Governor Perrot and M. de Sainte-Helène in June, 1684; here too that the Sheriff's officer reads the summonses, edicts and ordinances and posts them to a pillar; and it is here, in public, that criminals undergo their final punishments. On this market-place too is a wooden horse and a gibbet whose permanent presence and proximity are not exactly designed to instil feelings of merriment.' From 1715 onwards the population of Montreal grew faster than that of Quebec, and so did its activity. And it became the great centre from which the garrisons at the frontier posts were reinforced. The shopkeepers were sitting on a goldmine.

From a description based on contemporary accounts of the day it seems that 'the town may not perhaps appear gay, for the stone in this country which is used for construction work is of a rather dark grey. But the solidity and impregnability make up for any lack of elegance, and there are roofs of gilded metal to reflect the mid-day sun. Seen from the river or the coast Montreal is a lovely sight, with its encircling walls, its gables of stone or wood and its chimney-pots, its six or seven belltowers, unpretentious but well designed.' Lanctot the historian described the bustle of these people to and fro, never still: 'The wooden pavements are crowded with a motley and picturesque population; officers in coloured uniform coats over velvet waistcoats, swords buckled at their sides and tailed periwigs surmounted by tricorn hats embroidered with gold; tradespeople in clothes of fine linen and lace blouses, with striped hats; working-class people with their hair in little pigtails, in short pantaloons and waistcoats of every colour; soldiers too in white uniforms gaitered to the knees, ladies in hooped dresses, with powdered hair, with lace bonnets or with their hair dressed with ribbons; working-class women with coloured cloaks over short skirts—their hair done in workaday style. Here and there you come across a few Indians half naked, or with a blanket slung over the shoulder, faces daubed with vermilion or green, a feather in the hair. Heavy carts and wagons drawn by horses harnessed in tandem, their shafts groaning; carriages, high-wheeled, carrying elegant ladies fluttering their fans. All these people are extremely polite and the men constantly raise their hats to right and left. . . . Since the houses have seats at each side of the door, the street is alive with these ladies and gentlemen whose exchange of visits appear to go on through the whole twenty-four hours. There are many dinner parties and the meals are princely.'

This middle-class society, which lived in comfort and luxury, did not feel the effects of the resumption of war between France and England until they themselves became affected by shortages. Even then they did not lose their joie-de-vivre. In 1757 when the Inten-dant replaced the quadroon of bread with a ration of beef, and then later of horsemeat, the women gathered in protest outside the Governor's residence. The Governor himself threatened them from the windows with imprisonment; more alarmingly still, he de-clared that he would have half of them hanged if they did not disperse. In the course of the chapter on social life which appears later in the book, we shall see how, during these years of anxiety,

5 a. Seventeenth-century house in the Montreal region (Laprairie)
  b. House in the Quebec region (Ile d'Orleans)

6 a. The Blizzard (painting by Krieghoff)

b. An Habitant Farm (Krieghoff)

the people of Montreal yet found means to alleviate their own boredom.

THE COLONIST

Let us now look at the settler in Canada when he had had time to develop into a tangible entity in society, say towards the end of the seventeenth century. Through the preceding three or four decades his characteristics had been gradually taking shape, and from now on these were not to change in any significant way.

Twenty-five years earlier, when the seigneuries were being settled, he had acquired his grant of land which he would in future consider as his own farm. He had obtained it without payment. He paid his seigneur a minimum fixed rent every year. In return he was obliged to reclaim and to prepare for cultivation at least one acre of land annually. Frequently he did more than this, since he was entitled to retain entire the profits from his own labours. He worked hard. By nature he was a creature of the morning. Charlevoix observed that 'In this country everyone rises at dawn; the Governor, too, starts giving audiences at seven o'clock in the morning'. The colonist was only following the example set by those in authority. The bracing air of the early hours of the morning stimulated energy.

The regular working hours as stipulated by Pierre Boucher when he was Governor of Three Rivers were from sunrise to sunset. Citizens found this a logical and humane ruling. The colonist on his own land was not forced to conform with this timetable but following it came naturally to him.

And so by 1700 or thereabouts almost one-third of the average concession of eighty acres was under cultivation. The remainder was forest and was left to provide wood required for heating and building. Maples were carefully preserved to provide sugar and syrup. When the colonist received his grant of land, built a house with his own hands, together with his barn and other necessary buildings, he would find a wife. When his children were old enough to run the farm and to feed the stock, he would treat himself, as did his neighbours, to journeys to the districts around the Great Lakes, where he would traffic in furs. Then tiring of adventure he returned home once more to till the soil, which offered him the relative security with which he was content. Not exactly venturesome in his behaviour, at least he attempted to cultivate the wheat which produced so excellent a harvest in Canadian soil, with a view to export, as well as to rear more animals. But he soon realized how much he was wasting his energy. The authorities had provided no outlet for agricultural products from the country, notwithstanding the fact that as early as 1669, the King had ordered the Intendant Talon to 'Promote by every possible means the reclamation and cultivation of the land'. Such instructions were beside the point since the farmer had no outlet for his surplus produce. He thus contented himself with satisfying the needs of his own family and with working to supply himself with the small comforts he needed.

In due course some of his children would marry in their turn and settle down in the neighbourhood. Those who were left stayed to help him in his work. Strangers were full of admiration for the rapid and intelligent way in which he organized his new life. 'Farm-labourers who seem untiring in their work', wrote the Intendant Duchesnau to Colbert in 1679, 'enjoy an extremely good existence and are incomparably happier than those to whom we refer in France as the "good peasants".' La Hontan, Charlevoix and La Potherie thought in the same terms. The condition of the peasant in Canada was so enviable that, it was said, many members of the French nobility and gentry would have been glad to enjoy the same advantages—so long, however, as they were prepared to work hard. For the peasant in Canada was meticulous in his work, but meticulous in his own way, conditioned as he was by the vagaries of the climate. During the four months of summer he must lay in stocks of food for his family and animals, sufficient to last him through the whole lengthy period of winter. If he failed to do so they might all starve, particularly his animals.

The colonist's year was split up into different periods unequal in length and subdivided into cycles known as *temps*. During the summer months from June to September, there was seed-time, haymaking-time, harvest-time. These few short weeks meant days of unceasingly hard work, exhausting labour with no respite, particularly since cold or rainy days, the sudden and frequent thunderstorms in the dog-days, not to mention Sundays and the so numerous and rigidly observed religious feast-days, must be counted as lost. There were fifty-three such days during leap-years.

98

To the Sundays add the thirty-seven days of obligation, then there were eighty or ninety days in which manual labour could not be carried on each year.

The colonist knew that almost half the number of feastdays coincided with the periods of intensive work, and that between seed-time and harvest he had to make do with barely two-thirds of all possible working days. This meant that the remaining days must be filled to the utmost and that each hour was precious. Every member of the family helped with the field-work—women and children too. The woman of New France, observed Kalm, 'has a hard life full of suffering especially among the working classes. She is always to be seen in the fields, the meadows or in the stables, there is no form of work to which she does not turn her hand.'

Even the wives and daughters of certain seigneurs saw nothing unusual in working in the fields. The Governor, Denonville, him-self saw the Tilly family near Quebec, as well as the Saint-Ours family 'working in the fields every day'. They rose at dawn and worked till nightfall all through this brief period of summer. Meals were light and eaten in haste at irregular times. Sometimes when the heat was excessive the workers allowed themselves a brief siesta, of half an hour or more, taken in the shade of a wagon or a tree. When bad weather stopped the haymaking the farmer coped with all the little tasks which had to go by default when it was fine. He repaired the boundary fencing, greased the carts and wagons, sharpened the scythes, dug or cleaned out the drainage ditches. His wife and children worked at weeding the garden and the vegetable plots.

The ethnologist R. L. Séguin noticed how the peasant in Canada soon developed farming tools very like those used in European countries and in New England. At first they employed hand imple-ments only, but soon horse-drawn implements were brought into use. The first section of tools included the pickaxe, the hoe, the rake, sickle, bill-hook, scythe, the pitchfork, the flail and winnowing-basket. The first ground to be put under cultivation by the French in New France was turned over by pickaxes. Champlain tells us that the ship which in 1619 brought people, merchandise and animals to New France, also carried 'twenty-four labourers' spades'. In 1669 Michel Messier cultivated his land on which there were 'twelve acres suitable for ploughing with pick-axes'. Champlain was correct when he spoke of Guillaume Couillard, in 1628, cutting furrows with his plough, but this implement did not come into general use until several years later, since draft oxen were still as rare as were wheeled ploughs.

On June 25, 1647, an animal arrived in Quebec the like of which the Indians had never seen. It was a horse. It had been sent from France by the Directors of the Company of Habitants as a present to the Governor, M. de Montmagny, who had expressed his concern at not owning one. The Huron Indians, who were in Quebec at the time, never tired of admiring the docility and elegance of this beast. By the time twelve horses taken from the King's stables had been sent out by request of Pierre Boucher, the noble charger of M. de Montmagny was no more. Another consignment arrived in 1670 and these animals were given by way of reward to those seigneurs who had been most successful in promoting the reclamation and cultivation of land.

The French sickle was used to cut peas. This tool, enlarged to comply with local requirements, became the *crocheton*. Corn, rye and hay crops were harvested by means of a sickle whose edge was either sharpened or serrated, and also with the scythe. Forks were generally made of wood and had two prongs; branches of trees, ashtrees for choice, were also used. The three-pronged iron fork did not come into use until later. Threshing of grain was done with a flail; later it was winnowed with the help of a sieve, a winnowing-basket or a riddle. The first of these two implements was to be found on every farm, but the riddle belonged by custom to the seigneur or to the owner of the flourmill. For the use of it the farmer had to pay six *deniers* for each peck of grain winnowed.

The demands made on the space in the barn were so great that hay, clover, and other forage plants were made into stacks outside the buildings. Only the grain itself could be put under cover. Winnowing took place during the winter months as and when flour was required and this was one of the colonist's winter duties. In many districts it was customary to sow wheat in the autumn. The grain rested in the ground during the severe winter months, and this method produced such excellent results that some question arose of adopting it on the farms in France, a suggestion put forward in a letter from the Secretary of State in charge of the colonies, written in 1709 from Versailles to the Governor, de Vaudreuil, and the Intendant, Raudot. It was not always possible to sow the winter wheat. Often the frost came suddenly and froze the topsoil. Then the colonist's thoughts would turn towards his store of timber which needed to be cut, sawn and chopped up for the winter months ahead. Felling had to be finished before the heavy snowfalls, that is in October; and this too was the moment for repairing the farm wagons and implements, and for putting them under cover. After which the *solage* or stone base upon which the foundations of the house were laid, was carefully protected with earth rammed down, and straw—a process known as *renchaussage*. It was only when the first snow began to fall that the colonist came to realize that he had had no respite since June. Yet he was content, even if he were no richer than he had been a year before, since at least he knew that he could feed and keep his family warm through the long months ahead.

Winter was an important factor in the determining of the social entity into which the settler of Canada evolved. Little by little he became civilized, more shrewd, and more conscious of his worth. His existence was composed of his family life, his leisure, the sensible manner in which he performed his everyday domestic duties. Even the animals became tamer, since they were visited, cared for and fed three times a day in their stalls, where they were likewise confined until the coming of the summer days. When these tasks had been attended to, and when he was not obliged, as he was on stormy days, to clear the snow in order to avoid being cut off from his neighbours, the settler lived in the bosom of his family. He sat before his hearth, busying himself with little tasks which required a degree of skill, intelligence and thought. Sometimes he would develop his natural artistic talents in the making of furniture for his house; winter saw the fashioning of tables, chests, chairs, beds, cradles and toys for the children. In this sort of household where the settler was all the time developing a new outlook, his wife had an important part to play. If she were educated she would teach not only her children but her husband as well to read and write, for a colonist who was able at least to sign his own name had climbed a rung of a social ladder in the parish hierarchy. The woman of the house was also in charge of the daily devotions. She set an example for hard work by weaving, sewing and cutting out all the clothes and dresses for her family as well as the bedcovers and the carpets. She showed great ingenuity in cooking meals which had to be at once varied, substantial and appetizing, since a good table was one of the most important assets in these months of apparent inactivity.

Winter was also the season when guests were received and family celebrations were held. When a wedding took place the rejoicings would sometimes last for as long as four or five days. It was an occasion for parents and friends who had sometimes settled in far-off places to come together again after years of separation. Each night everyone went to dine at the house of the father of one of the happy pair. Afterwards there was singing and festivities lasting into the small hours. The meal which the guests began at around seven o'clock might last for four hours. 'The host, whether he be seigneur or freeholder, would be guilty of meanness if at the end of the meal the table was not still as groaning with food as it had been when the visitors sat down.'

After the meal there was dancing and the singing of popular songs supporting or modifying French traditions according to need.

It is possible to make an interesting comparison between the possessions of the Canadian colonist and those of a farmer in Normandy at the same date. At the end of the seventeenth century, Jean Collet, who was born in the outskirts of Gisors (Eure), signed on as a soldier in the Carignan regiment, and decided to go to live in New France. There he married a 'King's daughter', Jeanne Deschars, native of a village in Picardy, and they obtained a grant of land in the seigneurie of Batiscan. In 1688 his spouse died, and according to custom an inventory of her belongings was drawn up. On his holding, which was of the usual area, that is to say two acres wide by forty long, Collet had twenty-two acres 'of arable land, and pasture, a house, a barn and stables, the whole valued at twelve hundred *livres*. His possessions and farm implements were valued thus: two oxen worth one hundred and ten *livres* the pair; two young bulls, forty *livres* the pair; a cow, thirty *livres*; two other cows, twenty-five *livres* each; two pigs, eleven *livres* each. Then followed a list of the various implements, tools and kitchen utensils, three sickles, two ploughshares, one pair of plough discs, two choppers, a hammer, a trowel, three gimlets, two coffers with lock and key, a barrel of lard, sundry buckets and barrels, pots and cauldrons. The Normandy farmer who is simply referred to as

Pierre B. in the edition of *Revue des Questions Historiques*, which was published on the 1st of April, 1877, rented two farms; one of these at Etainhus, together with forty acres of land, cost 300 *livres* a year in rent, the other situated at Angerville—*L'Orcher*, comprised a total of 38 acres, and was also rented at 300 *livres*. The inventory lists the following: a wagon, 94 *livres*; a light cart for moving grain, 20 *livres*; a bushel of wheat, 1 *livre*, 5 *sous*; a mare, 65 *livres*; a two-year-old colt, 40 *livres*; a cow, 50 *livres*; a heifer, 5 *livres*; a pig, 7 *livres*; a sheep, 6 *livres*; 14 hens and a cock, 4 *livres*, 7 *sous*. If one takes into consideration the fact that Jean Collet had to pay an annual rent of only two bushels of wheat, a live capon or its value in money and two pennies of *cens*, or quit-rent, one realizes that responsibilities in Canada were very much less onerous than in Normandy.

The settler as a general rule led a simple and abstemious life, enjoyed a measure of security for himself and his family without wanting for anything. At the end of his life he was richer in kind than in cash. The inventory taken on his death nearly always showed numerous debts which he had not allowed to worry him, since, no matter what they totalled, his land at his death would always be worth more than they. A typical example of this was the case of Jacques Turcot, known as one of the most worthy colonists of his day. He was born a month after his father had been killed by Iroquois in 1652. His mother, Françoise Capelle, had been one of the original 'King's Daughters' from Normandy and was to remarry twice—Jacques Turcot embarked on his farmer's life when he was still very young, and when he died at forty-eight, worn out by work, he was seigneurial judge for Champlain. He owned four farms, one at Champlain, two at Batiscan, and one with an acreage of 200 acres within the seigneurie at Gentilly. He was one of the most important non-seigneurial landowners in New France. On the farm where he lived with his family he had forty-six acres under cultivation, a comfortable house which included 'two heated living-rooms, two closets, a kitchen, cellar and loft', farm buildings, barn, stable, outhouse, numerous animals, including eight bullocks and a horse. Jacques Turcot was comfortably off. Nevertheless the inventory of his possessions at his death revealed that he still owed money for the purchase of his farm at Champlain eleven years earlier; a sum of 800 *livres*, that is to say, more than one half of the purchase price. What is more he still owed 195 *livres* to the estate of the last two husbands of his mother, as well as various sums to tradespeople and individuals.

Colonists who chose, by reason of their taste for complete freedom, parts of the country which they thought belonged to no one, were much less solidly established.

Michel Gorron arrived from his own country of Vendée in 1655, and three years later was married in Quebec to a Parisian girl called Marguerite Robineau. They obtained a land grant at Saint-Charles-des-Roches, but after a few years crossed the river and went to settle down in Eschaillon, the seigneurie without a seigneur, where other colonists, Robert Ouy, René Maillot, Raymond Chesne, Jean-Baptiste and Pierre Lebœuf, Pierre and Charles François, went to join them with their wives and children and where all shared the same rough but free life without spiritual or material assistance. Nevertheless those who chose this way of life determinedly put up with all its difficulties.

The Canadian learnt at an early stage to live philosophically, content with small rewards, relying only upon his own ingenuity, organizing his existence to achieve some degree of comfort. Economic conditions were such that he was not able to save any money. The few sales he did succeed in making were paid for in kind. He allowed himself no luxury, save that of being free. La Hontan observed with accuracy that the settler paid neither salt nor poll tax, that is to say board nor lodging, that he was free to hunt and fish. In a word he was rich. His farm belonged to him. It had cost him nothing but his labour and now it was his most precious possession, and an inalienable right. 'The Canadian is proud,' remarked Bougainville disdainfully during the last years of the rule of France. Others before him had stigmatized him as being 'undisciplined, full of his own importance'. He was merely independent of character. Circumstances had ensured that he could depend on no one but himself, and now he only wished to live far away from any complicated problem.

By the time the settler had reached the age of fifty, he was already thinking of handing over his possessions, usually to one of his younger sons, if the latter were about to be married. The order in which this was carried out was very simple. The son undertook in a contract drawn up by the notary to support his father and mother, to care for them during their remaining years 'in sickness as in health', to give them a room with all the usual comforts of a home. This arrangement left the routine unchanged; the father continued to direct the work of the farm, and the mother to run the house. The parents had simply gained for themselves additional freedom and their true authority only came to an end when they decided to relinquish it. Once they knew that their line would continue, they could hand over their responsibilities. Some made demands which seem extraordinary, and which give us insight into the way of life they did not wish to lose or to surrender.

Confirmed bachelors and childless widows also thought it essential to provide for ill-health and old age. When they reached a certain age, they would adopt a godson, the son of a neighbour or a friend, to help them in the work on the farm. If this boy turned out well he would be set up with a legacy, if not the unmarried farmer would sell his farm and go to end his days with a family who would take him in on terms and conditions formally stipulated in a legal contract.

Death, when it came, was treated with religious respect. The local priest was immediately advised, as were close relatives in the parish and kinsmen of the deceased. A neighbour was usually asked to attend to the laying out of the corpse and, if the old man had died peacefully, to dress him in his best clothes. If he were poor he was wrapped in a sheet, for his clothes would come in useful for his eldest son. The body was then placed in a bed in the best room in the house. Every parishioner was in duty bound to view the corpse and to say a prayer for the repose of the dead man's soul. A jar of holy water and a little branch of pine needles were placed by the death-bed, and each visitor sprinkled the body after prayer. All through the evening and night rosaries were said aloud and the funeral took place in the morning of the next day. Often the old man would himself have taken the trouble to prepare his coffin, otherwise a neighbour would quickly put one together during the course of the evening. Before the deceased was taken from the house his body lay there so that all those present could sprinkle it for the last time. The lid of the coffin was only put on and nailed down just before it was taken away to the church. If it were only a short distance, then the coffin would be carried by friends or neighbours. Otherwise it was placed upon a cart or sledge, according to the time of year. While the funeral procession passed, everyone knelt with head bowed, made the sign of the Cross or murmured some last prayer. Burial in summer took place immediately after the religious ceremony. In winter the corpse was placed in a hut known as a charnel-house, situated next to the church. Burial of all those laid in this hut took place on the same day, when the ground had thawed in the spring, the date being announced by the priest during the sermon on the Sunday before.

CHAPTER SIX

RELIGIOUS LIFE

MISSIONARY LIFE

New France was created in the name of religion. At the time of his first voyage, Jacques Cartier set up a cross as symbol of possession, in the name of God and the King of France, of this new land of America. His companions kneeling on the earth behind him, their hands clasped, worshipped the cross. Moreover, Cartier's commission, signed by François I, had declared that it was his duty to work 'to increase the knowledge of the saintly and blessed name of God and of our Holy Mother the Catholic Church'. Cartier carried the word of God to the natives he met all the way from Newfoundland to Hochélaga, afterwards Montreal.

Some decades later, Champlain, for whom the French settlement in America was 'the only and unique way to make known the name of the true God, and to establish the Christian religion there', arrived in New France. The words he spoke before Louis XIII reflected his own thoughts and actions; he invoked the special grace of God who had chosen the reign of the Most Christian King to be the instrument for spreading the Gospel and for carrying the knowledge of God to these peoples who had never heard His name.

Prompted by Champlain, Cardinal Richelieu did not hesitate to grant legal and civil equality to all Indians who had been baptized; these became equal to the born subjects of the King, even in France, where 'if they so desire they can come and live and acquire there rights in property, can draw up a will, inherit and accept gifts and legacies'. Religion was seen as the keystone in the edifice that France was building in this country of America, and the spread of the gospel as the true aim of colonization.

Yet more revealing a phenomenon was that the religious imperative was recognized in France no less than in Canada. Under the reign of Louis XIII a code of prayers was laid down for furthering

107

the future of New France and its spiritual victory. Masses, prayers, penances by day and night comprised the offerings to Providence given to ensure Its approval of the work being done in Canada.

The outstanding contribution to the realization of these religious ideals in Canada was made by the missionary, a word newly minted in the seventeenth century.

The work of the missionaries in New France was of passionate interest to the world of this epoch. The Jesuits, who provided the largest and most active body for the Canadian mission, sent back to France a running account of their new activities, which were published under the title of *Relations*: here they were obeying Loyola's injunctions: 'What each performs shall be written down.' The heroic deeds of these missionaries were followed in France with the same curiosity, the same interest and enthusiasm, the same admiration, as were, much later, the adventures of the great nineteenth-century explorers.

The *Relations* served to attract as many recruits from the laity as from the clerics, despite the fact that the Jesuits depicted with perfect candour the rough and difficult life to which they were bound. They did not suppress the truth and portrayed with exactitude the thousand and one tasks of the missionary. Here is an example from the *Instructions to Fathers who are to be sent among the Hurons*, a directive which promises nothing specially alluring: 'Begin by making yourself liked and respected by the savages; try to win them to you by performing little services for them such as carrying a bright mirror about with you so that you can make a fire for them whenever they find the need to smoke their pipes. Strive not to appear revolted by their food, try to take your collation in the morning, for when the "barbarians" are on the move they only eat at sunrise and sunset. Be quick to take your place in the canoe, to disembark with haste and to draw up your habit to prevent it becoming wet. Above all do not become obtrusive in your relations with the savages; put up with their imperfections without comment. Should you have occasion to reprimand them do so with words couched in loving tones, and not in words of dislike. Do not forget that little gifts give great pleasure to the Indians, so provide yourselves with half a gross of awls, with two or three dozen little knives . . . so that you may buy your food in this way. When portages are made overland, try to help the Indians, carrying small things as far as you are able. If you lack the appropriate words, then give the Indians you meet a kindly smile. Do this for the sake of Jesus Christ who is our true King; He it is alone together with His cross whom we must seek as we go to gather in these peoples.'

The missionary accompanied the Indians on their expeditions. He was accepted by them and allowed to share their cabin or some rudimentary shelter, for the nights, but this exposed him to a thousand discomforts; cold, heat, smoke: his head touched the roof of the hut where the snow crept in; his feet, even when he slept with his legs curled under him, nearly reached the fire which burnt in the centre. The smoke was truly penitential, burning his eyes and making them water. Try as he might to read psalms from his breviary, yet he was often forced to lay aside his book 'seeing nothing there but confusion'. Meals were hardly a banquet; water to drink, foodstuffs based on flour made from maize and boiled in water, with the stiff consistency of glue.

Some aspects of the missionary's life can only be imagined; bedding down, for instance, on the bare earth, vermin always at hand, the impossibility of a moment's privacy to study or to meditate; the close proximity of ten or fifteen persons, of children of all ages who were never still, who cried or fought while the adults talked, and dogs which roamed around pushing their muzzles into everything. He was often hungry and there was no game; then the missionary had to content himself with chewing old mooseskins, 'which are much harder than the skins of eel', and with living on the buds of trees and the more tender barks.

In the numerous Indian tribes the medicine man watched with a malevolent eye the rival whose intrusion might weaken his own power over the people, and persecuted him relentlessly. He made fun of him, compared him to a dog, 'to the leader of the pack, to a bear'. He insulted him in public so that everyone, especially the children, shouted with laughter. Taking advantage of the scanty knowledge the missionary had gained of the native tongue, he persuaded him to write 'filthy things', and then made him read them aloud, to the great hilarity of everyone. Father Brebœuf added a further instruction for the missionary novices: 'Your life will hang by a thread, and what is more, you will be held responsible for the sterility or fecundity of the land, on pain of death. If you do not make it rain they will think nothing of discussing ways and means of getting rid of your presence.' But he rallied with the magnificent statement: 'I assure you that all this has only served further to confirm in me our vocation.'

Despite all its wretchedness, the life of a missionary was organized on monastic lines. He rose at four in the morning, meditated, celebrated Holy Communion unless prevented unavoidably, and read religious books until eight o'clock.

After which he would open the gates to the Indians. It was 'like an avalanche' of curious faces, beggars, converts about to receive baptism, newly-received converts making themselves thoroughly at home, settling down wherever they wished, prying into everything. One could not take one's eyes off them, for they would soon spirit away some object that took their fancy—food, or even furniture.

This kindly reception dragged on until almost midday. The missionary listened to grievances, cared for the sick, offered food, spoke of God and the holy saints to these people who understood nothing of his words. From twelve to two o'clock, the children were heard catechism; on certain days of the week the lesson ended at one o'clock and was followed by instruction of the potential converts. While this was going on another missionary visited the huts, 'seeking children and adults in imminent danger of death, teaching and baptising them'. This was yet further proof of self-denial for 'before reaching the end of the long encampment of Indians, one would be covered with vermin, sweat and filth'. The welcome was not always as warm as it might have been: in the face of abuse and insults the missionary had to be patient.

After an examination of conscience the Father lunched from two o'clock onwards, constantly forced at the same time to prevent the audacious savages from scooping his food out of the pot.

While he lunched he read the Bible. At dinner he read *Paradis ouvert à Philagie* by the Jesuit Paul de Barry.

Then the natives would crowd back on him and the tour of the huts began again. At four o'clock there were prayers, recitations from the breviary, correspondence, events of the day to be gone over, study of the Indian language. After dinner, holy meditation was followed by sleep.

On Sundays the day varied slightly. The missionary celebrated sung Mass and, after distribution of consecrated bread, prayers were said, catechism taught, and at five o'clock compline was sung, after which visits to the huts took place in any time that still remained.

Every effort was made to embellish religious ceremonies, and the fullest use was made of leaves, bouquets, garlands, and brightly-coloured materials.

The missionary's baggage was of extreme simplicity especially when he was travelling: a blanket on his back for the night, a bag in his hand in which, next to the articles used in the celebration of Holy Communion, he packed needles, fishhooks, trinkets of glass for offering as presents or in exchange for board and lodging.

Determined to overcome every difficulty, the missionaries set themselves to study native languages, and became pupils of the Indians. Not all of them managed to master these tongues, but some of them, notably Father Chaumont, excelled in them: 'There is no known turn of speech or subtlety of expression which I have not made use of—even including some which I have invented myself.'

Evangelization was organized from the start and founded upon the unbounded devotion of the missionaries. Apostolic zeal, whose four foundations are good humour, humility, patience and generous charity, was added to the desire to build up a nucleus of administration capable of ensuring the most complete and rapid spread of the gospel among the Indians.

There seemed to be two methods of accomplishing this, by imitation and by adjustment. The former required the Indians, particularly the young, to mingle with the French people and French children. This experiment was painstakingly attempted in 1668 after the opening of the little seminary of the Holy Child, where eight French and six Huron children were gathered together; it soon failed for parents did not like to be separated from their children, who in any case missed the forest way of life—which did not exactly fit in with the curriculum of the little seminary.

The method succeeded a little better with the girls, brought up by the Ursuline nuns in Quebec, who through intermarriage with the French became assimilated.

In Versailles many illusions were held about the assimilability of native peoples. Colbert himself charged the Jesuits with ineffectiveness: 'Their excuse,' he said, 'was that they believed that the sacred principles of our religion would flourish better if the savages, after conversion were allowed to continue in their normal way of life rather than being taught to think and behave as Frenchmen.' These criticisms appear slightly superficial when we know how deeply the Indians were attached to their own way of life. What in fact frequently happened was precisely the reverse: for obvious reasons it was easier to turn a Frenchman into an Indian than turn an Indian into a Frenchman. The geographical peculiarities of the country played their part.

Problems of adaptation presented themselves without end. In the beginning the missions were strictly of an itinerant kind. The missionary followed the Indians on their wanderings or stayed for a time in their villages. In such cases the missionaries were alone without supervision, often in danger. This system was opposed by Father Lalemant who advocated an organization of the kind set up by the Jesuits in Paraguay. There a central mission was established, from which missionaries went out to live among the tribes. In this way the missionaries were less isolated and were able to practise their calling more effectively.

The new idea was to persuade the Indians to settle in one place. 'One thing seems clear to me from what I have seen,' wrote Father Le Jeune to his Abbé, 'and that is that we must not expect very good results among the savages so long as they continue to rove about. Today they are sitting at your feet, but tomorrow your congregation will be gone, driven by hunger into the forests and up the rivers in search of their livelihood. . . .' To check their wanderings a proper village had to be established, a 'mission' where the Indians could learn to cultivate the soil and to become self-reliant without aid from outside. Missionaries attached to these posts had more time for instructing the Indians and creating a small Christian community. It was in this way that the mission at Sillery, near Quebec, was formed, starting with thirty families of Algonquins.

In Settlements of this kind the Jesuits were able to prepare their flock more carefully in the ways of piety and the Christian virtues. For though they continued to find their own food, to dress in their own way, to hunt and to fish, the Indians would also cultivate the land, practise various small skills according to their aptitude, and learn to read and write. They were discouraged from believing too much in dreams, from changing their wives or getting drunk, but these precepts were not always respected.

'Evangelization proceeds', in the words of a Jesuit Father. 'In

7 a. Type of Seigneurial manor of the eighteenth century

b. A military fort constructed in the seventeenth century, on the borders of Acadie

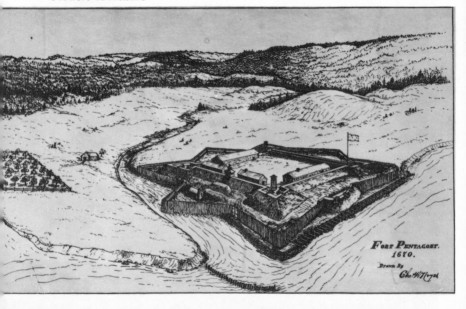

8 a. Three Rivers—houses of the French regime

b. Montreal—bastion of the seven-year war

this place, when we first came, we found not one single soul who knew the true God. Today, in spite of persecution, poverty, hunger, war and pestilence, there is not a single family without its converts. This is the result of more than twenty years' work.'

The missionary as evangelist had no easy task. He had to make allowance for the longstanding beliefs cherished by the Indians, and with some skill to put before them the truths of the Christian religion. Had they been browbeaten, their beliefs ridiculed, their faith in dreams derided, then all chance of converting them would have been lost.

One facet of the Indian character was an asset to the missionaries, and this was curiosity. Some of the Jesuits realized how this advantage might be exploited to good effect. After reciting a few Christian prayers in Indian dialect before his congregation, the missionary would ask for questions and answer them as best he could. The questions were diverse: 'Why do we die? Is nightfall the same throughout the world?' In their answers the Jesuits contrived to embody religious precepts. A great deal of skill was required, as well as tact and knowledge of the Indian mind, to get anything out of these dialogues. The requisite patience and pliancy of mind was not found in every missionary. Far too many of them wished to wield power over the Indians rather than persuade them and convince them. These were incapable of understanding the stubbornness of the Indians in the defence of their beliefs.

The discussion continued until it was the turn of the Jesuit to ask the questions. He took these from his knowledge of natural science which was of special interest to the Indians. He might ask them if the day was as high in the sky as were the stars, and what was the size of the sun. When he corrected their answers it was always with reference to 'the state of our beliefs', thus bringing in truths of Christian religion.

The missionaries threw themselves heart and soul into this apostolate: the satisfaction of converting one single savage was intense. They would rather achieve one convert than the 'conquest of an entire empire'. All difficulties were as nothing in the face of such a mark of favour from Heaven.

Even capture and imprisonment failed to diminish their ardour for evangelization. Thus poor Reverend Father Jogues, beaten, mutilated, his body covered with burning coals, preached to the Algonquins, fellow-prisoners of the Iroquois, and 'endeavoured to lead them to the knowledge of the Creator'. He disproved their stories of how the universe was created by showing them a tortoise, and he demonstrated to them that the sun has no life or learning: 'that it is in no way a God'. If they persisted in their belief that this heavenly body possessed divine meaning, then he tried to make them understand how much brighter was the light of its Creator.

The missionaries sought to bring the greatest possible dignity to their dealings with the Indians. Thus, when Father Brebœuf received the Indians from the village, led by their chief, he wore a surplice and a biretta. Everyone knelt to sing the *Paternoster*, 'paraphrased into Huron lines', after which the Father delivered a short sermon followed by questions, and rewarded those who answered correctly with 'a glass trinket'.

The reactions of the Indians to evangelization varied according to circumstances. If the moral lecture was of too austere a kind, the Indians would answer: 'Your ways are not our ways, your God cannot be our God.' The Hurons saw baptism as a talisman to good health or as a 'new interpretation of their customs to teach them to mortify the flesh' as Jesus did on the Cross. Huron women, fearing that baptism would not require men to become monogamous, were loud in protest against it.

The sixth commandment was extremely difficult to obey since chastity in women or girls was regarded as unseemly. The Huron chiefs led the field in licentiousness and immorality. Talk of Christian purity to them was taken as a challenge; it called for diplomacy of the most subtle kind.

Missionaries were always in danger, even amongst the most peace-loving and relatively civilized tribes. Thus in the frequent outbreaks of epidemics, the Indians sought supernatural causes for their affliction. Medicine men incanted spells and performed all sorts of rituals to exorcize the evil spirit. If it paid no attention to their pleas and promises, it was only because a more powerful spirit was guiding it. Suspicion fell upon the 'black habits' worn by the Jesuits, who professed to be so powerful. The medicine men were the first to voice these accusations which were quickly believed.

And so the threats grew louder, the Christian God was looked upon as being an evil spirit and he who had 'conjured' him up must be put to death. This sort of violence could arise even within the mission settlements, as when the Fathers Brébœuf and Chaumont were overwhelmed with insults, beaten unmercifully

114

and driven out of the village. Things could be even worse than this, and lead to the killing of the unlucky missionaries.

The Jesuits of New France were among the first French martyrs. When they embarked on their mission they understood the risks, and they accepted them; some even sought them out as being the natural climax of their vocation; to die as Christ had done.

And how they suffered. The Indians had developed, and practised constantly, methods of torture which would prolong suffering: with their garments torn off, their nails pulled out, the Fathers Brébeuf and Gabriel Lalemant were spirited away to the Indian village and beaten about the shoulders, the loins, legs, stomach, chest and face. Terribly bruised and swollen, they exhorted their fellow sufferers to accept their suffering to the glory of God. Their torturers, exasperated by their heroism and humility, lopped off one of their hands and pierced them with sharp awls and iron nails, tied tomahawks around their necks, trussed them up with thongs of bark soaked with pitch and resin, and set them on fire.

From the height of their suffering the martyrs continued to call upon God and to beseech these heathen to seek conversion, until the murderers, infuriated by their obstinacy, cut off their lips and noses. Remembering the ritual of baptism, which they had learnt from the Fathers, they mocked it by sprinkling their victims with boiling water.

The duration of such martyrdom depended on the whims of the women and children. It took six days for René Goupil to die, during which time he was repeatedly heaped with cinders and burning coals for varying periods. When Father Jogues was tortured to death, he was stripped naked and his flesh was cut away in strips before his throat was cut. Father Antoine Daniel was luckier to be killed by a bullet in the chest as he came out of the chapel.

Is it possible to judge evangelization as one does politics, by its results? From year to year the number of baptisms increased. Twenty-two baptisms were performed among the Hurons in 1635, a hundred and fifteen in 1636, three hundred in 1637. This throws a revealing light on the ardour of the Jesuits. Yet these new Christians were only rarely adolescents or adults. Father Charles Garnier baptized 100 Indians in a village which had been struck down by an epidemic. Forty-four of them died soon after, twenty of them still in infancy. The missionaries did not often meet with any opposition when they came to baptize old people at the point of death, or dying children, since at this stage baptism was regarded as a remedy or an insurance of a better life in the world to come.

When the Indian sincerely underwent conversion and became part of the Christian community, he often behaved in a praise-worthy fashion. He went to Church twice daily, in the morning to Mass and in the evening for prayers chanted aloud by the whole congregation. He listened with great attention to the sermons, did not fail to make his confession and share his joys and sorrows with the priest. When the Indians held a council they would send to the religious body to borrow one of their number to assist in the discussion, and the advice which the 'black habit' gave often helped them to make a decision. At banquets, the place of honour was reserved for the missionary. In some cases an Indian would be truly inspired by the Holy Spirit, and then life would take on the quality of the blessed in the Church. The Iroquois Saint Catherine Takakouita was one of these. Despite the menaces of her parents, and the importunities of members of her tribe, she retained the most complete purity; braving with dignity the heaviest sacrifices, rejoicing in being able to offer them to God. Some conversions achieved true fame; for example, the conversion of Garakontié, great Iroquois chief of the Onnontagués peoples. From the first he showed a natural sympathy with the French through his support of those objects associated with worship, which he sought to protect from blasphemous treatment. When he paid an official visit to Quebec, he underwent baptism and the Governor, de Courcelles, stood as sponsor to him, emphasizing the importance he attached to the ceremony by ordering a salute to be fired by every cannon in the fort, while a guard of honour paid homage to the Indian Chief. Garakontié showed himself worthy of these honours. He was a staunch upholder of the faith and of the peace. He addressed his tribe severely: 'Expect no support from me in the furtherance of your dreams of the maintenance of the super-stitious customs practised by your ancestors. I will not allow them; such practices are from now on forbidden, for they are contrary to the laws of God.'

Another Huron, Joseph Chihouatenhoua, was of the same

calibre. Before conversion he was already essentially a religious man, living an exemplary life. He had only one wife to whom he remained faithful in a milieu which regarded polygamy as normal. When Father Jerome Lalemant appeared for the first time in his village, and spoke to him of the mysteries of the Faith, he was immediately taken with a belief which seemed so exactly to conform with his own perceptions. When years after his conversion a missionary asked him how he imagined God to be, he answered that each morning he recited a prayer conceived in more or less the following terms: 'Creator, at last I know Thee; early in the morning I can talk with Thee; Thou it is who made this earth we see and sky we see; Thou madest us, we who are called men. Thou art master of us as we are masters of the canoes and the cabins we have built; Thou art our maker; it is nothing that we are masters for a very short space of what we have; for a very short time are we master of the canoe we have made canoe, and of the cabin we have made cabin.' The Jesuits were of course delighted with this happy and naïve conception of theology. But men like Garakontié and the Chihoatenhoua were exceptional.

The missionaries did not confine themselves to evangelism. Realizing the importance of the 'native' policy of France in Canada, they concerned themselves with other matters. They were skilful ambassadors to the Indian territories. On May 11, 1646, Father Isaac Jogues was sent 'on a peace mission' to the Iroquois whom he understood well, since he had been their prisoner. He knew them to be two-faced, that they tried to pretend their one desire was for peace, while for a long time they had been planning to exterminate the Hurons, who were friends of the French, in order to make 'one united people and one sole territory'.

The missionary also gave secret advice to the civil authorities: 'There are nearly three hundred harquebuses in this place, and seven hundred Iroquois who are very skilful in handling these weapons; they could sail into Three Rivers by way of various rivers,' wrote Father Jogues on a fragment of birch-bark for despatch to the Governor.

Again, the missionaries would use their sermons skilfully to further Government policy. Thus, to the Papinachois: 'You all know Onontio (the Governor-General), the well-known chieftain of Quebec; you all know how he is the terror of the Iroquois. The bare mention of his name makes them tremble since he laid waste to their country and set fire to their villages. Well, over the sea there are ten thousand Onontios like him, they are merely the soldiers of that great officer, of our great King of whom I have spoken.'

Missionaries were also to be found among the celebrated explorers of North America. Father Albanel made two voyages into Hudson Bay, sailing by way of Tadoussac and Lake St Jean in order to reach James Bay, overcoming exhaustion and the most incredible difficulties. Describing the countrysides through which he had passed, he wrote: 'There are two hundred waterfalls, which means two hundred separate portages to move canoe and baggage . . . There are four hundred rapids which can only be passed with the help of a long pole.' Albanel was already sixty when he made his second voyage with the sole object of bringing the gospel to the tribes in the North.

The name of Father Marquette is linked with that of Joliet and the discovery of the Mississippi. In 1673 they made their way south through totally unexplored country. They struck the river at 42° latitude and made their way down it until they reached 33°. During this voyage of discovery Father Marquette never lost sight of his evangelistic calling. He passed through the Illinois country where the tribesmen were harmless and gentle, returning to them to bring them the word of God, only to die a few months later.

The missionaries also made their contribution to scientific knowledge. Father Lafiteau, for example, discovered in Canada a medicinal plant—*ginseng*—already famous in China. It was found to be an excellent stimulant, to put on weight, 'to increase the vital forces'. The Indians knew it under its Iroquois name of 'garent-oguen', which had in fact the same meaning as the Chinese word *gin-seng* or 'man's thigh'. They also used it as a remedy against dysentery and to reduce fever, particularly in babies. It was some credit to Father Lafiteau to have recognized this plant which had become a favoured object of trade in Asia, and in a memorandum to the Regent, the Duke of Orléans, to have suggested that in future the plant should be developed for the benefit of New France, instead of relying on its importation from Tartary.

From the seventeenth century onwards, at the side of the missionaries stood auxiliary workers who were known as 'the given'. These auxiliaries were responsible for the material well-being of the mission. They did not take the community vows. Their agreement ended with a simple dedication; as in the case of Le Coq in 1639: 'I, the undersigned declare that of my own free will I have given myself to the Company of Jesus to serve and assist with all my power and capacity for work the Fathers of the said Company which is working towards the salvation and conversion of souls, particularly to those who are working to convert the wretched savages and barbarians of New France.' These lay missionaries in the Huron mission increased from the original seven to twenty-three in number.

The clergy in New France wished with all its heart to make this country into a Christian nation and to convert the Indians to true Catholicism. They believed their apostolate was justified by the undoubted benefits brought by religion to the 'savages'. They were appalled by the Indian way of life, by their complete lack of any moral sense, by the difficulties of their nomadic existence and the frequent incidence of epidemics and famine. The one and only remedy they could envisage which was directly related to the glory of God was to convert the Indians to Christian civilization.

Most of the Indians, however, were not ready for this sudden conversion from their ancestral customs, and the results were disproportionate to the sacrifices made by the missionaries who so gladly gave their lives to enlarge the Kingdom of God. Father Jogues was very much a case in point. Martyred for the first time by Iroquois, who cut off his fingers, he was only allowed to serve Mass with his mutilated hands after obtaining special dispensation from Pope Urban VIII. But he went again among the Indians and this time was tortured to death. The natives were infuriated by his bald head, since to them an abundant growth of hair was a sign of superiority.

It would have needed the passage of decades, prodigies of patience, and the endurance of infinite suffering to eliminate the superstitions so firmly rooted in native custom. And, to make matters worse, the missionaries had to struggle with yet another enemy which was imperceptibly crippling their efforts; this was the traffic in furs.

PARISH LIFE

Parish life in New France was slow to develop. The gradual establishment of villages made up of French immigrants called for organized religion, and colonists needed some sort of secular organization as well. This was built up only step by step and owed much to the impetus of Mgr de Laval.

From the very beginning pastoral work had also been the responsibility of the missionaries. But their conduct of this side of their duties had been perfunctory, and the settlers complained: the missionaries employed portable chapels and each Sunday celebrated one or two Masses in the homestead of a colonist. The Canadian church in its early days ran into two separate kinds of difficulty; in the first place the areas of colonization were scattered at intervals along the whole length of the St Lawrence from Tadoussac as far as Montreal. Secondly there was the Church's lack of effective workers, which meant it was impossible to establish a permanent ministry in each village. Thus in 1683 twenty-five priests and missionaries were expected to provide religious services in New France over a stretch of land of more than 1000 kilometres.

Most of the priests were young and strong but their work was exhausting if only because their parishes were so vast. M. de Saint-Claude, a Canadian aged twenty-eight, was responsible for the whole length of the south bank of the river which included the districts of Berthier, of La Durantaie, Beaumont, Lauzon, St Nicolas, Sainte-Croix, and Lotbinière; nearly 200 kilometres from one end to the other.

In the first stages the occupation of a presbytery was only intermittent and there was no permanent incumbent. From the seminary at Quebec priests were sent out to the various parishes for only a few weeks at a time. The civil authorities and the colonists were soon dissatisfied with this system. Frontenac the Governor asked the Court to issue formal instructions insisting that Mgr de Laval must establish permanent incumbents. The bishop agreed to this on condition that priests were guaranteed an adequate livelihood.

So it was that the basic plan for demarcation of the parishes was worked out at the beginning of the eighteenth century, providing for the establishment of twenty-five livings, and missions were set up. These parishes were very poor. At the time there were only nine stone-built churches, the rest were half-timbered, or simply log structures, roofed with thatch.

If there existed a presbytery, which was not often, for priests lodged in a settler's home, it frequently lacked even the barest essentials. Church and presbytery would be built on a small plot of land presented by the seigneur. Thus M. de la Bouteillerie at Rivière-Ouelle made a gift of four acres of land to 'be used to put up a church', and in 1685 a little wooden chapel was dedicated to Our-Lady-of-Liesse, patron saint of the parish whose first incumbent was the Abbé Morel. The priest opened a register for baptisms, marriages and burials.

Five years later, under the ministry of the Abbé de Francheville, a Canadian-born priest, the parish contained nearly 100 families, and in 1694 a church was built to replace the little chapel. This too was of wood, but the first priest to be appointed, the Abbé Bernard de Roquelys, a Frenchman, was lodged in the old seigneurial manor, restored and turned into a presbytery.

Above all parishes in importance was Quebec. The first priest to be appointed, M. de Bernières, who had come out at the same time as Mgr de Laval, had a presbytery built in 1661; a good solid stone house costing 8,500 *livres*, of which three-quarters had to be contributed by the parishioners. Since 1657, Quebec had possessed a fine church also built of stone and dedicated to Our Lady of Peace in memory of the peace signed with the Iroquois. It was built in the shape of a Latin cross and the chancel was apsidal. Fair-sized—just over thirty yards long and twelve wide—its wooden belfry rising above the transept held only one bell in 1657, but by 1664, it boasted three. The bishop was proud of his episcopal church, and wrote to the Vatican: 'Here we have a basilica built of stone, large and magnificent, where the divine services are held according to the ritual followed by the bishops; our priests and seminarists, as well as the ten or twelve choristers, are regular in their attendance.'

The various church ornaments were exceptionally fine; eight gilded chandeliers, together with chalices, cups, golden and silver cruets for the Eucharistic oils. By 1664 there was already an organ, brought from France by Mgr de Laval. The church might have belonged to any small French town, but the depredations of the weather, especially when the winters were so long, soon affected the roof. In 1664 there was a cry for help; 100,000 slates and 200,000 nails were needed for repairs. The work was to cost 2,000 *livres*, and the materials had to be bought in Nantes. The snow also had a disastrous effect on the wooden belfry, and for eighteen months the bells were silent, for fear that they might bring down the belfry. In the end Louis XIV himself supplied the money for restoration of the belfry to the tune of more than 10,500 *livres* over three years.

Income from the parish derived from various sources. In the first place from the pews, many of which were bought by families. In 1666 seventeen of these brought in 193 *livres*. In the same year more than 700 *livres* came in through the offertories. Surplice fees from the solemn Masses sung provided 200 *livres*. The finances of the church were administered by the Vestry; the assembly of churchwardens elected by freeholders. Present and former church-wardens nominated a Council of three of their members which dealt with the upkeep of the church, its repairs, purchases, loans, sales, as well as with the administration of property, and the collection of income.

The Vestry of Quebec possessed its own farmland; a farm at Cape Diamant which brought in thirty-six *livres,* and the house and farm at Cape Rouge. Sometimes the faithful fell behind with their rents and in 1661 an ordinance from the bishop stipulated that rent must in future be paid in advance because arrears amounted to more than 1,000 *livres*. The poor were exempt from this ruling.

Ritual observances cost a great deal of money. In 1668, the funeral of a M. Bourdon was marked by three religious services, followed by an annual High Mass for the repose of his soul, to be sung for twelve years in succession—High Mass with deacons and subdeacons, silks, silver, ten pounds of church candles. The total cost of all this was 197 *livres*, ten *sous*. But the priest's main income came from tithes, as in France. Until 1663 these taxes were not levied in New France. The Recollects and then the Jesuits had given free ministry to their settlers, but Mgr de Laval felt compelled to introduce the tithe in order to relieve the ever-increasing needs of the Church, and to provide for the existence of priests within the newly-established parishes. Contrary to practice in the towns, country tithes were not paid directly to the priests but to the Seminary responsible for the steady supply of priests and missionaries to those in need of them. The tithe was fixed at one thirteenth instead of one tenth.

The faithful, however, had acquired a taste for getting their religion for nothing. Complaints and recriminations poured in, supported, it seemed, by the deliberately ill-intentioned, and this despite a reduction of the so-called tithe to one twentieth. At Three Rivers they refused to post notices dealing with tithe laws. So violent was the opposition that the Abbé Morel at Beauprée stood at one time in physical danger. No tax was paid here until 1667, when an agreement was reached that the tithe should be reduced to one-twenty-sixth payable to the priest in wheat and delivered free to the presbytery door. A royal ordinance exempted those colonists who did not receive the holy sacrament from payment. In the course of this little war the secular power had sided with the settlers, obviously calculating that the Canadian clergy would become too rich and powerful if they received a thirteenth part of the country's total output.

Yet an inventory drawn up by the priest of Champlain, François Dupré, in 1687 indicated that the parish assets were by no means excessive: seven chasubles and six altarcloths, gifts of members of religious orders and of some ladies of the parish. A chalice worth 100 *francs* paid for by a 'door to door collection'. Another collection enabled the curé to obtain a tabernacle weighing 300 pounds. Chapels of the nobility were richer. The inventory of the goods of the seigneur de Portneuf, drawn up by notary Rageot, proves this. In the manor chapel were goods which would have delighted the heart of many a parish priest: 'a little pyx in silver, three little silver boxes for the Holy oils (known today as Holy oil stocks), a silver chalice with patina, thirteen frames large and small, gilded and with their canvases framed by bas-reliefs, two straw sprays (today found sometimes as "corn dollies"), a chasuble, the maniple and stole lined with Indian silk, and the whole lined with country cloth (probably buckram to stiffen it). A chalice veil of red damask edged with old silver galoon, a box for hosts (that is, a box to contain altar breads on the credence table for before the offertory), an altar cloth of taffeta, a chasuble, a stole, a chalice veil, and a lined burse with fifteen pieces of cloth for the altar . . .' The list goes on and on.

The beauty of ornaments and decoration owed much to the zeal of the faithful. The Abbé Navières, originally from Limoges, appointed to the parish of Sainte-Anne-en-Beaupré in 1734, could not get over the beauty and richness of some of the Canadian churches, though he himself inherited one of the places of pilgrimage which had already grown important: 'In our country parishes in France,' he wrote to a friend, 'most of our priests would be ashamed of the pitiable state of their churches and treasures, had they ever seen the cleanliness, the order, and the very richness of those in Canada. I know large parishes in Limoges which have not one quarter of the treasure and fine linen that I in my parish of Sainte-Anne possess.' The generosity shown by the flock of Abbé Navières was not the only example of this kind in New France. Throughout the country during the long winter evenings, women embroidered church hangings, while men carved statuettes or made small pieces of furniture for their Church.

The Swedish traveller, Peter Kalm, gave it as his opinion that many of the priests did not 'seem very strong in Latin, although the services are conducted in that language'. But daily duties of incumbents in the parishes called for moral and human qualities rather than intellectual gifts. It was a difficult task for a priest to integrate himself into the life of the parish.

At the outset, most of the priests had come straight from France. Unprepared for the harshness of climate and the general strangeness of everything, they usually limited their activities strictly to the observation of their spiritual duties. The colonists found them a little over-weight in their arguments, making too much of their own learning and not enough of local realities. They shrank from the cold, stayed at home during the winter months and only with difficulty acclimatized themselves. Some of them offended the Canadians by looking down upon them and their condescension did much to strain relations. Nicolas Bouquin, a priest from the diocese of Orléans, who took over the parishes of Champlain and Batiscan in 1692, was one of those guilty of this sort of superior attitude. In his sermons he would inveigh against his parishioners, accusing them of frivolous conduct, and borrow from the set orations of the great Lenten preachers as employed in the cathedrals of France. The poor colonists were bewildered and resentful. The only self-indulgence they were guilty of was one which they did not consider to be a crime; getting drunk once in a while. Other difficulties arose over tithes, visiting the sick during the winter months and over the timing of the services. Bouquin refused to bow to the seigneur Pézard de la Touche and his wife during High Mass, insisting that this was an honour due only to God and to His ministers of religion. When an edict from the Sovereign council, signed by a sheriff, ruled that he must pay homage to the seigneur, he demanded to be sent back to Quebec.

The Bishop, reluctant to give him another living, decided in spite of the shortage of priests, to allow him to return to France. It must not be thought from these observations that the Abbé Bouquin was typical of every French priest. Some were models of virtue and charity. Brother Nicolas Foucault was one of them. He had arrived as clerk to Mgr de Laval, was ordained in Quebec in 1689, and immediately appointed to a parish in which he soon became well regarded for his kindness and devotion. In due course he was sent out with the mission to Mississippi where he was killed by Indian tribesmen.

As time went on Canadian-born priests were ordained. The first of these was Germain Morin, grandson of Louis Hébert, the first colonist. This was an excellent omen, particularly when at the same time his sister, Marie Morin, became one of the first Canadian nuns. Next on the list were the twin brothers, Claude and Pierre Volant of Saint-Claude, of Three Rivers. They were sent out at once to work among the settlers. They may not have been very erudite, they were ill at ease in the maze of dialectic and theology, and they did not always know the answer to every question in discussion with the Jesuits, but they were humble and devoted and the settlers welcomed them warmly. They were easy to please, they visited the houses of the seigneurie and chatted to everyone. They brought news of distant parishes, acting in a friendly way as a sort of connecting link between the people of the various seigneuries in the territories under their ministry. What is more the civil authorities appointed them honorary officials in case of need in the parish. An ordinance from the Intendant, Bégon, authorized them to draw up wills in cases where no notary was available. In 1733 the King qualified them to draw up marriage contracts; later they were able to deal with bills of sale, contracts of all kinds, agreements, and deeds of gift. They set up powers of attorney, worded receipts, drew up official reports and their signatures took on a legal standing. This is the historical origin of the statute of authority held by the Catholic clergy of Canada to this day. Solid friendship and reciprocal understanding grew up in this way between the colonists and the priests who had grown with them.

The fair duty of a priest is to administer the sacraments. The first of these is Holy Baptism. It was the acknowledged obligation of all the faithful to have their children baptized at birth, and they were forbidden to practise private baptism at home on pain of being excluded from church for a month and, if they repeated the offence, of excommunication. The ordinances of Mgr de Laval were very clear on this subject. But the colonists were sometimes negligent, often unable to undertake the journey to church because of the demands of work, the danger of Indian attack, or the wintry conditions. The priests, with more understanding than the bishop, would compromise with these rules and make a note in the parish register of the reasons for deferment of the baptism: 'On December 7, 1710, in the district of St Peter's River, a daughter was born of the legitimate marriage of Pierre Masson and Catherine François, and private baptism was administered the same day by René Pinot, after which, on April 23, 1711, the child was brought to Batiscan, not having been able to make the crossing of the river in the first place, since it had not been sufficiently frozen.'

The practice of another sacrament also led to controversy. La Hontan, who served in New France, complained of the way in which the clergy conducted a form of inquisition under pretext of hearing confession. Confession was strictly compulsory. Before he could communicate, a man must show a certificate from his confessor. This certificate was demanded of those who wished to arrange a contract of marriage and especially before the Easter celebrations of Mass. It was set out in the following manner: 'I have heard the confession of . . . in the parish of . . . In testimony whereof I have delivered to him this certificate.' The faithful suffered this compulsion with a good grace, it seems. But such a practice of presenting certificates after confession led to difficulties between individual clergy. Some of them gave certificates to those outside their own parish. This 'trafficking' in certificates of confession was a frequent cause of dispute.

The parishioner who travelled about had to carry with him a religious 'passport' which showed that he belonged to a particular parish and provided proof of his eligibility to receive the sacraments, and of his good name as a practising Catholic. Penances imposed on the faithful took various forms: visitation of the sick, the keeping of silence, serving a number of masses, fasting, the restoration of wrongly acquired property (particularly among money-lenders). Absolution was often refused to tavernkeepers and those who made the natives drunk. Did the priests really practise inquisitions? La Hontan asserted: 'We have a priest who is a real bigot and his inquisitions are inhuman. It is impossible to deny that he is a spiritual autocrat. In his sermon he singles out individuals by name. He forbids his parishioners on pain of excommunication to read certain novels. . . . In his churlish view everything is shame and mortal sin. Can you believe it possible that he refused Communion to one of the most prominent ladies in Society simply because she wore a bow of coloured ribbons?' La Hontan himself had a bone to pick with the priest, who, according to the author's own account, was capable of bursting into his room without invitation and, discovering a volume of Petronius, would have thought to tear it into shreds, supposing it to be scandalous. It was true that M. le Curé was not reluctant to chide from his lofty pulpit those who had behaved badly.

Although some priests went out of their way to denounce unseemly behaviour, most of them performed a social service which was becoming more and more burdensome. As time went on the priest tended to replace the seigneur as the centre of the parish. The settlers would often meet in the 'salle des habitants' or public meeting room of the presbytery and there hold discussions with their pastor over parish problems. Tithes were a subject of much controversy. Gradually the priest, by setting an example and himself becoming a farmer, showed that it was possible through hard work to earn a livelihood. The parishioners, put to shame by his example, became more generous and willingly brought seed for sowing, farm implements, a pig, or a heifer. This enlightened dealing over the collection of tithes produced peace and a feeling of content.

It was halfway through the eighteenth century, when nearly every parish had its spiritual leader, that, according to one Canadian historian, the priest's status had reached its highest point of effectiveness. The parish was the link binding together a population often widely scattered. 'It was through the parish that the young Canadian realized that the interests of the group were of more importance than his own. The parish, guided by its priest, thus ensured family solidarity, fostered traditions and built up a moral and religious inheritance.'

The Canadians were sincere in their piety. In the words of Mgr de Saint-Vallier: 'Each house is a small well-disciplined community in itself, where family prayers are said morning and evening, where the rosaries are said, where individual consciences are examined

before meals, and where the fathers and mothers of families depu-
tize for the priest by superintending the behaviour of their children
and their servants.' These people regularly went to church. The
Governor, the Intendant, and members of the Sovereign Council
attended the cathedral services in a body. Afer the clergy, they were
the first to receive the holy bread, the incense, the kiss. After
religious festivals, processions were formed. So great was the crowd
for the ceremony of the translation of the relics of St Flavien and
Sainte Felicité, at which no fewer than forty-seven ecclesiastics in
surplices assisted, that the floor of the chapel of the Ursulines
sagged and gave way. Fortunately no one was hurt.

The Canadians were assiduous in their devotion. A papal bull
from Alexander III authorized the setting up of a sisterhood of
the Holy Family, the object of which would be to inspire a true
and firm piety in all Christian families and to help in the conversion of the heathen. The ladies belonging to the sisterhood
were to aspire to the following virtues: a sincere and heartfelt
affection towards their husbands, the practice of respect, obedience,
gentleness and patience towards him, his faults and bad moods to
be borne. To allow no native to die without first bestowing upon
him, when at all possible, the sacrament of baptism. To inspire
love by patience, gentleness and charity. In short, in the eyes of
those spouses who had to encourage their wives to join the sisterhood, the rules were perfect. Pictures of the Holy Family were
distributed throughout the colony.

Saint Anne was an object of particular devotion; she has
remained the patron saint of Canadians. In 1675 a fine stone-built
church was raised to Sainte-Anne-de-Beaupré, which became the
object of frequent pilgrimage, famous for its miracles. Marie de
l'Incarnation wrote that there paralytics walked again, and the
blind recovered their sight. In 1678 a new confraternity of Sainte-
Anne was established for working-class men. An entrance fee was
settled and an annual subscription; income from which was to be
used to say Mass for the souls of the dead of the confraternity.

The worship of the Virgin Mary was of prime importance in
New France. As early as 1536 Cartier himself had appealed to the
Virgin for help during an epidemic of scurvy. Throughout the
history of the colony, special acts of homage to the Virgin Mary
steadily multiplied, and when in 1638, by order of Louis XIII, the
Mother of Jesus became patron of France itself, Quebec went mad

with joy. Four Marian holy days stood out in the Church year; the Purification on February 2nd, the Annunciation on March 25th, the Visitation on July 2nd, and the Assumption on August 15th. The Jesuits, 'untiring promoters of the Marian worship', chose Mary as their patron at the church in Quebec and appointed December 8th as its day of celebration. The start of this day was hailed by a volley of artillery fire, followed by sung High Mass. In the afternoon vespers were held and the litanies of the Virgin recited.

Other brotherhoods grew up: of the Rosary, of the Little Congregation, and of the Scapular. Whenever difficulties arose, appeal went out to the Virgin for benevolent intervention. The catechism of the diocese of Quebec, which was drawn up by Mgr de Saint-Vallier, devoted much religious teaching to the worship and festivals for the Virgin. Huron women in the Island of Orléans paid special worship to the Mother of Jesus; they recited numerous rosaries every day, and at the end of each recitation 'they laid aside a porcelain bead to deck the crowns of the Divine Mother'. In 1660 when Phipps' fleet laid siege to Quebec the banner of Our Lady was raised to save the town, and Phipps sailed away. The piety of the Canadians was not a superficial manifestation; it served to influence their moral life. Until 1660, out of 674 children baptized, only one illegitimate birth was recorded. Father Charlevoix observed after his voyage to New France: 'We see', he wrote, 'in this part of America a generation rising of true Christians among whom the simple faith of the early centuries holds sway.'

EPISCOPAL LIFE

Canada was at first merely the seat of an apostolic curacy until, on the insistence of Louis XIV, who was supported by the efforts of the Jesuits in Rome, the Pope agreed to set up a bishopric, on condition that it was directly dependent upon the Holy See. The King agreed to nominate the Bishop, and demanded from him a solemn declaration of loyalty: 'I, François de Laval, Bishop of Quebec in New France, do swear in the name of the Most Holy and Sacred Name of God, and do promise to Your Majesty to be his faithful subject and servant so long as I live, and will attempt with all my powers to do his will and to work towards the welfare of his State and will eschew any counsel, design or undertaking which might prejudice the aforesaid. And if anything should come to my knowledge I will communicate it to Your Majesty . . .' This was a situation fraught with difficulty, the Bishop depended on Rome but owed loyalty and obedience to the King. There was bound to be misunderstanding between secular and spiritual authority.

Colbert set out in precise terms the role of the Bishop; he had to sustain in the settlers the practise of religion, and to keep them abreast of their duties towards God and the King.

While the Bishop's mission was thus limited to spiritual matters, the Government in Versailles, however, employed him to carry out the plans of the King; to impose French customs upon the natives was one such task. Colbert even imagined that Indian women 'once they have adopted civilization' would agree to marry colonists. Did the Bishop exceed the powers assigned to him? A letter from the Intendant, Talon, depicted the Church of New France as becoming more and more powerful, more and more formidable, with the prelate himself a creature of the Jesuits. From the very beginning there was a struggle between the Bishop who wished himself to carry out his proper apostolic duty and the French Government in whose eyes the head of the diocese was the agent of the King.

Many 'incidents' arose during these difficult years; from the beginning relations were poisoned by over-sensitivity. Such important questions arose as where to stand the Governor's pew in church. The Governor himself wanted to have it in the chancel in line with the Bishop's throne. This claim did not accord with Roman ritual. Neither Mgr de Laval nor the Governor, Argenson, would give in, and the Jesuits, trying hard to carry out their duty to the Bishop as well as their obligations to the Governor, decided to 'invite neither the Bishop nor the Governor to dine'.

There were other disagreements. For example, when the Bishop refused to attend meetings of the Sovereign Council because M. de Frontenac, the Governor, had appointed Councillors illegally. Or when Father Adrian, a Recollect, criticized from his pulpit, despite the expressed opinions of the Bishop, the political intriguing of the Governor and the Intendant: the religious bodies took the side of the Governor whereas the Intendant was supported by the Bishop.

A conflict of law was rudely provoked on the occasion of the

'Fénélon affair' when the Governor summoned to appear before the Sovereign Council that daring Abbé who had been so bold as to attack it from his pulpit. The Abbé refused to put in an appearance until Mgr de Laval had set up an official ecclesiastical court, which, according to him, was the only one competent to hear the accused. The King himself was obliged to intervene to soothe ruffled feelings; he called the fiery preacher back to France.

Further dealings embittered relations between the Bishop, supported by the Jesuits and the Governor, backed by a large part of the population. There was trouble over the traffic in alcohol. The Church flatly condemned the practice of selling alcoholic liquor to the Indians, whereas the State realized the essential need for trade in nascent Canada and was prepared to tolerate it as part of the barter-trade for furs.

On Ascension Day in the year 1660 Mgr de Laval declared the opening of hostilities: he solemnly pronounced from the pulpit of his church in Quebec the threat of excommunication against all those who 'will pay, sell, traffic or freely give either wine or spirits to the savages'.

As a consequence in the following year the Sieur Pierre Aygron otherwise Lamothe found himself faced with excommunication. The civil authorities acted in their turn on October 10, 1668; the Intendant Talon formally authorized trading in alcoholic drinks. Mgr de Laval promptly sailed for France to take the matter before the theologians at the Sorbonne, since it was a question of morality, at the same time laying it before the King in order to obtain a favourable decision. But he received only a meagre degree of satisfaction; decrees forbidding the sale of brandy were to apply only to the Indian villages far away from French settlements.

The Church of Canada was by no means free; it was directly under the tutelage of the political power at Versailles, which was determined to turn it into a submissive ally. But, in fact, its distant situation, its impoverished state, its desire to spread the gospel, the very nature of the apostolate in New France, which was nearer that of Christianity in its first century than that of Louis XIV, allowed it to develop a special entity imposed upon it by the Canadian climate and the methods used in colonization.

The diocese of Canada was enormous and communications were made even more difficult, sometimes impossible because of the long and rigorous winter. It was a hard life for the Bishop. He lived more like a missionary than a prelate.

The distance from Montreal to Tadoussac was 320 miles and the Bishop travelled by canoe in the summer, on snowshoes and by sledge in the winter. Mgr de Laval covered the whole vast stretch of inhabited land within his diocese on two separate occasions, in 1669 and again in 1681. By then he was nearly sixty. But the great distances failed to deter him and he appeared indefatigable, crossing the river several times in order to visit the seigneuries on each bank. He paid special attention to the mission stations among the Indians, and these latter rewarded the eminent Monsignor with a welcome which imbued him with new strength. On May 20th he visited the mission of La Prairie de la Madeleine, near Montreal, where a path had been laid for him from the river up to the chapel, and a little platform had been raised near the scene of his arrival.

When the prelate's canoe came in sight, the church bell began to ring, summoning all the members of the mission. As soon as he set foot on shore one of the Huron leaders addressed the Bishop respectfully: 'Bishop, pull in your canoe and listen to what I have to tell you!' Then followed welcoming speeches. His face alight with benevolence Mgr de Laval disembarked and, dressed once more in cape and rochet, he blessed the faithful who were on their knees. The chaplain of the mission, Father Frémin, intoned the *Veni Creator* in the Iroquois language, 'echoed by all the savages, men and women, as was then the custom'.

Then, clustering round the Bishop, who was accompanied by M. de Bouy, his chaplain, and M. Souart, Superior of the Seminary of Saint-Sulpice in Montreal, they moved singing in procession towards the first arch of leaves which had been erected by the Indians.

Monsignor paused beneath the arch in order to listen to the speech of an Indian, one Paul, the 'learned dogmatist' of the mission. After which he made his way into the Church where Father Cholénec, dressed in surplice, presented him with Holy water. Mgr de Laval then celebrated Holy Communion, while the congregation, both Indian and French, intoned in 'two bilingual choirs' the *Pange lingua*, the *Ave Maris stella* and the *Domine salvum fac regem*. After the ceremony, the congregation kissed the ring of the Monsignor who 'covered them with embraces', particularly the most fervently religious of them.

On the following day the Bishop baptized ten adults, and blessed the marriages of three couples, after which he said Mass. The Indians sang during the sacred service and received the sacrament from the prelate's own hand. When the Mass was over the Bishop proceeded to take a confirmation service. He allowed the French to be confirmed at the same time, but only after the Indians: 'It is for them alone that I have come,' he said.

At midday, following the custom of the Indians, a large feast took place at which the most beautiful coverings were laid out before the Bishop and his assistants. After which there were yet more speeches.

Monsignor then expressed a wish to visit the families of the Indians, which filled them with pride. They decorated their cabins with their most precious belongings, spreading blankets, skins or leafy branches on the floors. Mgr de Laval entered into each house, with kindly words for everyone. In the evening the Bishop baptized seven children and took the evening service. On the following day there was a Mass chanted by the Indians, and the pastoral visit of the Bishop was over. On the banks of the river, the whole congregation received blessing from the Bishop of Canada.

The total sum of the works of Mgr de Laval speaks for itself: thirty-three parishes set up, diocesan administration established, the founding of numerous holy fraternities, his presidency over hundreds of religious ceremonies, 126 of which were services of confirmation.

Not content with so much evangelizing, the prelate of Canada was also exemplary in his charity, visiting the sick and taking them sweetmeats. His devotion to the poor in the hospital was even more remarkable, and he did his best to encourage the work of pupils in the schools.

Sunday was the day above all others which belonged to the Bishop: he took every service within the parish, often preaching a sermon. At all the festivals of the Church he celebrated Mass and saw that everything was properly organized to further the solemnity and splendour of the religious ceremonial. Charity, modesty, fervour, were the qualities of this first religious leader of New France; he was the inspiration of the Church in Canada.

The Bishop was good at organization. The new diocese had need of solid foundations. Mgr de Laval believed that the Seminary should be the centre of the Canadian Church; the forcing ground for priests, the headquarters of spiritual training, the meeting house for the clergy who lived there in a sort of republic of religion with the Bishop as President. Priests and missionaries were sent out from this centre, where the regrouping and administration of all the assets of the Church in Canada were organized, to preach and spread the gospel to the Indians.

The ancient arrangement of *presbyterium*[1] according to the use of St Martin de Tours was unusual in diocesan life in France but was accepted by the King. It was closer in spirit to the usage of the primitive church than to the organization of the French Church, and it survived for only a few years, until the establishment of permanent livings under the authority of Mgr de Saint-Vallier. The parish of Quebec was to remain attached to the Seminary until the year 1768.

To fulfil his directives from Rome, Mgr de Laval had to set up a proper chapterhouse: the papal bull laid down that each canon should receive twenty-five gold ducats each year (and this when income from the diocese was very small). This requirement forced Mgr de Laval to divert the revenue from his Abbey at Maubec and to employ the services of the priests in the Seminary who graciously agreed to perform the duties of canons. It was thus with the utmost simplicity that the first chapterhouse was created on Canadian soil with five principal ecclesiastics, eight canons and four vicars. On November 12, 1684, the clergy assumed their offices in the course of a grand ceremony and in the presence of the Governor, his officers, the Intendant, councillors and other official bodies from the town. It lasted for half a day and ended with a solemn *Te Deum*, 'sung to the sound of bells and musical instruments, to the noise of artillery fire in the town', in the presence of troops and armed militia, ringed round by a great crowd.

Mgr de Laval also set up an ecclesiastical court; the ecclesiastical court of Quebec with a convenor and judge. Although the authority of this body was limited to offences connected with religious matters it often found itself in conflict with the civil jurisdiction, as when in 1661 one Daniel Uvil was condemned as a heretic, back-

---

[1] The manner of ruling a diocese by a system of 'collegiality' analogous to that evolved in the Vatican Council.

slider, blasphemer and profaner of the sacraments and sentenced to be shot with harquebuses.

Thanks to the energy, devotion and exhaustive work put in by the first Canadian prelate, the Church in Canada was in a flourishing state when Mgr de Laval's successor, Mgr de Saint-Vallier, appeared upon the scene. The clergy consisted of lay brothers who officiated in the parishes in the immediate neighbourhood of the seminary, a few country priests, Jesuits, Sulpicians, Recollects, and a few novices from the women's communities—Ursulines who ran a boarding-school for French and Indian girls, the nursing sisters who cared for the sick at their Hôtel-Dieu in Quebec and Montreal, and Daughters of the Congregation, who specialized in teaching under the direction of Marguerite Bourgeois. The chapterhouse in Quebec, the ecclesiastical court, the committees for care of the poor directed by the priest and assisted by laymen, completes this picture of religious life in New France.

The little town of Quebec was the religious centre of the whole colony. Peter Kalm, the voyager, was greatly impressed with the enormous size of this diocese which stretched from the mouth of the St Lawrence to the delta of the Mississippi. He observed that in Quebec alone there were eight churches all built of stone. The cathedral in the Upper town had a belfry with two partitions and two bells. The Jesuit Church was built in the form of a cross and its belfry was decorated with a sundial. The church of the Recollects had been founded by Mgr de Saint-Vallier, and was notable for its pinnacled roof, while the roof to the Ursuline church was domed. Finally there was the church attached to the hospital, which was the Bishop's chapel. The lower town had a church dedicated to Our Lady of Victories, crowned with a square bell-tower. To this list Kalm added the Governor's private chapel.

Ascending from the lower town, on the right one passed before the Bishop's palace: ' a large and beautiful building surrounded on one side by a spacious courtyard and a kitchen garden, and on the other by a wall'.

The Seminary was a very graceful building which enjoyed the best view in the town, looking over the St Lawrence river, and standing in its own orchard and kitchen garden. The Jesuits owned a magnificent property planted with fruit trees and with a garden in which grew 'every sort of herb and vegetable for the kitchen'.

Peter Kalm visited by special permission the large convent of the 'women of Quebec'. The nuns' cells were small, with bare walls but embellished with holy images and a crucifix; the beds had curtains and good quality blankets; a little desk and a chair made up the remaining furniture. The cell itself was unheated, but there was a stove in the corridor outside. Even so, the nuns sometimes slept in their shoes, so intense was the cold of their rooms. The communal rooms were upstairs. The sewing-room was 'spacious, well painted, with a cast-iron stove'. It was in here that the nuns sat before their embroidery; they also made artificial flowers. Kalm was much struck by the delicacy of the handiwork of the Ursulines. They worked in silence, while the eldest nun read aloud from the lives of the Saints. Meals, taken communally, were followed by readings from religious books. The lower storeys held the domestic offices; bakery, kitchen, dispensary. While in the loft 'the linen is dried and the grain is stored'. But the nuns were not recluses. Every day they took a little exercise on a gallery which surrounded their house.

LIFE IN THE COMMUNITIES

Three religious orders helped with the life of the Church in Canada. The Jesuits who arrived in 1625 specialized in missionary work; theirs was the largest order by the time Mgr de Laval arrived, having from sixteen to twenty-five priests. In Quebec eight Jesuit Fathers looked after their college of the *Compagnie*; others were employed by the Bishop in the parishes, and various missions; in Acadia, at Silléry, at Three Rivers, in Montreal and in the distant regions. Mgr was very full of praise for them: 'The Fathers of the Company of Jesus,' he averred, 'are a great help to me both in the ministry to the French and to the savages.' They took on every sort of apostolic duty; they heard confession, they preached, taught the catechism, visited the people to bring them the consolations of religion. They gave to the settlers more than they received. The Jesuits in France were their only source of help. 'They are in complete submission to me,' remarked the Bishop when the civil powers criticized them for dominating the head of the Canadian church. The Intendant, Talon, in a note addressed to Colbert in 1667, said that while he realized that the life of the Jesuits was 'very disciplined and exemplary' many of them, nevertheless, had 'disgraced themselves' because they had not obeyed their orders. The Jesuit Fathers, he added, were too much occupied with secular matters and 'encroach even upon the work of maintaining law and order, which is the business of the one and only magistrate'.

Frontenac, too, in order to keep watch on the activities of the Fathers, requested Colbert to ensure that the Jesuits were obliged to obtain permits for their journeys.

Peter Kalm awards them full marks for their learning, their politeness and their skill in handling people. Reluctance to be drawn into disputation meant that they rarely discussed religious questions. They preferred to devote themselves to the conversion of the heathen: 'In every village of Indians there is at least one Jesuit Father to teach them to live as good Christian people.'

Only selected persons were admitted to the Company. These did not usually stay indefinitely in Canada but returned to France after a few years. 'During my stay', said Peter Kalm, 'a priest resigned from his living with the Bishop's permission, in order to become a Jesuit.'

The Sulpicians had been interested in Canada ever since the foundation of their order in France by M. Olier. The latter had already been associated with M. de la Dauversière in the forming of the Society of Our Lady of Montreal which was established in Ville-Marie, the true 'City of God' in Canada. After twenty years the Society was no longer able to afford to maintain its work in Canada, and on March 9, 1663, the Seminary of Saint-Sulpice in Paris took over the ownership of the seigneurie of Montreal, together with the responsibility of running the Community of Ville-Marie.

In this way the Sulpicians six years after the death of their founder undertook to carry on his work. Colonists, artisans, *coureurs des bois* already came to join the few settlers who had been there from the beginning. Trading in furs was now centred irrevocably on Montreal, thanks to the strategic position of the island. A proper parish grew up, soon enhanced by a seminary and completed by two Indian missions.

M. Souart presided over the Montreal Sulpicians, who were recruited only from France. 'These aristocrats in cassocks', as they were called, enjoyed important political powers. They nominated the Governor of Montreal and were free to grant lands in fief and common. They did not, however, abandon their work of spreading the gospel to the Indians, and, like the Jesuits, their names are inscribed on the roll of Canadian martyrs.

The Recollects were the first Canadian evangelists. They had originally come over with Champlain, and then gone back to France during the English occupation of 1629. In 1670 they once more appeared in Canada and at once began to complicate the tithe problem by their promise to work for nothing. They were content to live on alms; as Kalm humorously observed: 'They take anything they can lay hands on.' The Recollects were an order of mendicant brothers, who allowed themselves no possessions and slept rough. The young monks went from house to house with their collecting boxes, begging for alms. In the parishes which held no resident priest they were received with kindness, since they were poor as were the colonists themselves. In due course the Bishop put them in charge of the parish of Three Rivers, which they were to retain until the Cession in 1773. They also worked as military chaplains in the distant forts. Kalm caricatured them unkindly when he wrote: 'They did not use their heads much while acquiring their learning.' Nevertheless they always enjoyed the sympathy and respect of the settlers and the soldiers, and their good-natured, charitable and unselfish lives are to this day proverbial.

At almost the same time as the first permanent colonists, the first nuns arrived from France. Three Ursulines from Tours, three nursing sisters from Dieppe and a lady of high rank arrived in Quebec in 1639. Two outstanding figures distinguished the group —Madame de la Peltrie, who had decided to devote her fortune and her life to the teaching of Indian girls, and Sister Marie de l'Incarnation, who had received 'personal visitations' about her mission in New France. Bossuet, when he had read her letters, was to call her 'the Saint Theresa of Canada'; they were so wonderfully written and at the same time a precious source of information about the early beginnings of the colony.

All these nuns gave themselves to their task with unlimited devotion. The Ursulines, once they had won the confidence of the young Indian girls who gathered round them, started taking their education in hand. The first task was 'to wash them from head to foot to get rid of the oil which covered them and of the vermin which lived on this oil'. One of the Sisters was specially detailed to this task. 'At mealtimes one often finds hairs or even an occasional shoe in the cooking-pot.'

So much for the Ursulines. The lot of the nursing sisters was no more enviable and they received their baptism into mission life 'on the very first evening after they had landed'. 'We begged,' writes the diarist, 'one of the priests, M. Le Sueur, to bring us an armful of tree-branches to make a bed; but we were soon crawling with the caterpillars which had been feeding on the leaves.' During their first winter the nursing sisters had to cope with an epidemic of smallpox among the Indians; 'a disgusting illness', and they had no linen, 'so we sacrificed our wimples and headbands. The dead we had to shroud in blankets or in beaver skins. Nobody would help us at all, until we all three of us fell ill ourselves and the Jesuits came to our rescue.' These nuns devoted themselves in a way that defies understanding, but even they sometimes wondered if they could carry on. Mother Sainte-Marie herself died during the winter of 1641. One of the two survivors made the following note in the community book, or what still remains of it: 'The number of savages sick and infirm having greatly increased during 1642, we have now as many as three hundred on our hands, and since we go to look after them in their cabins there is so much smoke and dirt that our habits do not look white any longer; the Jesuits have advised us to wear black or grey ones.' The sisters did not adopt this suggestion, firstly because they could not disobey the rules of their order, but also because these stains were only outward signs of their devotion.

In Montreal the same spirit of selflessness and sacrifice was demonstrated by Jeanne Mance and Marguerite Bourgeois. The apostolate of these nuns and of their companions can be summed up in three words: charity, teaching and devotion. The example they gave drew many to their calling; some of the first of those born in Canada asked to be received into their communities.

CHAPTER SEVEN

THE EXPLORERS AND THE *COUREURS DES BOIS*

THE EXPLORER

In less than fifty years, in three irresistible thrusts, the French had occupied more than half of the territory of North America from the frozen wastes to the torrid regions, the three principal towns of Quebec, Three Rivers and Montreal were the scenes of departure for incredible journeys.

The thirst for adventure, the obsession with the idea of exploration, and the attraction of a primitive life inspired hardy young men who, once they had moved out of the narrow band of settled territory along the banks of the St Lawrence, knew that the world belonged to them. They had only one thought; to thrust ever further into the boundless unknown to present first Louis XIII, then Louis XIV, with 10,000,000 square kilometres of new land— twenty times the whole area of France itself. This was a gift which the Government of France accepted without undue excitement, sometimes with active displeasure. Colbert was quite unmoved by the enthusiasm of Talon the Intendant, who after the first attempts at exploration wrote him a glowing report: 'I have the honour of informing you that Canada consists of a vast stretch of land, the limits of which on its northern coast I cannot know, since the distance from us is so great; but to the south there is nothing to prevent us from carrying the name and arms of His Majesty as far as Florida, and into New Sweden, New Holland, and New England too, indeed by way of the first of these countries one can reach Mexico.' Later Frontenac was to petition Versailles in the same vein. It was a waste of time; one after another these brave adventurers who had crossed thousands of kilometres and faced unbelievable dangers were to be derided, disgraced, sometimes imprisoned, when a Governor, an Intendant, or even the Court itself thought it a necessary measure for reasons of prestige or again for economic reasons. It made no difference. Every year the frail fleets of ships took on crews in the harbour of the St Lawrence, and those who came had often no precise aim, but only a will to discover these new territories of which it seemed, as Talon wrote, one would never know the extent.

Champlain was the first to fall under this spell. Quebec was to him no more than a base. He was fascinated by the passage up the St Lawrence. But others, first those who were his own companions, were to pursue his dream. In 1610 he gave into the care of the Algonquins a young boy, Etienne Brûlé, who had already spent two winters in Quebec and who was happy in this country and was clearly determined to get to know the Indian tribes. In fact Brûlé was to stay in these regions for the rest of his life. Others found themselves at home in the wilderness; Thomas and Nicolas Vignau, Olivier, Jean Richer, Nicolas Marsolet, and above all Jean Nicolet, who was able to resist the temptation to identify himself too completely with the Indians, and was to become not only the first great explorer of the new countries in America but also the first to mediate among the native populations.

As soon as he landed in 1618 this young Norman, barely twenty, set off to the Algonquin country where he was to live for two years. He accompanied his new hosts on their expeditions, showing great bravery, and shared their daily lives. Like them he sometimes went without food for a week on end. Once, in a period of famine, he kept himself alive on the bark of trees and moss. Back again in Quebec, he was soon bored with the life there and went off again, this time to a more distant region, the territory of the Nipissings. There he stayed eight years. He even became a voice in the councils of that nation. He observed, asked questions, took notes. When he produced the result of his discoveries and observations, Champlain (then Governor) was delighted and promptly gave him another commission, this time imposing no special limitations—the sort of life he would have liked for himself—to penetrate as far as he could into the interior of the new territories. So off once again went the indefatigable traveller. For weeks and months on end he journeyed by canoe, crossed rapids, explored. The lure of this enormous country was so potent that Nicolet did not rest until he had reached the uttermost end of the waterway, where it flowed out of Lake Michigan. Even then he was loath to return: so much unknown

territory lay beyond. By the end of this last voyage he had journeyed more than three thousand kilometres. He had spent twenty-
five years of his life in Canada in paddling over the lakes and along
the rivers. But he did not even know how to swim, as he himself
called out despairingly to his companions when his canoe was
upset off Quebec and he was drowned, foolishly, at the start of a
routine trip to Three Rivers to rescue one of his Algonquin friends
who had unjustly been condemned to death. It was left to Jacques
de Noyon to accomplish one of the dreams of Jean Nicolet, the
navigation of the great Lake Superior. He got as far as the region
which today is Manitoba.

Nicolas Perrot, who had at first been a faithful follower of the
Jesuits, put his thorough knowledge of the language and customs
of the Indians to good use. He became the great peacemaker among
the peoples of the interior. All admired him for his courage and
audacity. If a tribe threatened his life he would go courageously
to meet it, invite its chief to sit near him while he spoke to the
people. In 1682 he spoke thus to the Outagamis: 'Listen Outagamis! I have something to tell you: I understand you have a great
desire to eat the flesh of a Frenchman; I have come to fulfil your
desire with these young men you see with me. Put us into your
cauldrons and satisfy your hunger with the flesh you so long for.'
Then he quickly rose to his feet, drew his sword and added gravely:
'My flesh is white and delicious, but it is very salt. I do not think
that if you eat it it will pass through your gullet without making
you vomit.' When he heard this the chief held out the pipe of
peace.

By such methods, Nicolas Perrot succeeded in keeping the peace
among the larger nations west of Mississippi, of whom no one had
ever heard; the Miamis, the Maskoutechs, the Kikabouks and the
fierce Solokis. These peoples seeing white men for the first time
were told that on the other side of the great eastern sea lived a
peaceful nation over which reigned a chief called the Sun-King
who wished to be their friend. Perrot took advantage of their wondering amazement and built forts which were also to serve as
trading-posts, on top of which floated the flag with the lilies of
France. Never had a wanderer from France accomplished, nor
would any other wanderer ever again accomplish, such effective
work among the Indian peoples. When Father Gabriel Marest,

who was stationed at the Illinois village of Kaskakia in 1712, remarked that 'the Illinois are far less uncivilized than the other savages, Christianity and trade with the French has gradually civilized them', it was because the great peacemaker, Nicolas Perrot, one quarter of a century earlier had passed that way and had behaved towards the Indians more as a friend than a conqueror.

Yet in 1685 an order of the Governor, Denonville, new to his appointment, and in no way interested in the American policy, forced Nicolas Perrot and the other wanderers to discontinue their work. 'There are', wrote Denonville to the Secretary of State responsible for the Colonies, 'Frenchmen at present with Outaouais, who say they are under orders from my predecessor to journey as far as Mississippi. I know it is not your intention that they should go so far afield. I shall therefore endeavour to secure their return.' Denonville's action was the first sign of an attempt to check French expansion in the heart of this new world. Even though Frontenac wrote to his masters at Versailles that 'the Sieur Perrot, through his long experience and his understanding of the moods, manners and tongues of all the nations of the north, has acquired a very good name among them', this ambassador with his unique qualities had nevertheless to content himself with the cultivation of his little farm in the seigneurie of Bécancour, where he died in obscurity in 1717. Through these years of solitude together with his wife and children he relived his adventurous life through the writing of his *Mémoires sur les Outagamis, adressés a M. de Vaudreuil, Mémoires sur les guerres des tribus, Mémoires sur les mœurs, coutumes et religions des Sauvages de l'Amerique septent-trionale.*

The expedition led by Louis Jolliet and the Jesuit Jacques Marquette into the Mississippi was one of the boldest and most profitable expeditions ever undertaken. Since the days of Champlain it was the first voyage to be undertaken in the name of science alone. The Intendant Talon gave detailed instructions to the young hydrographer, then twenty-eight: he was to journey south and to try to determine into which sea 'the great river' of Mississippi flowed, and the river Mechessabe, 'the father of rivers', which it was thought might lead to the China Sea. Jolliet left Quebec with his companions in birchbark canoes and made his way to Michillimakinac where Father Marquette was waiting all ready for the great journey: 'They set out,' says the *Relation* of 1672–1674, with some solemnity, 'with five other Frenchmen to go into a country where no European had ever set foot.' This voyage of two or three months in the frail vessels which only Indians and experienced Frenchmen knew how to manage, gradually led them into the depths of a completely alien country, into a new continent. When they reached the confluence of the Wisconsin and the Mississippi rivers, the travellers were overcome by a strange and deep silence which they did not dare to break: 'For a whole week, no human figure appeared before them.' Were they really awake? Could this voyage so enchantingly easy to navigate, through a country which boasted such splendours of vegetation, really last? At nightfall they moored their canoes to the bank and pushed out into midstream to sleep in order to avoid surprise attack. One man in each canoe, anchored for the night, was constantly on watch ready to warn of approaching danger and to forestall the unconscious movements of those who were sleeping. For the slightest shift in their position could capsize the canoe. Thrusting ever further to the south, the wanderers arrived in the country of Illinois, where they were welcomed by the elders of the people, 'the most polite of all the native nations'. They learned that the great river, still as tranquil as ever, and always widening as it flowed, rushed not into the great sea which led to China, but into the Gulf of Mexico. The main object of the journey had been attained. Now it was time to return.

Jolliet returned to Quebec having covered more than 3,500 kilometres. He reported his findings to the Governor and to the Intendant, the most important so far to have come out of that mysterious country. Now it could be stated categorically that neither the Mississippi nor any other river led directly to the China Sea. Furthermore, they had found that it was possible to travel by way of the St Lawrence river to the Gulf of Mexico with only one large rapid where portage became necessary: the Niagara Falls. Still another fact had come to light: the large rivers from the west which emptied themselves into the Mississippi were broad enough to allow the passage of heavy boats. It was possible, if one followed these waterways to their limits, to find an exit to the western sea opening out to China. Encouraged by Jolliet's revelations, Frontenac sent to the Court a detailed report as well as a map of the new territory drawn from memory by the explorer.

When these explorers tried in vain to penetrate still deeper into the interior of the country, they nearly always found out that they were not the first to pass this way, but that other compatriots had been there before them. The names of those who left behind them letters or descriptions have passed into history, while the others are forgotten. For instance, a twenty-year-old Canadian, one Jean Fafard, knew the region of the great lakes better than anyone else, for he had travelled over it in every direction, as he had also explored the Mississippi. He was the best interpreter of the basic Indian languages, Iroquois-Huron, Algonquin and Sioux. It was thanks to the knowledge that Fafard possessed of these vast stretches of country that 'the gentleman *coureur des bois*' Daniel Greysolon of Lhut, was able to write: 'On July 2, 1679, I had the honour of placing the arms of His Majesty in the big village of the Nadoucioux, known as Azatys, where no Frenchman has ever been, which was equally true of the Sangaskitons and Honetoatons, who are twenty-six leagues (125 miles) away from the former, where I unfurled the arms of His Majesty in the same year of 1679.' Du Lhut was in no respect authorized to make explorations in the name of the King, but the gesture inherent in the planting of the flags, even if it raised a smile on the faces of the Frenchmen who had led him through these places which they themselves had known so long, made an impression upon the Redskins. Nevertheless Du Lhut had definite advantages over his travelling companions; he had the gift of leadership, was ambitious, and was also more an explorer than an adventurer. Furthermore he had received a confidential commission from Frontenac the Governor which he wished to carry to its conclusion. This was to make peace with the different Indian tribes, and to establish a centre for the delivery of furs; a task which he accomplished to the satisfaction of the Governor; he received all the kudos for it and all the honour, even if he, in fact, owed these favours to the wise choice he made in the intrepid *coureurs des bois* who had helped him to reach these regions and there to make peace with the natives.

Nearly every one of these explorers, who were perhaps the greatest that France could ever boast, died tragically or grew old in destitution and loneliness. Jolliet disappeared into the icy waters of the strait of Belle-Isle. Father Marquette succumbed to an attack of fever in an Indian village. Cavelier de la Salle was assassinated in the brushwood by his companions. Radisson spent his latter years in a modest lodging in London and silently departed from life. Jacques de Noyon returned to die in Boucherville 'very broken-down and infirm' observed the notary who took down his last wishes. Du Lhut continued to flout his inevitable destiny and reached old age; but his exploits had been forgotten long before his death, by which time he was crippled and almost blind, nursed by a Recollect, who prepared him for the final voyage into eternity. In 1690 the *coureurs des bois* who, during their journeying found their way to Fort Sainte-Marie, were intrigued by the strange behaviour of an old man who was always hanging around the residence of the Jesuits, an old man who walked with difficulty, bent, ghostlike, and troubled by a perpetual trembling which shook his limbs. This was Father Albanel, the great explorer of the North, who had paved the way for Radisson, and who spoke seven Indian languages and was renowned as the white man of the New World who had crossed the greatest distances on foot. As to La Vérendrye, who had travelled further than anyone along the route which led to the China Sea, that is to say the Pacific Ocean, he was thrown into prison for his pains, and his possessions were taken from him to pay his debts.

THE 'COUREURS DES BOIS'

Although the great journeys of the explorers took place several years before those of the fur traders and the *coureurs des bois*, it is not possible completely to separate one group from the next, so closely did their ways of life coincide. The trader had the inducement of immediate profit to sharpen his thirst for adventure and independence. But the explorer, too, almost always set out for his chosen goal armed with a permit for trading, obtained either as a means to finance his expedition or to enable him to barter with the tribes he met with on his wanderings.

We must never lose sight of the fact that the beaver trade was the only commercial activity in that whole great expanse of country. It was a fur in great demand in the principal countries of Europe, and the exceptional quality of Canadian beaver was very soon appreciated. Since pelts were easy to procure the trading possibilities were particularly attractive to those companies who secured monopoly over it; the profits sometimes reached a figure of a thousand per cent. It was quite a usual thing, especially in the early days, to barter a superb pelt from the Indians in exchange for no more than an ordinary needle, a looking-glass, a glass necklace; articles which threw the women into ecstasy. Gradually the Indians became more and more demanding and wanted articles of a more useful kind such as knives, axes, tins, cauldrons, blankets. Until, in the end, they would insist on alcohol, in which they over-indulged to such an extent that its ill effects were to endure up to the time when the beaver trade was entering its decline.

For, like all trade which wins too easy a reward, this one fairly soon began to decline. The great fur fair in Montreal was soon no more than an excuse for exploiting the gullibility and drunkenness of the Indian tribes. The European wars and the Iroquois blockade also played their part in diminishing the Canadian fur trade. When in 1660 Radisson arrived suddenly in Quebec with a cargo of 400,000 pounds of furs which he had collected in a region, as yet undiscovered, around Hudson Bay, he opened at the same time a new door to Canadian youth, always eager for adventure but used to stagnating for many months in enforced inactivity. Now these young men could journey far to seek the furs which the Indian tribes no longer brought back to the trading posts in the 'Lower' countries. For this reason, economic activity now soared higher with an unprecedented burst of vigour. It helped to create a new social clan, the *coureurs des bois*, bold yet uneducated, the spiritual heirs of the explorers.

The principal attractions which took the youth of Canada into the land of the beavers were the passionate longing to travel and the taste for adventure, rather than the desire for money. In the low lands they had no other resources than agriculture, but the administrative authorities made no effort to increase the centres of colonization or to find markets for farm products. Worse still, they prevented the new colony from establishing industries, which, as they thought, would threaten to compete with similar industries in France. This country with its area forty times the size of France must supply France with nothing but furs. This was the line of thought which guided the authorities, and their policy was to confine this vast new world and its great natural wealth to the limits of a colony which the *coureurs des bois* only wanted to expand.

When an expedition was planned the person who held the

permit to trade in furs formed a partnership with two or three companions. They bought goods, engaged boatmen, and equipped two, three, and sometimes four canoes. Conditions for the journey were laid down in a notary's contract which seldom varied. Those who signed on were equipped at the expense of the partnership, undertook the voyage at their own risk and venture, and would receive on their return a percentage of twenty to twenty-five of the profits on the furs they brought back. The expedition set out from Quebec, Three Rivers, or more often from Lachine, below Montreal, where the merchandise and the canoes were transported in wagons to avoid long and difficult portages. The men then loaded the merchandise into the craft and the long voyage began. Since he was not sure whether he would return the wanderer took care to put his spiritual and secular affairs in order. He drew up his will before a notary. He specified that the journey was to be 'with God's help', of twelve, fifteen, or perhaps eighteen months' duration. In case Providence should decide that he should never return, he dictated his 'last wishes'. He entrusted the parish priest with a sum of money so that Masses should be said for the repose of his soul. His property would go to his wife who was to care for their children until they married or reached their majority. If he were unmarried he still drafted his will, and a copy of the document was preserved together with his other important effects in 'a locked casket', which was then usually deposited with a relation or close friend.

The moving example of François Frigon serves to illustrate the irresistible fascination of the Northern lands. Like the other colonists, he had obtained a land grant which he set out to cultivate and to improve. In 1670, he married one of the 'King's Daughters', and children were born. By 1685 there were six, and in this year too Marie Chamois learned of the death of her last surviving brother which, she believed, meant that she would inherit the family fortune. She made her way to Paris, only to be confronted with a rapacious mother-in-law. To enable her to undertake the voyage, François Frigon had got into debt and now he had to pay up. He thought that his profits from the fur trade would enable him to do so. Leaving his children with neighbours, abandoning his farm, he set off each year for unknown country. But, to judge by the documents which allow us a glimpse of his affairs, he was not enriched by these repeated journeys. In 1692 he mortgaged his land to help settle his more pressing debts. A few months earlier he had obtained from the procurator of the Jesuits, Father Raffeix, a reduction in the amount of rent and tax payable on his land at Batiscan. About the same time the judge at Champlain ordered him to pay according to his contract a sum of 200 *livres* to the two trading partners of a fruitless expedition. Was he to do better in this journey of 1695 for which he was preparing in June of that year? For the first time his elder son, Jean François, accompanied him, and two neighbours whom the notary appointed 'partners cum employees'. In Montreal they bought merchandise to a total of '8000 *livres*, 10 *sols*, 8 *deniers*' from the merchant Antoine Trottier-Desruisseaux: the sum to be reimbursed 'on their return from the voyage which would—'with God's help—be the following year—1696'. Antoine Trottier for his part contracted to provide food and clothing for Frigon's children while the voyage lasted.

An anonymous *Mémoire* dating from 1705 described these voyages by canoe: 'The *coureurs des bois* convey themselves in little sculls of hardwood, very light and convenient. The man in the stern steers, the two others paddle in the bows. A properly-manned canoe can do more than fifteen leagues a day in calm waters, more if it is going with the current of the river; when it is paddled upstream it does less. When you meet waterfalls or rapids which cannot be crossed by canoe, you go ashore, unload the baggage, carrying it on back and shoulders, together with the canoe, until the falls and rapids are left behind and you come once more to waters where you can re-embark. This is called portage. When there is a favourable wind the passage is considerably easier, for you put up the sail which is supplied with each canoe, not only for this purpose, but also to be used as a tent on dry land, to which you resort every evening for eating and sleeping. It was in this kind of canoe that these three men embarked at Quebec or Montreal to make their way over a distance of 300, 400, or even as much as 500 leagues, seeking out beavers among the savages who had often never set eyes on a white man before.'

Anyone who had seen the fur-hunters at work was lost in admiration of the untiring endurance of these men of iron, who combined the astuteness of the Indian with the natural ingenuity of the Frenchman. Frontenac, who observed them closely, was struck with wonder when he realized the robustness, the thick-set

149

sinewy strength of all this breed of men: 'Unless one had witnessed it', he wrote, on his return from a voyage to Lake Ontario, 'one could not believe the exhaustion of those men, dragging the boats, most of them had been in the water a great deal of the time up to their armpits and balancing on rocks so sharp that some of them had legs and feet running with blood, yet their gaiety was undiminished and as soon as they got back to camp some of them began to jump about, to perform gymnastics, and all manner of games. They smoked without ceasing, sang the songs of their country which their fathers had taught them and which came from their French ancestors. Every two hours they left their canoes and rested for five to ten minutes. They calculated their distances by the number of pipes they smoked between two stops.' Moreover, the taste for danger was inherent in them: 'In the great lakes they are bold enough to cross the wide bays in a direct line, even over a distance of several leagues, to avoid increasing the distance of their route by hugging the coast.' In these inland seas they acquired the experience of true sailors. One look at the horizon and they could forecast the temperature twelve hours ahead, a secret they had won from the natives of the region, and one which was almost infallible.

The winter voyage demanded special techniques and a great deal of endurance, since the cold, the storms and the possible scarcity of game all had to be taken into account. Two indispensable parts of equipment were snowshoes and sledges. With this meagre equipment some Frenchmen, together with Thomas Godefroy and a missionary, accompanied a detachment of Attikamègue Indians in 1651 to a mountainous and hitherto unexplored region. It was a fairly short expedition of less than 1,000 kilometres there and back. The departure took place in the midst of winter, but an unduly early spring brought unforeseen complications. The Jesuit wrote in his notes, which were carefully preserved in the pocket inside his breviary, the daily details of his tour: 'The weather is good but it has not been very good for us by reason of the fact that the strong sunshine has begun to melt the snow, which holds back the progress of our sledges and clogs our snowshoes, and could even lead to our falling into the water. I was deceived by some ice which broke under my feet—if a soldier had not come to my assistance and taken my hand I should not have been able to save myself from drowning, for the water underneath was like a strong torrent. The route on this first journey led through continual and torrential rapids, and among waterfalls which fell from the top of precipices, producing treacherous ice, very dangerous and irksome because we were forced to walk in the water while still wearing our snowshoes, which then became slippery when we had to climb over the icy rocks under the waterfalls and cliffs.'

Every day brought its blessings and its unpleasantness. On the third day, when the wanderers had been on the march since dawn without having eaten at all, a mirage transformed a clump of trees into Iroquois. In the evening the Jesuit and his companions set up their camp on an island to protect themselves from possible attack. Nobody knew where the next meal would come from. In order not to overload the sledge, only the strictest essentials had been carried: maize flour, dried peas and ships' biscuits. They had been counting on being able to hunt and fish, but game and fish were both scarce. To assuage their hunger they were reduced to digging up roots of trees from the frozen soil. 'The fifth and sixth days were both very different, and yet similar in that both were equally fatiguing; the first was rainy, and the second fine, but both were extremely difficult because of the snow which melted in the rays of the sun and clogged our snowshoes and our sledges; in order to avoid this we were forced, during the next ten days, to set out very early in the morning before the ice and snow melted.' To travel in the early morning meant 'from three in the morning until one hour after mid-day'. At the end of this march of ten hours, in which they were able to advance by thirty kilometres, each voyager 'comforted himself with ominy, or *sagamité*, a pancake boiled in water, and half a smoked eel'. The thirteenth day was the worst going of all: 'We set out again at three in the morning by terrible tracks through scrub so thick that at each step we had to search for a place to put down our feet or our snowshoes. Several times I took the wrong turning because it was impossible in the dark to follow the tracks of those who went ahead. Then we came upon lakes covered in slippery ice where it was extremely dangerous to proceed in snowshoes, because of uneven ice and melted snow.' At mid-day the group came to an exhausted standstill, having covered, in these distressing conditions, a dozen miles, that is to say twenty kilometres. The only food available was a share of the beaver we had killed that morning. It was only by the end of a fortnight that the travellers arrived at the goal of their expedition—the encampment of the Attikamègue

Indians. By this time they had covered almost 320 miles, and it was time for them to return.

The scenes observed by the contributor to the *Relations* vividly illuminate the extraordinarily successful and rapid adjustment of the explorers and the *coureurs des bois* to the life and customs of the country. Although the missionaries complained constantly of the lack of comfort and hygiene in the Indian encampments, they nevertheless seemed to adapt themselves to both with some ease. They liked the atmosphere of the wigwams. They saw young people only recently arrived to stay for years among the Indian tribes— among them those young Canadians who had taken refuge in the forests during the English occupation of 1629 to 1632, and had won the affection of the Indians—they shared their lives, their customs and ideas. An Indian chief challenged one of his captives, Godefroy, to a race in snowshoes over a distance of five kilometres. Godefroy won. The following summer the challenge was repeated: this time they were to race on foot. Godefroy was again the winner and went up to embrace the loser, a sight the Indians had never seen before.

Gifted with lively intelligence, full of initiative, wise and observant, most of these young men not only benefited from the experience of the Indians in making do with their own scanty resources, but also improved on it. They took easily to native methods of transport, the canoe in summer, snowshoes in winter. They modified their clothing to make it more practical for marching and journeying. Their intelligence helped them to swift mastery of forest lore, and soon they were past masters in this way of life.

Radisson and des Groseilliers were suddenly caught by the winter in the depths of unexplored forest on their way to Chagouamigou Bay in the Hudson region. They needed all their experience and skill to keep themselves alive. First of all they had to build a shelter in two days. Radisson himself has described it for us. It was built in the shape of a triangle, on the edge of a stream, with its base towards the water. The walls were the trunks of trees with the bark still on; the roof consisted of branches interlaced. The fire was lit in the centre on the earth floor, and the smoke escaped through a hole which served as chimney. To the right of the hearth two squared blocks of wood covered with branches of spruce served as beds. To the left stood another squared block which was the table. The rest of the furnishings did not amount to much; firearms, clothes and some goods for barter. An isolated post in a place of this kind needed special arrangements to ensure its protection. Carefully, lengths of twine were laid around the circumference of the shelter and carefully hidden in the grass; to these were fixed little bells taken from Radisson's assortment of small wares intended to be used for barter. Now the two companions were able to sleep soundly without being surprised. Any attempted attack would be announced by a carillon calling them to arms. Radisson, as the youngest and most agile, had the job of replenishing the larder; he would go out into the surrounding forest to snare hares and to fish through holes in the ice of the river. Des Groseilliers kept watch over the hut. It was essential at all costs to avoid gunfire. Often in the middle of the night the wanderers would be suddenly awoken by the ringing of the little bells. Indians? No, merely wild animals attracted by the smell of humans, who had broken through the barrier. But in fact the Salteu and Ojibway Indians in the surrounding country had soon come to learn of the presence of strangers in their hunting territory. They prowled round the fort, quite silently, and then drew nearer. Radisson realized that his system of defence could have been more efficient. Using tubes made of birch-bark he scattered gunpowder in a circular trench dug around the fort. One night when the Indians came very close, he seized a firebrand from his hearth and hurled it into the trench; immediately an uncanny belt of flame sprang from the earth lighting up every aspect of the frail shelter. It had a magical effect on the Indians. These two foreigners were without doubt gifted with mysterious powers which must be respected.

A troop of Indians from the country of the Cris offered to escort these mysterious long-bearded demi-gods to their own country further to the west; today the country of Manitoba. The travellers had already put more than 2,000 kilometres between them and their starting point, but they had no hesitation about pushing further. Still secure in the powers of magic with which they had been endowed, they were of such particular interest to the Indians that Radisson was later to recall with satisfaction: 'We were true Caesars! It never occurred to anyone to disagree with us. We marched free of burdens, since these poor wretches deemed themselves lucky to be allowed to carry our baggage in the hope of earning a copper ring, an awl or a needle . . . they were more lost in admiration of our actions than the crowds of Paris doing homage to their King. They kept crying out; we were gods, we were devils! For four days through the woods we journeyed. It was magnificent country, parts of which resembled our own French parkland. At last we found ourselves only a league away from the homesteads of the Cris. There we spent the night, to prepare ourselves for a grand ceremonial entrance next day. The fleetest runners among the Indians ran ahead to warn the people of our coming.'

At the Indian encampment the travellers were received with all solemnity. Young Redskins walked ahead of them bearing gifts for every member of the tribe; needles, combs and above all looking-glasses for the women and girls. The Indians in their turn displayed their treasures; bales of beaver pelts surplus to their own needs. These the Frenchmen accepted with delight and emotion which they scarcely troubled to hide. Suddenly it was winter. The lakes and the rivers froze; the way became impassable with such a load on hand. They must wait until the spring in order to take back the precious harvest to Quebec. From now on they would also have to share the life of the tribe with its privations and discomforts. The Indian women were obliging enough, but it was also necessary to eat. And game became very scarce in the face of those hundreds of mouths needing nourishment. By January, they were starving. Hundreds of Indians succumbed to famine during these winter months. The Frenchmen, strengthened by the knowledge that they would soon be on their way, managed to hold out. Then at last the spring came: game was plentiful once more. They built up their strength, and took the way home with their precious cargo of furs.

While those wanderers in the countries of the North had to defend themselves from cold and starvation, those who reached the Mississippi encountered an enemy much more insidious and ill-intentioned; an invasion of mosquitoes. Father Gabriel Marest, who had had some experience of life in the North (he had been with d'Iberville in Hudson Bay in 1694) averred that the cold was far easier to bear than the mosquitoes, and other insect plagues. His successor in the country of the Arkansas, Father Paul Poisson, who came like him from the province of Champagne, has given us a picturesque and detailed description of the havoc wrought by Canada's mosquitoes: 'The greatest torture of all which makes all the rest seem like a bagatelle, is one which is beyond belief, unimaginable to anyone in France unless they have experienced it; the special Canadian mosquitoes, with their cruel torment. I really believe that the plagues of Egypt were not more agonizing: *dimittam in te & in servos tuos & in populum tuum & in domos tuas omne genus muscarum & implebuntar domus Aegyptiorum diversi generis & universa terra in qua fuerint.* There are *frappe-d'abords;*[1] there are horse flies too, and gnats—tiny flies, whose sting is so lively, or rather so burning, that it seems as if a little spark has fallen where they bite. There are mosquitoes like midges, even smaller than gnats, so minute one can hardly see them, which go above all for the eyes. There are wasps, there are hornets, *omne genus muscarum,* in a word. But the others are not worthy of mention beside the true Canadian *maringouins* (mosquitoes). This little animal has inspired more oaths from the French since they have been in the Mississippi than have ever been uttered in all the world until now. A cloud of mosquitoes accompanies the traveller every morning; when he moves through willow or the canes, as he cannot help but do, another horde throws itself furiously upon the canoe, and refuses to go away. You have to wave a handkerchief continuously, but this does not in the least deter them; they fly off for a second, and then return to the attack. Your arm gets tired sooner than they. When you relax to eat your midday meal and rest from ten o'clock till two or three, you have to do battle against a whole army of them. You have to 'make smoke', that is to say you kindle a big fire which you then smother with green leaves. You have to put yourself in the thickest part of the smoke if you want to avoid the torment. I do not know which is the worst, the cure or the disease. After the meal it would be pleasant to sleep for a while at the foot of a tree, but this is absolutely impossible. Your whole time is spent in continuous battle with the mosquitoes. You return to the canoes still in their company, and when the sun sets you lie down to sleep on the earth with them. Then there is no longer a single army but several armies, all to be fought against. You are eaten, devoured, they get into your mouth, into your nostrils, your ears. Your face, hands and body are covered with them. Their sting penetrates your clothes and leaves a red mark on the skin which swells until you get inured to their stings. After a hasty supper, you cannot wait

---

[1] In modern America *no-see-ums.*

to shroud yourself in your tent[1] (baire), although you know you will suffocate in the heat. Whatever skill and subtlety you employ in sliding into your tent, you always find that some of these insects have come in with you; very few are needed to ensure a restless night'.

The *coureur des bois,* like the explorer, was satisfied with very few clothes, those proved to be most suitable and common to all; *mitasses, brayet,* and moccasins. *Mitasses* were a sort of gaiter made of canvas or the skin of roedeer. Being very strong they were better than stockings. The imaginative wanderer embroidered them with signs and symbols of every sort, which he showed off proudly as if they were trophies, when he finally returned from his voyage. The *brayet* was of native origin, a short pair of trousers usually of thick canvas, reinforced at the seat and knees with inserts of supple leather. To protect oneself from mosquitoes or the cold, one could lengthen the *brayet* in such a way as to fasten it under the *mitasses.* The moccasin was a shoe without a sole or a heel, made of cowhide or mooseskin, specially treated to keep its suppleness in the cold or damp. Of all the articles in daily use copied from the Indians, they were the most indispensable for the French. They were used not only by the *coureurs des bois* but also by the settlers. Nowadays, they are made in various styles; of cowhide or of 'beu', as it was called, tanned or untanned boots and shoes. The moccasin is like maize, a true product of America. The Indians had found a process which was at once economical and practical for giving the skin of moose or elk the desired elasticity; their women chewed the skin.

The *coureurs des bois* used their ingenuity to improvise various technical processes for making waterproof the leathers used to make moccasins. They perfected the *babiche,* a fine thong of reindeer skin which the Indians were using at the time as a substitute for thread, while the French preferred dry eelskin, a tougher material, at the same time thinner and more malleable.

Any other clothes were extras and individuals followed their fancy in choosing things to take along for idle moments—perhaps

[1] Author's note: name given to the material used for sleeping tents in the Mississippi region. Here the word refers to the tent itself. The first thing done on landing, 'is to make one's tent carefully'. (Letter from Father du Poisson, 3rd October 1727.)

a jacket of wool or cotton, always in some bright colour so that a hunter would not unthinkingly mistake his companion for a forest animal. When paddling his canoe the *coureur des bois* preferred to strip to the waist, and his skin was gradually baked by the sun and the wind and became less sensitive to mosquito bites.

The equipment of every voyager was kept to a minimum, to leave the greatest possible amount of space for the merchandise. When he went ahead of la Salle to the Fort of Frontenac in order to prepare the expedition into the Mississippi, Father Hennepin's baggage consisted of 'a portable altar, a blanket and a palliasse'; he did not even carry a spare habit. There was a rifle to every canoe and a blanket of wool or bearskin or mooseskin which was used only when someone fell ill. The same applied to the brandy ration. For brandy was precious, intended only for the Indians, and carried with all possible care: when it rained and it was necessary to sleep out-of-doors, the men sheltered under their upturned canoes, propped up at each end. In winter they dug a hole in the snow, the frozen earth below being covered with spruce or cedar branches against the cold. The roof of frozen snow was usually enough to give protection from the cold and the winds.

The wanderer was no less sparing with the food he took along. He limited himself to emergency rations. Even so, the white explorer was more generous to himself than the Indians. At least he always made sure of a supply of basic foodstuff—always the same; wheaten biscuits, salt bacon, peas, and maize cakes. It was just the same with the most extended journeys. When Cavelier de la Salle was preparing for the expedition which was to take him to the Mississippi, he ordered a sack and a half of flour, half a peck of grain, half a tablet of soap, a small cauldron to make soup in and a quarter of a peck of ground Indian corn to be taken to the quayside. 'If the savages have any fresh meat then I would ask you to have some of this delivered to the boat, and to tell those in charge of its transport not to eat any of it; to ensure this you should attach a note of its weight.' In the same letter we find another piece of advice: 'That all members of the expedition take the minimum of provisions possible, any surplus to be conveyed, if necessary, overland, and I beg you to advise them once again to be as sparing as they can.' Thus fishing and hunting were the order of each day, particularly shooting and trapping hares and beavers: the latter provided an oily meat, which was not only nutritious but also pleasant with a flavour of pine. The Frenchmen quickly adapted themselves to the Indian philosophy where food was concerned. They could live for a week on end solely upon lichen and bark. They revolted only against one thing, on which the Indians were happy to feast in times of famine; rotten meat. Rather than bring themselves to eat this, the starving *coureurs des bois* would chew the leather of their moccasins and their jackets for hours on end.

The silver birch, modestly hidden in the midst of the rich and splendid forest, was the Indian traveller's true friend, and became so too to the *coureur des bois,* when he came to realize its manifold uses. We have already spoken of its use as the chief material of the Algonquin canoe. But it was also used to construct wigwams, those conical huts which the nomad population managed to render fairly water-tight, and in which they spent the winter months. The *coureurs des bois* were to fall back on the same device to protect themselves from the cold. They also adopted the Algonquin custom of protecting their foreheads with birch leaves while undertaking portages. The soft spongy texture of the leaves absorbed sweat and kept them cool. The bark was used by the French for another purpose, also recognized by the Indians; it took the place of papyrus. Trappers used it for the notes they made of their journeys, writing with a lump of blackened clay baked in the fire or the charred root of a tree; they also outlined maps of newly discovered regions, added up their sums, and on the point of death wrote down their last wishes (if they could write at all), to be sent home to their families.

POPULATING THE AMERICAN INTERIOR

From the middle of the seventeenth century, the strategic position of Michillimakinac was both the prescribed meeting-place for travellers and the point of departure for new explorations. It was situated to the south of the strait which linked the Lake Huron and Lake Illinois (today Lake Michigan), not far from Lake Superior, and about 2,000 kilometres from Quebec.

Coureurs des bois who intended to push on further in pursuit of furs were also obliged to halt at Michillimakinac. In 1683, after numerous requests, the Governor of New France agreed to install a permanent military garrison, and from now on, surrounded as it was by the Great Lakes (Superior, Huron, Michigan, Erie and Ontario), a great ring of water, almost 2,000 miles round, it was known as 'the Gibraltar of the American Interior'.

In the neighbourhood of the post the Indians raised their tents, so that Michillimakinac became a general meeting-place. It was a village of perpetual change, its population increasing and dwindling like the flood and ebb of the waters which surrounded it. There were moments when the little township held more people than Quebec itself and then it buzzed with incessant activity. It was there that in 1671, the delegate of Talon, the Intendant, one M. de Saint-Lusson, assembled representatives of fourteen nations to a ceremony at which he solemnly took possession in the name of France, 'of every country as far as the southern seas'—countries already traversed by tough traders and explorers.

The Indians and the Whites pooled their technical skill and in a few years fortified the position. When the edicts appeared ordering fur traders to confine themselves to the banks of the St Lawrence, many of the *coureurs des bois* preferred to keep their freedom and decided to establish themselves at Michillimakinac, at Pontchartrain or at other posts in the region.

It was at this time that a new social feature of Canadian life began to emerge, the outcome of the promiscuity of the Indian tribes, whose way of life and customs had already been adopted by these wanderers. There were some inveterate wanderers who abandoned their wives and children, leaving them to live as best they could in the settled seigneuries, while they remained in the south to pursue their own adventurous lives. But most of the champions of the free life were unmarried, and these living together with the Indians were the first begetters of the hybrid Canadian. The passing missionary had no hesitation about regularizing these unions and baptizing the children. The village atmosphere was entirely respectable, bourgeois even, except for those occasions when the bartering of furs gave rise to public orgies of drinking. The wanderer would instal his 'squaw' in a single-roomed cabin supplied with essential amenities: a stone hearth, a bed of birchwood, a cradle if she were pregnant. The wanderer knew that the Indian whom he had 'adopted' would be more a servant to him than a wife. She ground the maize and cooked the *sagamité*. She helped with grading the furs, made moccasins, repaired damaged canoes. She had never lived the soft life, and she knew very well that if her companion left her she would have to go back to a drearier existence among the people of her tribe.

The Michillimakinac pattern gradually spread almost everywhere. Many travel journals, as well as correspondence between the Governors and the Intendants, show that Frenchmen all over the central American territories were living in Indian fashion. 'We hear', wrote the Intendant, Bégon, in 1715, 'that a hundred Frenchmen who secretly embarked at Michillimakinac, two years ago, having used up the merchandise of the traders who equipped them, made their way to the Thamarois by way of the Mississippi river, where forty-seven of them are already settled!' This statement was confirmed in a letter from Father Gabriel Marest who observed the presence of numerous Frenchmen among Indian tribes living in that region. 'The Illinois are much less barbarous than the other savages; Christianity and trading has gradually civilized them. This is very evident in our own village where the inhabitants are nearly all Christians. This is also the reason why several Frenchmen have come to settle down among them, and only recently we have married some of them to Illinois girls.' In spite of repeated repatriation ordinances, the intermarriage of the races increased apace, with the approval of the local chiefs and the broadminded missionaries who themselves were there to observe with some gratification the swift growth of the plant which sprang from the seed of their apostolate.

Thus, only a few decades after Champlain and then Colbert had demonstrated their faith in the formation of a new race by bringing together the French adventurer and the resident Indian, their dream began to come true. Unfortunately this evolution was going on thousands of kilometres too far away from the headquarters of the short-sighted authorities. The Governor was determined to administer New France from Quebec at a time when the vital centre was far away in the heart of the new country. Thus it was that little by little America slipped from the control of France.

While, at the request of her colonial representatives, England was stepping up her policy of encouraging emigration to her American possessions, France not only restrained her own would-be colonizers under the pretext that her main interests lay in European expansion; she went further still and attempted to recall to Quebec those hardy pioneers who were already established in the heart of the great continent.

9 a. Quebec — Ursuline monastery, the old foyer

b. A farm at Boischatel near Quebec

10 a. The death of General Montcalm (Picture by Watteau)

b. The death of General Wolfe (Picture by Benjamin West)

When in 1763 France surrendered her Canadian territory to England, it was not only a question of the small settlements on the banks of the St Lawrence, with their 60,000 settlers. She also unknowingly gave up more than forty advance posts and trading forts established in the very heart of America, which would have given her, if only she had equipped them and supported them, a powerful and more positive contribution to the economic and cultural development of the land.

THE TRADE IN ALCOHOL

Brandy, at least in the early days, was not only the most favoured article of barter in the fur-trade, it was the regular tender for moosemeat and other necessities of the day; snowshoes, soft shoes, *mitasses*, blankets. It was, in short, the recognized currency in all transactions. It is not surprising that its abuse grew so rapidly in the parishes of the low country frequented by Indian tribes, that the authorities had to take severe measures to deal with it. The archives have preserved for us interesting extracts from these local enquiries.

Nicolas Gastineau, Sieur du Plessis, erstwhile civil and criminal judge at the Cape, a big trader himself in the northern countries as well as along the southern rivers, declared with disarming frankness that he had certainly seen the savages on occasions drunk, and that it was possible he could have contributed to this; but the trouble was that it was impossible to tell which of them had already been drinking elsewhere. This meant that, speaking for himself, he had sometimes dispensed beer to the said savages according to the regulations, and it happened that some of them had had more than they should—at least it seemed as if they had. He went on to observe that those who had reported him for giving drink to the savages, Messieurs Barthélemy Bertaut, Michel Gamelain (his brother-in-law), Jean Perè, Benjamin Anseau, for example, had themselves been guilty of the same offence, and especially a Mme de la Poterie, the wife of the local governor. During most of the preceding summer, he said, this important lady had traded beer to the savages, 'so freely that they swarmed round her house in droves, drinking, fighting in general disorder, urinating and spitting in the house, continuing their brawling as they made their way home. Further, that the said noble lady had collected chests full of *pourselines,* great quantities of moose and beaverskins, piles of shoes and other wearing apparel belonging to the savages, tongues of moose and hunting trophies. In a word the said savages had handed over to the said demoiselle their all.'

Many hitherto unpublished details of the way in which these small traffickers traded and lived, are to be found in the records of investigations conducted between 1665–1667. Father Druillettes had visited every dwelling in the Indian townships and villages in the region, and was able to assess at first hand the ravages produced among his flock by the brandy distributed by these traders. His attitude throughout the formal enquiries seems to have been discreet but firm.

On February 3, 1667, he succeeded in persuading an Indian woman called Christine to leave her village 'to give testimony in the matter of the traffick in drinks, which, he found, she herself had witnessed in the forest'. Christine, 'after she had been warned by Father Druillettes to tell the truth', told how, on the preceding Tuesday seven Frenchmen, some of who were militia and some civilians, met by the river at Three Rivers with the men of her tribe and handed over various vessels containing alcohol—a small gourd, an earthenware flask, a bottle of moose-hide holding a pint, and two other receptacles each holding half a pint. 'Asked if they had made any trouble she said no, they had only drunk, her son-in-law and his wife were the only ones who had fought.'

The evidence of these witnesses made it quite clear that the Indians themselves would only trade with those who offered them drink in exchange for their wares. Frenchmen, whose outstanding quality was not their honesty, also made good profits and their example soon encouraged others. It was foolish to be surprised if under these conditions the loads were heavier and the merchandise more varied on the return journey than on the way out; there were barrels, bottles and gourds of brandy which were often topped up with river water when the Indian encampments were reached. As for the return journey, let us hear what the traffickers themselves have to say: Jean Cusson saw Michel Gamelain's servants coming back from the post of the Sainte-Anne River, with 'good fat meat, about two sacks full, three or four moose tongues, as many heads, and a fine black beaver skin'. Nicolas Dupuis saw brandy being exchanged by Martin Foisy for Indian shoes and lard. The Sieur de Bellerive's valet sold the Garaot natives a pint of brandy diluted with an equal amount of water for two *louis* and four *francs*.

It is easy to see that shoes, silver or meat were not to be obtained without pains or even suffering. The snow, the cold and the great spaces were no less hostile to these local hunters and traders than to the long-distance travellers covering their thousands of kilometres. In 1669, during a census taken by Bouteroue, the then Intendant, the settlers in Three Rivers, of the Cape, and of Champlain declared to this official that traders, settlers and soldiers were out trafficking in brandy with the Indians forty or fifty leagues away. Such shorter excursions also had their incidents and accidents. For example, in the Three Rivers district, Michel Gamelain was bitten by an Indian in the arm and leg after drunken scenes and a bloody affray.

The true responsibilities for this sort of thing often lay with prominent citizens, who were punished all too lightly, despite the bad example they were setting. We have to remember, however, the imperative need of the settlers to keep on good terms with the Indians: they dared not risk losing their fur-trade. Thus the Sovereign Council which on June 20, 1667, condemned Nicolas Gastineau, Jean Le Moyne, Michel Gamelain, Jean-Baptiste and Nicolas Crevier, Benjamin Anseau and François Fafard for trafficking in brandy with the Indians, did not charge them with encouraging drunkenness and public scandal. It condemned only when the law insisted, and under moral pressure from the missionaries. It was in the following year, on November 10, 1668, that the right to sell and barter brandy to the Indians was given to all the French of New France. It is not difficult to imagine the consequences of this action.

CHAPTER EIGHT

ECONOMIC LIFE

At the outset the Canadian economy depended exclusively on private companies whose principal aim was to trade in furs. Champlain added to this, firstly on his own initiative and later with the aid of the King, a plan for colonization.

Louis Hébert, an apothecary by profession, became the first colonist in New France. He disembarked at Quebec, in 1617, and found 'a beautiful country where there is good land'. Soon the cultivated fields 'were filled with fine grain, the gardens were laden with every sort of green thing, such as cabbage, turnips, lettuces'. But for more than twenty years agriculture as such was to remain confined to the land cleared by the Hébert family. In 1634 Giffard and the hundred colonists from Perche arrived in Canada. They were skilled farmers able to judge the fertility of the soil and to determine where which crops would best grow.

The way in which these colonists acted was to decide the whole future. In the course of a very few years, they were to set up a model for the organization of land and agricultural techniques for Canada.

The original grant of land to Giffard made by the Company of One Hundred Associates consisted of 'a league of land to be taken from along the sides of the St Lawrence river, one league and a half in width'. How could this property be shared with his companions? Realizing that the river provided the only highway, and judging by the experience he had acquired in his native province, where the fields were laid out in narrow strips giving on to the road, he decided to divide the territory into oblong portions sited upon the steep banks of the river, and reaching deep inland. In this way each farmer would have access to the river, and could reclaim his land by working further and further away from the river and at right angles to it. This form of holding in *rang*, peculiar to Canada, and which may still be seen in the land registration plan of the province of Quebec, came to give a special character to the territory of New France.

The first settlers were established on good land of fine alluvium or clay. The population grew rapidly, encouraged by the large birthrate, and it was soon necessary to reclaim other stretches. These were carved out immediately behind the original holdings. A second line of farms was developed on the model of the first. Soon the colonists filled the banks of the St Lawrence as far as the outskirts of Quebec, and then as far as Montreal, with their *rangs*. The richness of the soil encouraged a large population on the slopes of Beaupré, and in the parishes 'beside the water'.

Giffard also laid down techniques for cultivation. It was first necessary to clear the dense forest vegetation from a large part of the *rangs*. Away from the river the settlers felled the trees with axes, laid aside the straight trunks to build their houses, and burned the remainder on the spot. In this virgin soil, further fertilized and enriched by wood ash, the colonist sowed wheat, barley, and oats; later hemp and hops. For three years at a stretch the ground produced cereals for use as household food. More burnings of timber and work with the plough ensured a further period of three years' cultivation. A simple system based on the division of fields into two equal parts, one planted with cereals, the other remaining as grass for cutting and grazing, following a three-year rotation, was sufficient to feed both men and animals. But by this rhythm the land became exhausted. So then the axe was used again to push back the forest, yielding new plots where burnings gave several more years of cultivation. Gradually production diminished. The only solution now was to extend the area under cultivation.

Stock-rearing completed the farm economy; horses and oxen for draught, cows for milk, pigs for meat and bacon, sheep for wool. In 1734 the censuses showed a total livestock population of 71,008, nearly half being cattle. The stock provided manure to enrich the soil.

The farm house stood in an orchard and kitchen garden; above it lay yellow and green strips marking the fields of ripe wheat and pasturelands. An agricultural economy concerned only with food production led to a state of self-sufficiency, for every household need was satisfied. Some districts did, however, supply the towns with wheat, vegetables and fruit.

The Intendant, Talon, wishing to teach by example and to encourage the export of agricultural products, put his own farm, 'les Islet' under cultivation; land sited on the banks of the St Charles river. He grew cereals, flax, hemp, hops; he raised cows, calves, horses and poultry. In this way he was able to set up a small freight service for some of the twenty vessels which left each year from Quebec to Acadia, or the islands of the Antilles, carrying flour, biscuits, peas and vegetables in their holds.

But Talon's efforts did not bear fruit. The colonist went on cultivating for his personal use the 'French' produce to which he added native crops, such as maize or Indian corn, potatoes and tobacco.

Wheat was of prime importance in New France, providing the main food for the colonist, who, according to the Intendant, Raudot, ate two pounds of bread daily. Because of the long winter freeze, wheat was generally sown in the spring and harvested at the end of the summer. It grew well, and produced fifteen times the weight of its seed.

Since the farmer usually limited his sowings to his individual needs, if there were a bad harvest he became buyer instead of producer, and ran the risk of incurring debts. The farmer who produced any surplus produce sold it at an inflated price. What could he do with his money? He hoarded it in the good old-fashioned way under his mattress and did not re-invest it to increase the size of his farm.

When there was a shortage of wheat, bread became expensive and many families starved. In 1751 the Intendant Bigot organized the free distribution of bread, peas and meat to assuage the hunger and resentment of the sufferers.

An enquiry held in 1712 by Gédéon de Catalogne showed how little intelligence went into the agricultural plan for Canada; fields were too large, cultural methods too much subject to tradition —nothing had changed since Giffard's day—and there were too many holidays between the months of May and September. Moreover, the settlers did not attempt to extract from the soil more produce than nature was prepared to put in. There were other more attractive activities in New France to which the colonist could turn.

NATURAL RESOURCES

Canada contained important natural resources. In the first place there were fur-producing animals. The trade in furs, originally monopolized by the companies, began to interest the whole colony, and took various forms: barter with the Indians who visited the colonists, 'permits' authorizing hunting outside the settled territories, the fairs in Montreal, where every year, as we have already seen, the Outaouis gathered with more than 200 canoes piled with over 100,000 skins.

Beaver outweighed every other fur in importance; the five different sorts of skin from this animal were used in the manufacture of clothing, especially hats. The wholesale slaughter of these fur-producing animals caused hunting territories to extend the whole length of the valley of the St Lawrence up to the Great Lakes. Every year more than 40,000 beaver pelts were brought ashore at the Montreal Fair.

The forests of deciduous and coniferous trees were some of the finest in the world. The main species, such as oak, red pine and spruce were very valuable. Timber was derived from the reclamation of land, and especially from fellings carried out on the orders of the shipbuilders. Felling was particularly extensive in the region of Montreal, and in the valley of the Richelieu—to such an extent that in 1722 two citizens of Quebec, Jacques and Joseph Carcy, offered to supply the King with deal beams, ash planks, turned and twisted wood, squared logs of oakwood, the whole totalling 40,000 *livres*. As well as being used in the naval shipyards of Canada, timber was also produced for export—a matter of interest to the French Navy since in 1724 a naval commander was sent to carry out an inspection of the timber forests.

A great deal of effort went into the search for metals, since the principal aim of all the expeditions to the New World had been a quest for gold. Failing gold deposits, New France was forced to content herself with copper, lead, coal, and iron.

Talon urged the exploitation of mineral wealth as being 'essential to the King's purpose, and for the settlement of Canada'.

There were great hopes of discovering copper, but several expeditions were sent out to prospect along the banks of Lake Superior, and no worthwhile deposits were revealed. From the attempts made by Lesueur which led up to the explorations made by Denys de la Ronde, employing German workmen, nothing but disappointing results were obtained.

Indications of lead at Gaspé and in the Bay of St Paul were never exploited. Prospects for coal were better. The mine at Cape Breton in Acadia, which was easy to work and which contained good quality coal, provided cargo for the ships returning to France. Colbert was urged by Talon to abolish the tax on Canadian coal entering the Kingdom, in order to encourage further mining. But there was a shortage of skilled miners and export prospects were limited to a few ships moored at Cape Breton. No impressive results were gained.

Iron was the potential trump card. The indefatigable Talon discovered the presence of pyrites in the black sands of Three Rivers. When Colbert received enthusiastic reports of this, he decided to send an iron master to New France, in the person of the Sieur de la Potardière. The Intendant was not mistaken. At the first trial, 150 pounds of ore was excavated; it yielded fifty pounds of metal. As a result iron works were constructed on the banks of the St Maurice.

The gulf and estuary of the St Lawrence provided excellent fishing-grounds. There was an abundance of seabass and white porpoise which provided fine quality oil; dried cod was an important addition to the diet of the colony, especially to the army.

Eels were regarded as a special delicacy. In 1646 forty thousand of them were caught and resold for half-a-crown[1] a hundred. They were the staple food of the lower classes.

Talon wanted the settlers to establish fisheries; he observed wistfully that 'confronted with such riches they behave as if they were paralytic'. Fisheries were established which kept the Antilles islands provided with dried and smoked fish. From Point Lévis to the Labrador coast various stations were set up sometimes under the patronage of the religious communities. But it was difficult to get the best out of them despite a Royal grant of 400 *livres* a year. The fishing ground most regularly worked was the one at Saint-Paul where white porpoise was caught with the help of barriers to keep the fish in at low tide; one hundred and sixty porpoises could supply twenty barrels of oil, but how was it to be exported?

[1] An obsolete French coin formerly worth 3 francs.

INDUSTRIES

In Canada there were artisans, often nomadic, who went round from village to village offering household utensils of their own manufacture. They were perfectly content to take board and lodging and a few coppers in exchange for their wares. Since no permission was necessary to open a shop or to practise a trade, anyone who was able to do odd jobs or had some trading skill could set himself up to make clogs, shoes, hats, furniture or canoes.

Work was carried on at home. Peter Kalm noticed that a great many of the houses in the villages belonged to artisans.

In 1771, with some degree of over-optimism, Talon observed: 'This year from the wool of His Majesty's sheep, which he has had grazing here, I have made bouracan, canvas, bunting, *serge de seigneur*, almost a third of all shoes are made from this country's own leather; at the present time I have sufficient products of Canada to dress me from head to toe.'

The Intendant expressed his aims in the following terms: 'People must be able, without leaving the town, to find everything necessary to the comfort of the settler; food, lodging, and clothing.'

There were workshops for weaving, a tannery, factories for shoes. Hemp and linen, and wool were used in weaving, and shoes were made from cowhide and moosehides. Production depended largely on the persuasive power of the Intendant. While Talon and Raudot Hocquart directed the economy, manufacturing output soared; under other administrators, it merely ticked over and was in danger of stopping altogether.

M. Bissot's tannery, at Lévis, made 8,000 pairs of shoes a year, many of them intended for the army. Charest, who succeeded Bissot, was no less energetic. The three hatters in Quebec made almost 1,500 hats a year, until in 1736 they were forbidden to work for fear of prejudicing the industry of the mother country.

Weaving was notable for the activities of a forceful personality, Mme de Répentigny, who was the first to set up a mill for the manufacture of sheets and textiles. Short of experienced workers, she learned that the Indians had taken eight English prisoners who understood the techniques of weaving and the secrets of dyeing; whereupon she bought them their freedom, and hired them herself.

Since flax and hemp were still fairly rare, this woman had the

169

ingenious idea of using the bark of certain trees, as well as nettles, wool from goats, and the wild cotton flowers which grew in the uncultivated fields. After some experiment, she discovered new dyeing elements based on 'blue earth'. She used part of the hair of Illinois cattle to manufacture *serge sur fil*, and she perfected a process which softened the hide of moose without treating it with oil.

Other women followed the example of Mme de Répentigny. Twenty-eight looms in Montreal wove twenty ells of canvas every day. These weaving mills were destined to a short life since the colonists' wives themselves sewed clothes at home to fill the family wardrobe. Besides hemp was expensive. It was worth sixty *livres* the quintal (100 kilogrammes), and in Brittany it cost only eighteen.

From the first years of the colony beer was brewed. It is known that the settlers of Quebec possessed a brewery co-operative from 1634 onwards. The Jesuits in 1646 commissioned Brother Ambroise Cauvet to make the '*cru* and beer'. The seminary of Quebec brewery was set up in 1680. All were following the example of the first Recollect missionaries who brewed beer at Nôtre-Dame-des-Anges in 1620. The making of this popular beverage had become nationwide by around 1666, when the Intendant Talon conceived the idea of a state brewery. He established it not with the purpose of encouraging the settlers to drink more beer, but for economic reasons: to dispose of the surplus harvest of wheat and to cut down imports of wine. The brewery could produce four thousand barrels of beer, of which two thousand were designed for export. It used twelve thousand pecks of wheat and this provided the settlers with an outlet for their cereals. Beer was expensive at 25 *livres* the barrel, and Talon's praiseworthy idea was only half successful.

This great Intendant of New France focused all his attention upon the shipyards, which he considered to be the firmest basic industry. It did, in fact, give rise to the establishment of other related enterprises such as tarworks, rope-making, nail-factories and iron foundries. The raw material came from the enormous forests of oak, pine and spruce.

A brigantine for the use of the King was constructed in Quebec in the year 1664. Three years later, Talon ordered a ship of 120 tons to be built. Colbert sent him instructions: to 'build three or four good warships within three or four years'. Work was started on the construction of a ship of 400 tons, armed with forty-six guns. It was 1738 before the ship-building yards in Quebec received any important orders from the navy.

The first was a cargo-boat of 500 tons, named the *Canada*. White oak and spruce from the district around Montreal was used in its construction; the nails came from the forges at St Maurice, the masts of red pine had been felled near the river Chambly. The builders worked with a will under the direction of Levasseur the master-builder sent by order of the King. Soon the tackle which had been imported from France was fitted, and the crew of eight seamen arrived from St Malo.

The *Canada* put out to sea and crossed the Atlantic to Rochefort, where its construction and fittings were passed as satisfactory, even if the cost of their manufacture did seem excessive at 217,707 *livres*!

Other vessels followed suit. The *Caribou* for which curved spruce was used, the *Castor*, a frigate carrying twenty-six cannon. Work speeded up, and a new shipyard was planned in Cul-de-Sac for the construction of the *Saint-Laurent* with its sixty cannon. The last order was for the *Algonquin*, a ship armed with seventy-two guns.

But in 1752 a decision was taken to allow no further naval construction to be carried on in Quebec. The reason for this was that inspection showed the two ships which had been launched from Quebec, the *Caribou* and the *Saint-Laurent*, to be built of poor quality wood. This wood had been transported by flotation down the river and it had been dried too quickly, causing it to deteriorate. After this setback the naval shipyard confined itself to a modest line of private contracts.

A by-product of wood, tar obtained from the stumps of trees, was first manufactured by specialized workers. The cost of making it was too high here at fifty *livres* the quintal, when at Rochefort it cost no more than twenty *livres*. But the Canadians relieved the specialists of their task and produced it more cheaply so that large quantities could be exported.

The iron ore recovered from Three Rivers was found to be of excellent quality and a company was formed known as the 'Forges du Saint-Maurice'. The first stages were not easy, and production was insufficient owing to the shortcomings of the experienced iron-masters. A skilled iron-master 'Olivier de Vézin' arrived in Three Rivers in 1735. In spite of his experience, results remained disappointing, for there was not enough water for regular supply to the furnace.

The company went into bankruptcy, and the Royal Government then took over the working of the enterprise. From 1746 onwards the works began to thrive. The workers at the forge manufactured during the course of one year 400,000 *livres* of iron for the State and for the colonists, as well as seventy-seven *livres* of steel (by way of experiment, but the grain produced was too coarse), ten anvils, 300 mortar bombs, 5,500 cannon balls, four great cauldrons, 358 cooking-pots, thirteen hammers and 200 stoves. Six cannon were cast and sent to France where their construction was said to leave much to be desired. In 1750 the forges showed a deficit of 25,000 *livres*. Peter Kalm, visiting them, found one grave fault in the enterprise: it was badly administered, the result of numerous abuses, and the excessively high cost of manpower. From now on the orders undertaken were to be limited to everyday objects employed by the settlers of New France themselves.

Every one of these attempts at industrialization, most of which were doomed to failure or at the most to partial success, nevertheless gave some Canadians a chance to launch forth into business, and to foreshadow the pioneers of American 'business'. One of these was Abbé Lepage. Originally from the Ile d'Orléans, he became a seminarist in Quebec, and was subsequently appointed priest of Jesus Island, near Montreal.

Like many Canadian parishes, his was impoverished. The Abbé was not content with ensuring spiritual administration, he wanted also to provide work for his flock. He bought the seigneurie of Terrebonne for 10,000 *livres*, and borrowed 8,000 *livres* to build 'flour-mills'. He was raised by the bishop to the dignity of canon, but instead of taking his seat in the chapterhouse, he worked on his business affairs. When reprimanded by his superiors he gave his answer by reducing his ecclesiastical work, and by increasing his industrial activities in proportion. He had fellings made in woods in accordance with orders sent by the King for provision of planks of oak and pine. He manufactured tar, launched out into cod-fishing, put a slate quarry into production, and had plans for constructing ships for the use of the navy. He became financially embarrassed because production from his mills slowed down—the water level had fallen—but this did not prevent him from planning ironworks within the seigneurie. However, the authorities in

Quebec, on orders of the King, opposed the plan, after which Abbé Lepage offered to make himself responsible for operating the iron-works of Saint-Maurice. Once again his offer was turned down.

Under pressure from his creditors, by 1745 he was forced to sell all his business enterprises for a sum of 60,000 *livres*. Undeterred by this, and in no mood to seek retirement, he built another saw-mill, which he worked until his death seventeen years later.

TRADE

Trade within New France fell off. There was not enough circula-tion of goods, for most objects in general use were manufactured at home. What is more money was scarce, prices high, and mer-chants did not hesitate to take from fifty-five to 120 per cent of the profits for themselves. Yet customs duties on imports were only applicable to wines, liqueurs and brandy. Exports consisted almost entirely of furs.

Companies holding a monopoly of the fur industry had made substantial profits. In the five years from 1632 to 1637, the Com-pany of the One Hundred Associates made a profit of 60,000 *livres*, during the first year, of which fortunately eighty per cent remained in the colony.

In 1669 free trade was granted. Merchants who sent goods to their agents in La Rochelle had to disburse the 'one-half of a quarter'[1] to the King as commission on beaver pelts, and of one tenth on moosehides. In 1670 this tax brought in 70,000 *livres* despite the fact that the price of beaver in French markets had fallen.

Rents, permits, monopolies, smuggling, forest expeditions, Indian raids on farms, and the Montreal fairs all served to con-centrate the export of beaver skins from the port of Quebec.

Taxes levied on beaver should have provided a proportion of the colony's budget, but agents of small groups secretly conveyed cargoes of pelts to France, in order to escape the duty of 'half of a quarter' imposed by the King's warehouse.

In addition Canada exported corn, catfish or porpoise oil, tar, timber for building; mostly masts and planking for the navy.

The export of 'gin-seng', which could have been such an excellent source of revenue during the seventeenth century, came to an end

[1] Twenty-five pounds weight.

because it had been seasoned too rapidly, and the quality was not good enough for the Chinese importers.

The captains of ships would sometimes refuse to load certain goods, such as masts, with the excuse that they lacked proper facilities for transporting them or sometimes they would shorten such masts as they did accept on board.

Bills of lading of three ships sailing from Quebec in 1669 listed the following cargo: planking, wet and dry fish, salt eel, salted salmon, porpoise oil, wood, beer, five barrels of flour.

These ships put into Cape Cayenne, Ile de la Tortue and Guadeloupe. Talon thought that these Canadian wares would sell well in the Antilles and cargoes of such colonial products as sugar and tobacco could then be transported to France. Then the ships would sail once more to Quebec with canvas, cloth, wines, brandy, household articles, hardware, armaments, medicines, and construction materials. In this way the Intendant hoped to reduce the deficit balance of trade in New France, which had by now reached a figure of more than 500,000 *livres* a year.

This three-sided trading began to fall off. The lust for money displayed by the small group of merchants in Quebec, exclusive owners of the retail shops, and their selfish concentration on immediate profit, served to weaken the trade of New France.

The growth of a healthy financial structure in New France was retarded by the system of barter. At the beginning the *de facto* currency had been beaver, whose pelts provided money for imported articles, food, and even for the acquisition of land or to endow a daughter. . . . This explains the vital importance of the fur-trade to every settler in New France.

Talon admitted that the system had its merits in that it 'obliged everyone to turn his hand to work in order to survive'. But the price of beaver pelts fluctuated. It went down in 1665. The French traders would no longer accept payment in kind. They demanded hard cash and the colony had none.

The Sovereign Council in Quebec and the Royal government then took steps to attract gold and silver coinage to New France. French money in Canada was worth twenty-five per cent more than in France, and the West India Company minted a 100,000 crowns of 'Canadian coinage' for use only in the colonies. This, however, was regarded with the greatest suspicion by the French merchants, mainly the trading community of La Rochelle, who only very reluctantly brought themselves to accept the copper coinage from across the ocean.

This lack of currency seriously affected trade between France and Canada. There were, however, two sources of liquid currency to improve the situation. From 1664 charges payable to the Intendant, and pay for soldiers of the Carignan regiment were made in cash.

The subsidies sent each year by the King for administrative expenses, rose well above 100,000 *livres* and helped to fill the country's coffers with new coinage. But the Royal funds did not arrive until the autumn, well after the budget had been settled, while expenses dated from January. It was therefore necessary to seek out other methods of action. In 1685 the Intendant, Jacques de Meulles, had the notion of using playing cards for money. He cut these into two, signed them, sealed each half with its number, and guaranteed repayment when 'the King's funds' arrived.

This was only a temporary expedient but so successful was it in restoring confidence that it was regularly used. The public were so enthusiastic that it began to hoard the cards, which of course undermined the system, so that the Intendant was forced to issue new cards to make good the deficit, thereby exceeding the value of the King's funds available for re-imbursement. Issue after issue was made until in 1714 the circulation of this currency reached a figure of almost 2,000,000. It was inflation.

In 1729 the public demanded that the card system be reinstated. 400,000 *livres* were made, of which 150,000 were to be used for trade within the colony.

The Intendant used another method to recover the gold and silver pieces. This resembled the use of bills of exchange. He signed *billets de caisse* or cash orders for traders in exchange for payments in ready money. When the ships came in, the merchants paid for their products with these orders which were later repaid in Paris by the treasurer of the Admiralty. It could have been a good plan, had it been used with care, which it was not. In 1747 the Intendant signed 2,600,000 *livres*' worth of bills of this kind, and a further 30,000,000 in 1759. It was a bottomless pit!

The reason why the monetary system fell into disrepute was because of the shortage of cash. When money did circulate inflation followed, since the currency itself was suspect and trading was adversely affected.

Clearly this situation did not improve the collection of taxes nor the balancing of the budget. The Canadians had always been hostile to the idea of paying taxes. Mgr de Laval was confronted with every sort of difficulty when he tried to obtain tithe payments of a twenty-sixth.

The population paid its 'quit-rent' to the seigneur but refused to perform any statutory duties for him or to lodge soldiers without remuneration.

Compared to the charges the State incurred, revenues it received were minimal; charges rose to six times the amount of income. The King constantly attempted to raise taxes, but the settlers, through the Intendant, each time objected to the King's demands on the grounds of their own poverty. The deficit rose to such an alarming height that Louis XV was forced to impose a slight measure of taxation which still caused recriminations. He laid down a customs duty of 3 per cent which was collected equally on imported and exported goods. This tax brought in 600,000 *livres* to the Royal Treasury in 1755.

The Canadian economy was based on shaky foundations. Agriculture was neglected: the Canadian colonist worked only when he was forced to. Serious work on the land meant facing the daily threat of ambush by the Iroquois. The farmer was not going to accept such grave risk except to satisfy the basic needs of his own family.

Industry and the export trade were unable to absorb any overproduction. Moreover the colonist preferred to concentrate upon trade in furs which brought in an income sufficiently high to compensate for danger. There were among the settlers in New France, many former soldiers of the Carignan regiment who had not finally decided to exchange the musket for the ploughshare.

Natural resources and industries were neither worked nor developed in any rational fashion. There was always a shortage of skilled workmen and of capital. One or the other should have come from the mother country; but in this field the Royal Government seems to have possessed no real long-term policy, and grants had been misused by some administrations. The inadequacy of the monetary system meant that the economy of New France was endangered.

11 a. Jeanne Mance 'the cloistered nun'

b. A citizen of the eighteenth century, Mme Trottier-Desrivières (Picture by Frs. Beaucourt)

12 a. Madame de Frontenac at
the Court of Louis XIV
(Musée de Versailles)

b. Bigot's lover, Madame
Peau (Angélique de
Méloizes)
(From the archives of the
Méloizes family)

Why were the necessary measures not imposed? It appears that beaver was considered as inexhaustible manna, the one thing worthy of concentrated effort. This error of judgment caused the soldier workers to turn away from the potential richness of the soil, and what lay beneath it.

By 1760, when the colony was threatened, its economy was weakened. The English victory changed the colonist's natural inclination; trading in furs was taken over by the victors. The Canadian finally resumed occupation of his farm, forced by want of any other activity to become a farmer at last.

CHAPTER NINE

METHODS OF TRANSPORT

THE ATLANTIC CROSSING

The little ships of the 16th and 17th centuries which succeeded in crossing the Atlantic carried passengers who surely must have questioned whether this unknown land, whose coast they glimpsed from off Newfoundland, could possibly threaten them with greater dangers than those they had just undergone. The sheer rocks, the turbulent waters and strong currents of the straits alarmed them. Yet in front of them lay the great waters at the mouth of the St Lawrence river, and as they approached its banks, they finally breathed again. They realized perfectly that the risks they might encounter in the rivers and forests of New France could never approach those of the Atlantic crossing. The sea route to Canada or the islands was, according to sailors, the most dreaded of voyages: 'I have been to Canada seven times,' wrote Captain Vaudron in 1716; 'and although I managed to survive, I can promise you that the very best of these voyages gave me more white hairs than any others I have ever undertaken elsewhere. It was a perpetual torment of mind and body.'

From the home port to Quebec the crossing could last for almost any length of time and be subject to every kind of peril: climate, adverse winds, gales, icebergs and pirates. One of the shortest crossings, in fact probably the shortest of this period, was undertaken by Champlain in 1610: his ship set sail from Honfleur on April 8th, and arrived in Tadoussac nineteen days later, on April 26th. In 1687 a ship carrying the Chevalier de Vaudreuil made the crossing in twenty-seven days. On the other hand voyages could last for more than three months; one is reported as having lasted for 112 days. The return journey to France was both easier and calmer given the prevailing westerly winds.

At the beginning of the seventeenth century, ships were never more than 200 tons in weight, 90 feet long by 30. A hundred people, together with their equipment, could be accommodated under

178

conditions which could hardly be described as comfortable. Huddled in the steerage between the hold and the upper deck, the passengers slept higgledy-piggledy on thin mattresses. Unmarried men lay in the bows, 'married couples' were amidships, and the stern was reserved for women. In good weather the hatchways and portholes were left open to provide ventilation, but as soon as the weather or raging seas forced the sailors to batten down it was barely possible to breathe. A few ships had narrow cabins along the bulkhead, with curtains to close them off, sparsely furnished with a narrow bed. Important people and nuns were placed here, or those in feeble health. The captain of the ship which took over Marie de l'Incarnation and her companions in 1639 lent them his own cabin 'which is splendid and spacious'. Father Le Jeune on his voyage of 1632 occupied one which was much less so: 'It was such', he wrote later, 'that we could neither stand up nor kneel nor sit, and which was worse, when the weather was bad, rain would at times run onto my face.'

A passenger who made the passage in 1632 had this to say: 'To begin with we had beautiful weather, and in ten days we had sailed 600 leagues, but for the next thirty-three days we were barely able to cover 200. . . . We were three or four days hove to, as the sailors say, our rudder lashed, and our ship at the mercy of the waves and currents which at times raised her on top of mountains of water, and then as suddenly lowered her once more into the abyss.'

A young nun, Sister Cécile de Sainte-Croix, accompanied Marie de l'Incarnation and her heroic companions in 1639. The ship which took them sailed from Dieppe on May 4th, and did not arrive at Tadoussac until the following July 15th. Thus more than seventy-two days were spent at sea, and Sister Cécile, writing later of the chief vicissitudes they experienced, was still in a state of terror: 'We had a furious storm which lasted a fortnight with hardly any respite, and this meant that for the whole of Rogation Week as well as on Ascension Day, we were unable to celebrate Holy Mass, or to take Holy Communion . . . the ship tossed so much during this time that it was impossible to remain standing nor take the smallest step without assistance, or even to sit down without holding on to something, since this could lead to one being thrown uncontrollably from one side of the cabin to the other. We were forced to take our meals flat on the floor and for three or four

179

of us to hold the plate, and even then we found it very hard not to upset the food . . . I myself was very uncomfortable during this time because of the vomit which flowed uncontrollably from my mouth especially when I lay down, and I am not exaggerating when I tell you that I must easily have thrown up a bucketful, which made me look upon my bed as the most distasteful of furniture. Besides, during these great storms I did not sleep at all; I should have been better leaning against something, since there was no way of holding one's head up.'

When the nuns reached the Gulf of St Lawrence, where the wooded slopes of the New World came into view, they thought the end of their trials must be in sight. But the ship did not sail into Quebec; it lowered anchor at Tadoussac. The rest of the voyage was by fishing boat where all, monks, nuns and other passengers, were packed together on deck: 'the only space available since the rest was full of cod which gave off a very unpleasant smell. During the several days and nights that we were on board we necessarily suffered a great deal,' the diarist observed unemotionally: 'There was no bread, and we were obliged to pick up crumbs from the hold, where there were more rat droppings than biscuits; we took care to examine them minutely in order to supply ourselves with some sort of food, which we then ate with dry cod, raw, having no means of cooking it.'

Nevertheless, the voyagers were less frightened of storms, icebergs and barbarian pirates than they were of epidemics. The terrible conditions of hygiene bred dysentery, scurvy and boils. Very often numerous deaths were recorded. When the vessel carrying Mgr de Saint-Vallier, the new Governor, Denonville, and a force of 500 officers and soldiers, arrived in Quebec, many of them were already dead, and those who did reach port were ill. They were immediately taken to the Hôtel Dieu 'and they had to be laid in the chapel, in the outhouses and henhouses'. In his account, 'from Quebec to New Orleans', Father Schlarman recorded that in 1732 a ship had to stay at sea for the whole of twenty-four weeks, and that 100 passengers out of 154 succumbed.

TRANSPORT BY WATERWAY

For a long time the only routes available for travel were waterways, especially the St Lawrence River, and no one was dissatisfied with the situation. Travel by waterway was in such general use that no efforts were made to construct a route overland. Many years earlier the nomadic tribes of Algonquin had conceived a true masterpiece of versatility and lightness of weight—the birchbark canoe; the French colonist adopted it immediately, and was soon able to manœuvre it as deftly as the Indian. Horses were rare when colonization first began, and oxen were used only for grubbing out trees and for ploughing. The authorities had, it is true, ordered a public road to be made, but for a long time it remained incomplete. At best there was an uneven path or two in some places leading through the shingle and sand along the river banks, and these could only be used for the transport of heavy loads over short distances. Besides no one worried at the thought of traversing great distances: 'These people set out by canoe or on foot to journey from Quebec to Montreal, or to the two furthest points of the great lakes, in such carefree spirits, and with such cheerful faces that one would think they were only visiting the homestead next door.'

The canoe, lightweight yet tough, was in need of constant care. Its sides were at the mercy of any rock at water level or the branch of any drifting treetrunk. Repair kits were always carried, and these consisted of a roll of birchbark, strips of skin or root, and resin from the pine or spruce. If damage resulted from a rocky passage, a daub of ochre made it watertight.

Birchbark, which was free of knots, was also used as a sail; in a favourable wind the skilful canoeist was able to sail his frail craft from Quebec to Montreal or over the lakes, and his paddle hardly entered the water. Sailing boats were fashionable around 1660 as the population increased. La Hontan remarked that on leaving Quebec in 'a little sailing boat' he arrived in Three Rivers five or six days later. Owing to the tides and difficulties of sailing round obstacles, it was only possible to travel by day. 'I was not sorry when we dropped anchor each evening,' remarks the same passenger, 'since darkness did not prevent me from seeing an enormous number of settlements along both banks of the river, and barely a musket-shot away.'

Another method of water transport was the *cajeux*, a form of raft made out of pieces of wood solidly bound together, roughly constructed, and easily fitted with sails. It was used particularly for the transport of heavy goods, and when crossing lakes and those

181

rivers where the rapids were especially dangerous. 'Our canoe was swept away by a gust of wind,' says the author of a *Relation* of 1669, 'and we were brought in by another, just as we were wondering whether to construct a *cajeux* to rescue ourselves.'

These *cajeux* were too heavy to be carried over the rapids and were often left abandoned on the bank, which saved later travellers from having to make their own. *Cajeux* made from cedarwood were used as fireships against enemy vessels lying off Quebec, during the Seven Years' War. Loaded with flaming logs they were left to float with the current or the tide. This was a hopeless procedure, for such flimsy rafts were very quickly sunk by a single cannon ball from the enemy.

TRANSPORT OVERLAND

The first vehicle for transport overland was the sledge, which was used in summer as well as winter for heavy loads. Usually constructed from ash-wood, its size depended on the use for which it was intended. Sledges on runners were different from the native sledge copied from the Indians, and used on trading expeditions, drawn by men or by dogs. The cart and tipcart came into use later, usually built on the farm itself, except for the wheels which were made by the wheelwright who belonged to the seigneury. The settler used carts for hay-making, for harvesting grain and taking corn to the mill rather than for long journeys.

When in or around 1735 the roads became more or less fit for traffic, the *calèche*, or barouche, a sort of open carriage, made its appearance. It had already enjoyed a certain vogue in Quebec and Montreal, being favoured by the Governor, the Intendant and other lofty officials. At first it was no different from the barouche used in France, but for passage over the royal road the circumference of the wheels was considerably increased to avoid getting stuck during the thaw. Journeys over short distances were made in a simplified form of open barouche, known as a *cabrouet*, consisting of a seat without any back, merely fixed to a shaft on wheels.

The barouche soon reached the countryside and was adopted for everyday use. As and when the road was levelled and it was possible to drive at a greater speed, the vehicle became lighter and more graceful, more elegant—which qualities were observed by foreign travellers. In 1735 an officer, d'Aleyrac, observed that 'all the settlers have a summer carriage or barouche, a little resembling the cabriolet. However short the distance they intend to travel, and whatever the time of year, they never go on foot.' The settler was already beginning to make use of the light barouche, rather than of his horse. When in 1756 Montcalm had to disembark some ten leagues below Quebec because of unfavourable winds, a settler drove him into the capital 'in one of those little carriages of the country known as carts or barouches, which resemble our cabriolets, and are drawn by a single horse'. Montcalm remarked upon its liveliness and smartness: 'Their horses are very like those of the Ardennes in strength, stamina and even looks.'

The carriole like the barouche was nearly always open. Despite the vagaries of the climate, there were very few with enclosed seats. The latter were not normally employed except when persons of high society were driving to their smart parties and were afraid of spoiling their clothes. These carriages, furthermore, were scarcely ever seen on the main roads. Travellers preferred to dress in such a way as to defy the cold and the *poudrerie*, ready to shelter where they might if overtaken by a thunderstorm.

Although there were stages and inns every 30 or 40 kilometres, the countrypeople were ready to receive travellers at any hour of the day or night and they always gave them good welcome. For them it meant an opportunity for the country people to hear news from Quebec, from Montreal, even from France—news, from their point-of-view, was well worth the board and lodging they so willingly gave. The legendary hospitality of country dwellers in Canada dates from this time.

Throughout Europe and especially France, if the dictionaries are to be believed, the word 'carriole' was derogatory. The word signified an 'ugly carriage', and an inelegant one. In New France where it was used only in winter it was, by contrast, the most popular and elegant of vehicles, and the one which could best be adapted to transport over snow. In the provinces of Northern Russia it became identified with the 'tarantass', but the latter could be adopted equally well to wheels or runners and could be used in summer over bad roads. The 'carriole' in Canada had at first been only a sledge, roughly put together and made by the owner himself. Later on carpenters and wheelwrights pooled their skills and designed a vehicle with some degree of elegance. The runners were thinner and higher, thus allowing them to cut more easily through drifts of snow. Then the army adopted this form of transport which until now had been confined mostly to the use of country people and well-to-do artisans. In 1753 some officers from the garrison in Quebec were invited to a wedding thirty miles away: they drove to it in a carriole and afterwards swore that their journey had given them more pleasure than they had ever known throughout their campaigns in Europe. Senior officials themselves found this means of locomotion practical, and possessed of an elegance which suited this country of snows. Bigot's deputies, during the inflation of the last months of the Seven Years' War, authorized the carriole for use only for the Court. On March 19th, that is to say, six months before the country surrendered, Bourlamaque described the arrival of the Sieurs Cadet and Péan into Montreal: 'They made their entry like Ambassadors, with six carrioles. Six more of them had gone ahead to Répentigny, fortunately the Chevalier de Lévis was not one of these. Fresh horses were awaiting them in the *place*, and while these were being changed, Cadet gave an audience to the settlers from inside his carriole.'

In this way the carriole became the winter carriage of the nobility, as well as remaining the normal means of transport for journeys made by the ordinary settler. Officials ordered carrioles with upholstered seats, and heated bricks were placed on the floor and covered with a linen cloth. The settlers covered the seat with a bearskin or moosehide, known as the 'carriole skin', and heated logs were laid at their feet.

The stamina of Canadian horses and the lightness of the carriole enabled an almost unbelievable speed to be reached, so that distances of as much as 100 kilometres a day could be covered. On April 29, 1716, the Intendant Bégon had a notice fixed to the door of every Church: 'We forbid all persons, drivers of carrioles as well as those on horseback, to allow trotting or galloping while the congregation leaves the church, until they are ten *arpents* from the church, afterwards they may give their horses their heads provided there is noone ahead of them on the road.' This was the first road safety rule to be imposed in New France.

For taking his whole family to church on Sundays, the settler used a heavier type of sledge, usually fitted with walls of removable planks, and used for the transport of timber during the rest of the week. This was called the 'berlot' or 'berlin' in which one usually stood upright and which was able to hold ten or more people. A draught horse or an ox rather than some more sprightly animal was

184

used to pull this heavy load. In intense cold the back of the animal was covered with a light blanket, which was replaced by a fur rug while it waited outside the church. The berlin was not in any way elegant, but its broad low runners made it 'incapable of upset' on the bad roads.

Travellers were unanimous in their praise of the Canadian horse with his ability to endure the winter. Although descended from a French breed he had acclimatized himself to the rigours of the climate just as well as any human being. 'These horses are like machines, so impervious are they to the cold,' wrote La Hontan. The Englishman Isaac Weld was equally impressed: 'The same horse can, when harnessed to a carriole, cover more than eighty *milles* (about 125 km.) a day; the snow feels so light beneath his strong hooves.' Racing horses on the ice on the St Lawrence or other large rivers, became one of the most fashionable winter sports.

Nevertheless, use of the horse remained the privilege of the authorities, seigneurs, and well-to-do settlers. Missionaries, the *coureurs des bois*, poorer colonists in the heart of the country, still used dog teams to draw their loads. La Hontan observed that from Montreal to Quebec sledges or sleds, 'drawn by great dogs', were much in use on the ice or frozen snow of the river. These dogs were reputed to be as tough as horses and just as impervious to cold. 'The Recollects', wrote Lebeau in 1740, 'use another form of sledge which they have drawn by dogs, when they go out collecting alms. Very often the St Lawrence river has ten feet of ice upon it, and if the wind sweeps the snow over it, the settlers can move with great ease between Quebec and Montreal. Otherwise they make use of snowshoes as do the savages.'

In fact, snowshoes were of Indian origin, as was that indispensable adjunct of a long-drawn-out winter, the toboggan or native sled. Every French traveller in turn was equally impressed by the use of this ingenious method of progress, and many were able to describe the construction and operation of both articles as used by the Indians: 'It is not possible', observes Charlevoix, 'to wear snowshoes without ordinary shoes; the native shoe must be used; a sort of slipper made of smoked skin, folded underneath at the toe and bound with cords.' The toboggan was not complicated to make; thin planks of pliable wood were used, ash or maple, and the front was raised and the back bound with crosspieces of much thicker wood. When shod with snowshoes the traveller could

185

pull his sledge by means of a rope fixed to his leather braces or belt.

The upkeep of roads during the winter was strictly and con-scientiously supervised by the different seigneuries, because of the constant risk of straying off the road and being swallowed up in deep snow. The most complete and detailed ordinance on this subject was given out by the Intendant Dupuy in 1727: 'Roads which are impassable at this time of year because of the great depth of snow on the ground, as well as on the frozen rivers and streams, put travellers to constant risk of losing their way if the roads are insufficiently marked with poles. It is therefore necessary to order the settlers of the lands administered by the Governments of Quebec, Three Rivers and Montreal, whose homesteads are sited on the larger roads, to mark them, each person doing so according to the area covered by his homestead, in such a way that travellers are in no danger of losing their way, failing which a fine of ten *livres* is payable by those contravening the ordinance, to the vestry of the parishes through which the main roads pass.' The ordinance further laid down that poles must stand at least 8 feet high and be placed at intervals of three to each 200 yards of frontage. These poles were usually small fir trees, often spruce which, because of their sombre colour, and thick bushy branches, could easily be spotted from a distance. The same ordinance forbade the grubbing out or cutting of these poles, 'upon risk of corporal punishment, and the statutory punishments for stealing'. It was also laid down that 'on pain of the same punishments, every person whoever, or whatever he may be, is to bring his beasts up the road every morn-ing, and after every snowfall to beat the snow down on the road between the poles bordering their homesteads'. At the end of his ordinance Dupuy expressed his astonishment at the way in which the settlers neglected the upkeep of roads which must surely be of the utmost use to them. 'This seems to have no relation to sense or reason in a country where snow falls every year in such great quan-tities, and stays for so long on the ground. The settlers must be made to think for themselves each winter and they must take the same steps without waiting for ordinances from ourselves.'

It was not until the year 1747, that is 140 years after the founda-tion of Quebec, that a reasonably passable road was built to link the capital with Montreal. Land grants laid down in definite terms the obligation of the colonist in maintaining a road through the whole of his holding 'for the convenience of his neighbours'. But this obligation ended at the boundary of the seigneurie, and the colonist laid out his roads according to his own convenience and whim. When the chief surveyor of New France, Pierre Robineau de Bécancour, was ordered to visit in 1706 the three Governments of Quebec, Three Rivers and Montreal, to complete the laying-out of roads, he realized that practically nothing of the work had yet been done. Most seigneurial roads were impassable; narrow, twisting, at the very best fit only for carts and tip-carts. Along the south bank of the river, great stretches of land lay uncultivated with no road at all. The chief surveyor also suggested that the authorities should first construct a road on the North bank, which was nearly all populated. But he did not accomplish a great deal, and in 1715, for all his labours, he had nothing but a few reports to show.

His son succeeded him, but was hardly better qualified than his father. And how was one to compel the settlers in the seigneuries to construct roads and bridges in their respective parishes? The colonists had no intention of giving their services for nothing, especially at harvest or haymaking time. Moreover, neighbouring settlers did not always agree on the route to be followed. The chief surveyor no longer dared to appear in the countryside where the settlers greeted him with forks, sticks, and axes. In short, by 1730 only sections of the road had been laid out, unsymmetrically, and with no bridges across the streams. The important rivers, of which there were fifteen, were not all provided with ferries; they had to be crossed by canoe, and another means of transport had to be picked up on the opposite bank. Dupuy, the Intendant, took a month to get to Montreal and back, even as late as 1727.

At last a competent and forceful leader of men took the chief surveyor's post. When Robineau de Bécancour died in 1729, he was replaced by an engineer called Jean-Eustache Lanouiller de Bois-clerc, until now controller of navigation and fortifications in Quebec, and he, in the space of the first three years, was to complete more work than his two predecessors had done in all their sixty years. Strenuously supported by Hocquart, the Intendant, he put into force the 'corvées du roi' or statutory services due to the King, enjoined the officers of militia in the parishes to obey under threat of severe sanction, and then set about reconstructing existing

187

bridges with a new technique suited to the climate. The pressure of descending ice floes in the spring meant that supports could not be used in midstream. Therefore it was not feasible to use bridges over rivers wider than forty feet, the maximum length of the joists which were fixed to each bank on stone foundations. Where bridges could be used, they had to be shielded with planks against sudden changes in temperature and the drifting of snow.

When this work was accomplished, the chief surveyor took over the restoration of the road itself. During the summer of 1733 he had built a road 24 feet wide and 60 miles long between Portneuf and the Pointe-du-Lac. He chivvied the owners of riverside properties, rushing from one parish to another with inexhaustible energy: 'remaining anything up to forty-five days in the saddle, from May 9th to October 1st'. Lanouiller was an enthusiast. By 1737 he was certain that by the following year the royal road would be open over its entire length from Quebec to Montreal, and that it would be possible to make the journey in four days. It was too much to hope. His scheme was not finally realized for another ten years, when he could write to the ministry that at last he had been able to make the journey in his barouche from Quebec to Montreal in the month of August. But the road was still by no means perfect, and he himself admitted it: 'This road would be accessible to carriages if there were ferries on the main rivers. The section between the river Maskinongé and Berthier has to be almost entirely reconstructed since the land is boggy and during wet weather has to be relaid with pontoons and cedarwood stakes.'

This overland road was in no way a popular route, and was used along its whole length only by the authorities. The Comte de Malartic of the Béarn regiment drove out of Quebec in his barouche on the 1st July for Montreal in order to arrange billets for troops. He described his method of travel: 'Every two leagues we change horses. It costs twenty *sous* for each passenger, and forty *sous* for two; there is no inn nor village but the road is lined with houses, most of which are habitable, where one is welcome and can find something to eat and drink.' Malartic did not mention the state of the road, but he chose to return to Quebec 'in a little canoe'.

In fact the river was still the most practical and easy link between Quebec and Montreal, and was used throughout the year for journeys of an urgent kind. When the ice held on the river it was possible to travel on skates with steel blades; a faster, more prudent and economical method. The Governor used skaters to deliver orders to officials in Three Rivers and Montreal. Experienced messengers were able to travel a distance of 125 miles on smooth ice with a favourable wind, hardly pausing for rest. On one occasion such a skater reached the limits of endurance. He was despatched with an urgent order from Montreal to Quebec, and covered a distance of 180 miles (175 km), in 18 hours. On arrival he died, some said of exhaustion, others that he had dined too well *en route*.

No regular postal service was in operation until the beginning of the eighteenth century. Until then those who wished to send letters had to wait upon the goodwill of some ship's captain or a passing traveller. Moreover letters often did not arrive for a considerable time after despatch, if ever. 'For us Frenchmen and Fathers in Huron country,' wrote Father Le Jeune in 1635, 'we must expect no answer inside two years to letters sent to France.' Very often such letters were forgotten somewhere or mislaid *en route*. In order to be certain that important communications arrived at their destination, their writers made two or three copies which were sent off by different routes. The archives in Quebec contain three absolutely identical letters written by the same person, and all three were received by the addressee. When vessels from Europe put into the port of Quebec those who awaited news of relatives still in the mother country rowed out to the ship where the Captain handed to the first arrivals all the letters and parcels in his charge. In their haste to know whether someone from France had written, the people wrangled and quarrelled. To prevent this situation, the Intendant Hocquart put out ordinances forbidding the Quebecuois to board ships until the captain had landed. The letters and packets were then handed to a person specially appointed to the duty, and to whom those interested had to apply. It was the beginning of an organized postal service.

Around 1690, a Portuguese naturalized-Canadian, Pierre Dasilva, offered his services in exchange for a modest wage as regular postman between Quebec and Montreal. 'His diligence and loyalty' were noticed from above, and the Intendant soon gave him an official post as 'ordinary messenger for the carriage of letters from M. the Governor-General and ourselves in the King's service, throughout the whole area of the colony, responsible for the letters of individual people in order to take them to their destination and to return with replies. We have imposed a tax of ten *sous* on the carriage of each letter from Quebec to Montreal, and the same sum for their return, and any other article so sent will be charged for according to its ultimate destination.' The Intendant also warned against attempted interference with the postman's work, and enjoined officials and soldiers to give him 'help and assistance'. When the intrepid postman died in 1717, after a quarter of a century of service, he was replaced by his son-in-law. Their journey, like all journeys, was carried out on snowshoes or with a dog-team in winter, and by canoe in summer.

CHAPTER TEN

THE STRUCTURE OF A NEW POPULATION

The first signs of French courtesies in this deserted country were of a touching simplicity. Even from a distance of 2,000 miles the customs, manners and traditions of the mother country were spontaneously observed. Tradition, for instance, demanded that the good wishes expressed at the dawn of a new year be accompanied by a gift, however modest. By some ingenious means this tradition was observed in a colony where even the ordinary necessities of everyday existence were lacking. The anonymous writer of *Journal des Jésuites* for the date of January 1, 1646: 'M. Giffard was presented with a book by Father Bonnet on the life of Our Lord; a small book for M. Deschatelets; for M. Bourdon a Galilean telescope. M. le Gouverneur was greeted by the soldiery with their harquebuses, and a whole group of settlers. The nuns sent letters at a very early hour of the morning, presenting their compliments. The Ursulines sent beautiful gifts, and two splendid pies for dinner. I gave them two pictures, one of St Ignatius and another of St Francis Xavier, in enamel.'

The custom was repeated each year. On New Year's Eve the Governor held a reception. His guests consisted of the Jesuits, leading citizens, and a few tradespeople. This was the term of office of M. de Montmagny, Champlain's immediate successor, the great seigneur, father, friend and confidant of all, who brought to New France a distinctive atmosphere and habits which were rooted for all time. When the missionaries travelled to far-off territories, M. de Montmagny accompanied them down to the quay from which they would depart, and there he stood until the canoes had faded from the horizon. When the nursing sisters and Ursuline nuns arrived on August 1, 1639, he himself went down to the shore in his ceremonial robes with his entire suite, in which the principal assistant was Antoine Bréhaut de l'Isle, himself a Knight of Malta. The Governor wished to be the first to offer his hand to the new arrivals, and to sound off cannon in their honour. These small details help to illustrate how much splendour and grace attached to the life of M. de Montmagny. Even in a lost and distant country the King's representative must at all times, whether in public or in private, show himself worthy of his honourable post.

As is its wont, worldly sophistication grew to replace the kindly grace of these years of struggle. The danger of any serious war with the Iroquois faded, and everywhere was felt a great joie de vivre. The governing class has been accused, not without reason, of being one of the main causes of the loss of Canada to England. Certainly this society, with some rare exceptions, was devoted more or less exclusively to pleasure, and its behaviour cannot be called serious. Officials, and those in administrative posts, likewise tradespeople who moved in the entourage of the Governor and the Intendant, and who helped to create the prevailing atmosphere, had never looked upon New France as more than a temporary post. They had never dreamed of settling there and adopting it as their own country.

Those who had been born in Canada rapidly set the tone of life in society there. The girls were pretty, well-educated, gay, ambitious, and travellers loved to sing their praises: 'Canadian girls,' said Bacqueville de la Potherie as early as 1700, 'are witty and refined, they can sing well, and love to dance. They do not seem to be either provincial or middle-class, indeed they are proper women of the world, and Parisian women of the world at that.' The ecclesiastical authorities also noticed how they were disposed to show off their assets. 'Some of them,' remarked the Bishop of Quebec in 1690, 'have no hesitation in exposing both neck and shoulders when they are in their own houses; we ourselves have met them in this condition.'

The arrival of Frontenac as Governor, with his suite, helped to invest society with something of the atmosphere of a miniature royal Court. Frontenac wished to imbue the post of Governor of New France with all the protocol and ostentation he could devise. This warrior with his surly manner loved the atmosphere of the salons and throve on flattery. He very much enjoyed the company of the society ladies of Quebec. These elegant creatures were at his feet, especially since each one of them realized that in Versailles Madame de Frontenac was in the very same position vis-à-vis the King. In 1689, just after his return as Governor, de Frontenac 'was visited by all the ladies, whose ill-concealed delight was as apparent in their faces as in their words', remarked La Hontan, himself exultant since he was now able to make use of the Governor's purse and to eat at his table.

And so it was that from the second half of the seventeenth century there were moments when one could imagine one breathed the atmosphere of Versailles rather than the air of the streets of Quebec. One sensed the same climate in Montreal, where the reigning Governor was only faintly interested in society, and when the Intendant was in residence. One of the features of this minia-ture Court was the weight which everyone gave to the privileges attaching to his or her own position in society. An everyday event, not only in the towns but also in the most modest of the seigneuries, was the ceremony of the marriage contract, presided over by the father of one or other of the engaged couple, or less often by the notary. Invitations to attend the signing of the contract or religious ceremony, which usually took place on consecutive days, were sent off several weeks ahead, because the distances were so great and the postal services so infrequent and slow. It was necessary to produce some exceptionally good reason for refusing the invita-tion. Guests thought nothing of travelling hundreds of miles, even in winter, and in making the most strenuous efforts to attend. The supreme ambition of every family was to secure the presence of the Governor and the Intendant. When these guests accepted, the duties of the notary increased greatly, for it was his job to settle the order of precedence to be enjoyed by the guests. 'The sensible notary prepares his list of guests a long time in advance, and when, after the contract has been read, he invites the guests to sign, he is able to call upon them in a confident voice and in their correct order. Despite all these precautions sensibilities are frequently offended and resentment often incurred. The poor scrivener is hard put to it to please or make amends to the injured parties. Every kind of mistake may be forgiven, even the extravagant behaviour which sometimes follows over-indulgence in drink, but a slight in protocol is never forgotten.'

This fierce protection of social prerogatives gave rise to ridiculous incidents, which have rightly been called 'quibbles of precedence'. The Governor claimed the right to be saluted by the pikemen 'just like the Marshal of France'. The Intendant demanded that he be ranked as the Governor's equal at every public ceremonial. The King's Lieutenants from Quebec demanded the same standing as the Governors of Montreal and Three Rivers. Commanders of forts proclaimed their right to demand that the chaplains bow to them before taking Mass. Officers of the militia were offended because their equivalents in rank in the Navy treated them as inferiors and were distant in their behaviour towards them. To add to all this churchwardens made it known that they were not prepared to allow officers of the law to precede them in procession. Finally the beadles were offended 'because the choristers of the parish take their places in the choir-stalls while they themselves remain in the sacristy'. Class prejudices, rivalry over social distinctions, became ever more rife in this sort of closed circle whose members were so constantly in each other's company.

There is a classic example of one of these 'quibbles of precedence' in 'the affair of the *prie-dieu*' which took place in 1694 and divided into two camps, violently opposed, the adherents of Mgr de Saint-Vallier and those of the Governor of Montreal, M. de Callières. The Recollect Fathers, wishing to inaugurate their new church with all solemnity, invited the Bishop, the Governor, the Intendant, the Sulpicians, and every other person of note at the time in Montreal. Rules of precedence required the Governor-General of the country to be given the right to a *prie-dieu* inside the church, next to the Bishop. Then M. de Callières demanded similar treatment in the absence of the Governor-General. Mgr de Saint-Vallier had no intention of allowing this, and he gave orders to the Superior of the Recollects to remove the *prie-dieu* assigned to M. de Callières and to have it placed further back. When the punctilious Governor entered the Church he noticed the change that had been made, and he signed to two of his officers to return the piece of furniture to its previous position. Monseigneur immediately turned on his heel and retired from the ceremony.

The Intendant Raudot revived in Quebec customs he had acquired during his long attendance in Paris circles. He was a man of great culture, who gathered at his home a set of musicians and men of letters, and here he often received the small nobility of Quebec. The diarist of the nursing Sisters, to whom he often went for conversation, has painted an extremely agreeable picture of him: 'He is an old man with plenty of wit, easy and pleasant to talk to. He can converse on any subject. He knows the history of every country, and gets on famously with everyone, however unimportant, as well as with children. He is very fond of young people and excellent at amusing them. His usual form of entertainment, and one he is anxious to share with his guests, is a concert for voices and instruments. Since he is so anxious to please, he likes us to listen to this symphony, and he often sends his musicians to sing motets in our Church.'

It was quite usual, especially when there was threat of war, for everyone to throw himself into a whirl of social distractions. Claude de Bonnault wrote with some justification: 'It is as if no one were sure of what tomorrow might bring, and as if these people flourished on the threatening danger that daily surrounded them, and therefore they hastened to enjoy life to the full. They wanted to make the most of every minute; they read, wrote as much as they could, danced, played cards frenziedly, made love. There was a great deal of lovemaking in Canada at this time . . .'

These accurate commentaries were inspired by their author's reading of the lively correspondence of Mme Bégon, which he himself discovered and had published, and which allows us to share intimately in Montreal society during the last years of French rule. There were endless balls, receptions, dances, orgies, drinking. But all of these paled beside the parties held in the Intendant's palace in Quebec where the Intendant Bigot held the limelight. Montcalm described a ball at the Intendant's palace where 'more than eighty ladies and young girls, all charming and very well-dressed', could be seen and admired. These receptions were succeeded by revels, by dancing and gaming. Junior officers were ruined. Montcalm stood by ineffectually at these orgies. He went to them to enjoy himself but he discovered they bored him. After a particularly noisy turn at the tables in the Intendant's residence, he could not resist writing a description of the evening to General Lévis: 'I thought they were mad, or at least that they were suffering from fever.'

The salon of Madame Hertel de Beaubassin, in the little street, the Parloir, was the favourite place of assignation for Montcalm when in need of comfort, friendship and understanding. This woman, still young and fresh-looking, reserved in her manners and sure in her taste, became the General's confidante. Although the

house was open to the whole of the aristocracy of Quebec, nevertheless visitors arrived only at infrequent intervals, especially since
they feared to interrupt an intimate tête-à-tête. For this reason they
found their way to the equally hospitable, though perhaps more
formal and less relaxed, drawing-room of Madame de la Naudière.
Here too recent events were discussed, including the dissolute
behaviour of the Intendant.

Nobody really believed that Bigot played to gain large sums at
the expense of his officers; he played because he adored it and the
distraction it offered him, although 'ill fortune pursues him too
often for justice'. On Christmas night in the year 1756 Bigot played
and 'lost with regularity'. One evening in February, 1758, he had
1,500 *louis* taken from him in the space of three quarters of an hour.
Like all unlucky and distracted players, he ordered an endless
succession of new games, and when the stock was exhausted, he
invented new ones. Dealings became so outrageous and dishonest
that the Court heard of them, no one knew by what means. An
ordinance went out prohibiting: 'Dubious games, especially the
one known as Three Cards, Tope and Tingue, Passedix, the Two
Cards, Quinquenove, Mormonique, Hoca, Bassette, Pharaoh,
Lansquenet, Dupe, Biriby, Roulette, Odds or Evens, Quinze, Petits
Paquets.'

Montcalm was of the opinion that Quebec enjoyed an atmosphere of rejoicing, 'by comparison with the dreary way Montreal
is governed, where nevertheless one must resign oneself to staying
during Lent'.

Was the Government of Montreal really so dreary? Clearly
General Montcalm understood the city less well than did Madame
Bégon who lived in it and was very much of it. She loved to gossip,
and would write whenever she felt like it to her son-in-law who was
forced to accept her somewhat overwhelming affection. 'There
was a great banquet at the Intendant's,' she wrote, 'you know, my
dear son, how the ladies in our country flock to the house of M. the
Intendant. Great dinner-party at M. de Longueil's for ladies and
officers.' In another letter she confides: 'I think the city of Montreal
is less awake than I am this morning, for the ball did not end until
six o'clock. Every lady in the town must have danced until dawn.'
Madame Bégon could not, of course, resist the temptation to
observe that women who had always been considered prudish had
not managed to resist the contagion: 'Would you believe', she

wrote to her son-in-law, 'that that fanatic Madame de Perchères danced through the whole of last night?' and here she added her own comments: 'Our priests are going to preach very hard after this. And what is even better is that there is a ball tomorrow at Madame de Valtrie's and another the following day at Madame de Bragelonne's. There is something for M. le Curé to wring his hands about.' Indeed the priests were frantic and not without reason. But in the midst of the so universally reckless behaviour, they were almost the only people to tremble at the thought of the holocaust that would soon engulf them all.

LOVE AFFAIRS

The history of New France is strewn with lovers and adventurers. In this new country, full of unforeseen happenings, with risk an inherent part of everyday life, passions of all kinds throve, and freedom blossomed. Uncertain of what tomorrow might bring, these people wanted to make the most of today. Vast schemes for conquest, for exploration, for putting down the Indians, the feverish excitement of living in a new world, all played their part psychologically in causing people to overstep the limits of pleasure and often through their blind excesses eventually to come upon faith of a sort, though by a very different path from the one which the founders and missionaries had trodden before.

The *Journal des Jésuites*, a kind of daily chronicle of the first days of the colony, was soon full of discreet accounts of romantic adventures. 'Courville arrested *propter raptum imminentum* of Mlle d'Auteuil,' we read in the entry of May 1, 1651. The following May 7th: 'Mlle d'Auteuil has been sent to Beauport to M. Giffard', and again in November: 'Courville has embarked for France'. Some curious spirits, anxious to piece together these intriguing scraps of information, investigated the original and found there a genuine love story. Charles Cadieu otherwise known as Courville was an adventurer who had developed connections in the high society of Quebec. 'Mlle d'Auteuil' was really the wife of Denis-Joseph de Ruette, the Sieur d'Auteuil, a well-known civil servant, whom she had married in Paris on November 18, 1647, and who held the post of Councillor and Procurator-General of Canada. While her husband and her mother were away on a voyage to France, Claire Françoise, perhaps not unwillingly, fell victim to abduction by

Charles Cadieu, otherwise Courville. To shelter her from danger, the young woman was shut up with the nuns in the Hôtel-Dieu, and from there she was taken to Beauport, while her lover was thrown into prison, and then sent back to France. This, so far as we are concerned, was the end of his part in the story. As to Madame d'Auteuil, we are told from the documents that in 1657 she obtained a judicial separation and was given permission to go to France in order to deal with a family lawsuit. While in Paris she gave birth to a son who at four years old was taken away by his father. Madame d'Auteuil never wished to return to the country she had been forced to adopt, and she retired to some property at Ville-l'Evêque. When in 1674 her son returned to Paris to study law, she refused to see him, and set in motion procedures by which she might disinherit him. This is clearly a slice of real life which would delight any novelist.

In the career of d'Iberville, among the tales of conquest and adventure there was at least one weakness, and this was an undue attraction to women. In 1686 a young girl of good family from Montreal, Jeanne Geneviève Picoté de Belestre, accused him in public of having seduced her. The matter was taken before the Council of Quebec. D'Iberville was accused of the crime of 'rape and seduction' which was punishable by death or sentence to the galleys. But he was not to be found: the affair had taken place before the expedition to Hudson Bay had sailed, and this voyage did not end until October, 1687. When the ships at last returned, the seducer would be caught; but then it was learned that he was in France, where, by request of the Governor, he had gone to 'convey to His Majesty an account of the happenings in the bay "in the North"'. He was found guilty in his absence and a sentence, mitigated somewhat by reason of his connections within the Council, was to support the child entirely until the age of fifteen and to give the mother complete freedom of access. In her heart, Mademoiselle de Belestre had always hoped that eventually d'Iberville would marry her. When at last in 1693 she heard that he was about to share his future with Marie-Therèse Pollet, she retired to live with the nuns in the Hôtel-Dieu in Montreal, where she died in 1721, aged fifty-four. She had never been able to forget the dishonour she had brought upon her family.

This looseness of morals, though not infrequent, was mostly confined to certain circles. But since it attached often to high strata of society it was, as we have seen, remarked upon and given publicity in public condemnation from the pulpit, which merely succeeded in exciting the passions. To denounce vice in this way only serves to inflame it to further excesses. It is merely fanning the flames in order to extinguish the fire.

The affection of a handsome officer, François Jordy de Cabanac, for Marguerite Disy did not escape the eagle eye of the Bishop. Marguerite Disy had married Jean des Broyeux in 1677, at the age of fourteen, when he was twenty-seven, and a well-known *coureur des bois*. Madame de Broyeux was left alone in her house in Batiscan with her young son François, and her house became a meeting-place of fur traders, adventurers and soldiers. François Jordy soon became a friend of the lady, and conducted the affair with such indiscretion that the priest of the parish was alarmed. Letters passed between the Bishop and Frontenac the Governor. The latter, in order to avoid probable scandal, sent the Sieur de Jordy to a billet in Sorel. At the same time, Mgr de Saint-Vallier published a mandate forbidding the lovers, the Sieur de Jordy and Madame des Broyeux, to attend the churches of Batiscan and Champlain. Hearing of what had happened Jordy returned in haste to Batiscan together with his friend Bourgchemin, where they arrived, seemingly by chance, one Sunday morning. They entered the church with as much noise as possible. The priest, Foucault, realizing that something unusual was taking place in the nave, turned round, recognized the intruders, interrupted the service at once, and retired into the sacristy.

Like all passionate infatuations the feelings of the officer and Marguerite Disy were short lived. All these events had taken place in 1694. Two years later Jordy de Cabanac married a girl from a well-known family, Marie-Anne Nolan. He became Mayor of Three Rivers, and Knight of St Louis. In 1722 M. de Vaudreuil could say of him: 'He is of good character and well-disciplined in behaviour.' As to Madame des Broyeux, when her husband died in 1701 she must have learnt wisdom, since the chronicler does not again mention her name. According to documents of 1720, it seems she became a midwife; a humble profession indeed.

This frenzy of independence and freedom in affairs of the heart was given free rein, especially in marriages 'à la Gaumine'. This was a stratagem which had first been used in New France in the first years of the eighteenth century. A couple who for some reason or other had been refused the right to marry would make their way to Church in secret, together with two witnesses, at the hour when Mass was to be celebrated by the parish priest. Then, at the solemn moment of consecration, the couple would declare aloud their intention to take each to husband and wife without further ceremony. This practice became so fashionable that the Bishop, this time supported by the administrative authorities (since the male partners in most such marriages were soldiers), excommunicated those who had contracted marriage in this way. Some such unions of this kind caused scandal in society and in legal circles.

The most spectacular of these marriages 'à la Gaumine' was one which threw two families of some authority in ecclesiastic circles into violent opposition. Alexandre Joseph de Lestringan, Sieur de Saint-Martin, a captain in the Navy, and member of the guard on duty at the Château de Saint-Louis, and his wife, Madeleine-Louise Juchereau de Saint-Denis, a Canadian by birth, wished their daughter, Marie-Anne-Josette, to marry a young officer who had just come over from France, one Louis de Montéléon, the son of the King's butler, Paul, and born in Paris. They applied to the Vicar-General, M. Charles Glandelet, who had indicated that before they could obtain permission to marry all couples, 'particularly people newly arrived from France into this country, must furnish authentic documents to indicate that they have never previously been married'. Montéléon thought this was a reflection on his character, whereupon he insulted the Vicar-General, and encouraged by his future in-laws would have physically injured him, 'and no doubt would have done so, so carried away with rage was he, had he not been restrained by the said lady of St Marin who begged him out loud to desist, and stopped him'. On January 7, 1711, in the little church at Beauport, near Quebec, the marriage took place of two modest working people, Thomas Touchet and Geneviève Gagnier. M. de Montéléon accompanied by his fiancée and her mother attended the nuptial Mass; at the moment of consecration 'Montéléon challenged the priest to marry him and the said Demoiselle de Saint-Martin, and then declared aloud that he would take the said demoiselle in marriage. She in the same tones declared that she would take the said Sieur de Montéléon for her husband, and thereupon took all the congregation assembled there to witness the same.' This caused a great scandal among the population of Beauport. The priest hastened to draw up a detailed description of the proceedings in order to issue a summons, which he then sent to the Bishop and the Intendant. After studying the document, a fine of twenty *livres* to be given to the poor of the parish was imposed and the marriage was made valid from the following fifteenth day of February.

This sketch of sentimental life under French rule would be incomplete without a reference to Madame Péan, the great love and inspiration of the Intendant, Bigot. One of Bigot's first lieutenants was Michel-Jean-Hughes Péan, of whom a chronicler of the time said: 'His merit lies in the charms of his wife, who pleases M. Bigot, and with good reason, she is young, lively, full of wit, with a sweet and easy nature; her conversation is gay and amusing; in fact she enchanted the Intendant, who, during all his stay in Canada, was interested only in her and was so good to her that everyone envied her good fortune. He went regularly to her house each evening. She built up a little coterie of people of her own kind.'

The Intendant, Hocquart, to whom we are indebted for a description of the adventures of yet another young and headstrong girl, Louise-Catherine André de Leigne, wrote of the Canadian girls of his time that 'they are witty, which gives them in almost every way an advantage over the men. They all love fine clothes and in this there is no difference between the middle-class wife, and the wife of a gentleman or an officer.' Had they been less beautiful, less witty, less flirtatious they might not have aroused so much passion as they undoubtedly did.

Still more numerous and more romantic too, at least at first sight, were the unions of the whites, especially the *coureurs des bois* and the military, with Indian women. Very few could resist the easy attractions of these women, when every moral law and rule of humanity was thrown over or forgotten in obedience to the diplomatic gesture which called for the bridal couch or the daughters of the tribal chieftain to be shared, in order to ensure the friendship of the latter.

The restlessness of adventure and of the nomadic life soon seized hold of young people, some of whom, impelled by their rejection of a more ordinary existence, became inveterate adventurers and *coureurs des bois*.

In the country near the Great Lakes, which was the stronghold of the *coureurs des bois,* and where intensive trafficking of furs went on, the villages did not take long to grow up. And since these villages contained very few white women, the *coureurs des bois* soon became friends with the Indian women. Missionaries when they happened to be in the district would hasten to regularize such unions, which became so general that the authorities very soon thought of forming parishes. The children born of these marriages grew up and quickly helped to increase the population of the villages. Thus the authorities at last came to realize that the products of these marriages had little in common with the new strong and virile race of which Champlain had dreamed.

INTELLECTUAL LIFE

Between 1635, the year in which Champlain died, and the end of French rule in 1763, four generations grew up. Only the first of these received an entirely French education. Such was the spirit and originality of feeling in this new country that succeeding generations strove to throw off old ways with great rapidity. Nevertheless, the quality of these immigrants of the first generation was such that those who came after retained the main features of their way of life, such as their language and their customs. Artisans, labourers and tradesmen were from the very first neither illiterate nor ignorant. The contrary has been too often alleged because various acts drafted by notaries have been preserved in which witnesses had declared themselves unable to write or to sign their name. But these witnesses were in fact neither illiterate nor ignorant. Too often the wrong conclusion was reached after merely a cursory look at notaries' acts containing the testimonies of witnesses which affirm, 'not knowing how to write nor to sign their name'. But those who signed these contracts were fairly numerous and those who 'made their mark' either by means of a cross or by some other distinctive and original means, had mostly at some time learned the alphabet. They were often uncomfortable and shy in the presence of educated and distinguished people, and also the fact that they only rarely had occasion to practise their writing obliged such humble people to reveal their awkwardness. They avoided the humiliation of a clumsy scribble laid beside imposing flourishes. The colonist, Jacques Aubuchon, in a document drawn up in 1665, declared he 'did not know how to write or sign according to the rules'. Nevertheless he did sign with writing which was perfectly legible a year later, and he later still signed many other documents. Others, such as Pierre Dandonneau and Nicolas Dupuy experienced the same feeling of shyness when they came to hold a pen in their workworn hands. They were intimidated in the presence of a strict scrivener, and told honest lies with seemingly no unpleasant consequence. But statistics themselves did not lie. During the period from 1634 to 1680, which deals with the first generation of New France, about 800 different signatures of colonists were found, out of a total population of only 2,500 settlers. And of these 800 signatures those of important personages, who by reason of their status and position must have known how to write, are not included, and nor are signatures of religious bodies.

By 1635 adjustment had begun. The settlers in Quebec asked the Jesuits to instruct their children, and with their own hands built the school. These religious bodies began to teach and were amazed to find themselves 'surrounded by so much youth at such an early stage'. Four years later the Ursulines opened their first convent for the forty or so girls in the neighbourhood. In 1655 courses designed for study of the classics were fully booked at the college in Quebec: these were courses devoted to literature, lasting five years, whereby three years were assigned to learning letters and grammar and one each for the humanities and rhetoric. The whole was completed by a two-year course in philosophy designed for those who were to enter religious orders. This teaching of the classics by the Jesuits in their school in a wild country soon invited attention from outside. One traveller, Lebeau, spoke with enthusiasm of their 'literary games', games which the governors themselves would watch and sometimes take part in. On July 2, 1666, the first 'disputations' in philosophy took place: 'All the powers are of the opinion', observed the author of one of the *Relations*, 'that Monsieur the Intendant put his arguments very well. M. Jolliet and M. de Francheville answered him astutely, with every sort of logic.' One of the professors, Father Beschefer, was able to write with enthusiasm: 'We have Philosophy, and seven pupils have sustained theses. You can see from this that Kébec is something very special.' Yet there were barely three hundred settlers, some fifty families.

During this time, the Bishop of Quebec, Mgr de Laval, set up both a small and large seminary, to train a native force of clergy.

Like Champlain he thought it was possible to gallicize the Indians, to impress upon them as they sat at their desks in college some notion of Latin and of history and philosophy. He was soon disappointed. Only one of the first of his chosen pupils was even faintly interested in these novel happenings, and this only because he was an orphan and was able for once to eat his fill and to sleep under cover. The five others seized by home-sickness made off on expeditions into the forest. Henceforth the Bishop of Quebec concentrated his efforts on the education of the children of his fellow countrymen. He modified the rules and stiffened discipline. From the time they entered the school the children had to undergo a general inquest into their lives. For the future they were to have a spiritual leader who would listen to their confession every Saturday. On that evening recreation was replaced by self-examination. Every day the pupils had individually to recite the prayers for the Blessed Virgin. Those unable to read well recited the second rosary instead. Outside the hours devoted to religious exercises, every pupil had to apply himself to learning a trade, or else do manual work for the seminary. Each pupil had a room of his own for which his parents were asked to supply a table, a bed and a chair, the only pieces of furniture allowed.

A shortage of professors meant that the pupils were forced to attend some of their classes at the Jesuits' College, and vice versa. The length of study varied according to the intellectual ability of the scholars. It usually lasted for from five to seven years. If we study the roll of scholars which has been preserved, we are struck by the fact that there is mention of a clerk, an apprentice, even of soldiers, who in their own country would never have had the chance of beginning studies of the classics.

Encouraged by this success, the Jesuits inaugurated lessons in hydrography and mathematics to train land-surveyors, map-makers, navigators and engineers. The usual course of studies lasted two years, and those in their twenties and thirties, wishing to improve their minds, were not ashamed to sign on for it: 'I have pupils with beards on their chins, to whom I am teaching naval techniques and fortification skills as well as other things to do with mathematics. ... One of my pupils is at the helm of a ship bound for the North,' noted Father de la Chauchetière in 1694, with obvious satisfaction. Since navigation of the St Lawrence was both delicate and complicated, captains of ships received special practical instruction, and their services were very valuable when surprise attacks were made on Quebec from ships at sea, especially during the Seven Years' War. Experienced pilots, compelled to guide enemy ships upstream were easily able to steer them onto the reefs or let them run aground. The course in hydrography achieved such success from the outset, that Talon was inspired to establish a proper Naval Academy in Quebec. The most famous pupil to come out of this school must certainly have been Louis Jolliet, the great explorer, who was later to succeed his own professor Franquelin, as King's hydrographer of New France.

While he supervised the progress made in his seminary, instituted above all to train priests for the colony, Mgr de Laval improved the standards of his school of arts and trades designed for the sons of the lower classes, who were not always suited to classical studies, but who, either through heredity or natural inclination, wished to become apprenticed to some basic and indispensable trade. For their special benefit he created scholarships for students giving free board and lodging and instruction in the trade of the scholar's own choice. Teaching in the arts concentrated on painting, sculpture, gilding and cabinet-making. As for trade, young men could learn to be carpenters, joiners, slaters, cobblers, tailors, builders, makers of edge-tools or locksmiths. Later a section for teaching agriculture was added to these faculties.

At Montreal in these early years Gabriel Souart, the Sulpician, was in charge of teaching the boys while Sister Marguerite Bourgeois and her companions taught the girls 'to read, to write and sew, as well as their prayers, their Christian duties, how to speak correctly and easily, how to behave elegantly and to train themselves in the upright ways of the wisest and most Christian girls in the world'. These lessons took place during the summer, for the severe winter prevented the girls from leaving their houses from November until April.

The Jesuit, Chauchetière, whom we have already encountered in Quebec, was Pro-Regent in Montreal in 1694, where he had 'twelve to fifteen scholars'. Furthermore he taught mathematics to officers in the army.

The 'brother hospitallers' in Montreal, who were also teachers, followed the initiative which had been given to teaching in Quebec by Mgr de Laval. One of the principal aims of this community was, according to Royal patents, 'to bring in poor orphan children, the disabled, old people, the sick and other male people in need, to be housed, fed and cared for according to their needs, as well as providing them with the sort of work to which they were suited, and to teach trades to the said children, and give them the best education available'. This institution to which a whole generation of young Canadians in the district around Montreal owed its learning, failed sadly because its directors, who came from the fraternity of Charron Brothers were hopeless organisers. After their departure the settlers of Montreal demanded support from the King to set up a college to be run by the Jesuits, as in Quebec: 'All who are under the protection of the Government of Montreal, officers in the army, the middle-classes, tradespeople and settlers, rightly aware of the ignorance and idleness of their children, seek recourse to you to beg you to support their good intentions by making available anything that will help to organize the youth here.'

A quarter of a century after Raudot, the Intendant Hocquart realized that such education as was given to the children of officers and gentlemen amounted to very little: 'They can hardly read and write; they have no idea of the first principles of geography or history. It is much to be hoped that they will become better educated . . .' This was the opinion of the Intendant. He would have liked the youth of Canada to be instructed in geography and European history, since he himself had no idea of American history. His knowledge of the country did not extend further than Quebec and Montreal. He had heard talk of Michillimakinac and of Lake Ontario, and the post at Detroit. He would have been hard put to it to find these places on the map. The Canadians knew it. D'Iberville's spelling was pathetic. He wrote by sound. But he knew North America better than anyone else and defended it with his own methods, which were inspired more by instinct than by his education. The explorer, Nicolas Perrot, admitted that he had learnt more in his life among the Indians and on his expeditions into the forest than he had ever learned at his desk. Jean Nicolet, who owned an important library in Quebec, was only happy in the forest, when he was breathing the air of Indian civilization. These people required no more than a grounding. Their education was completed by the vastness and richness of nature.

A new spirit, whose significance was somewhat beyond the grasp of the authorities, began to take shape. 'Indiscipline' was the word they gave to a phase of adjustment of which the finer shades escaped them. Apart from the instruction supplied in the three government capitals by the Jesuits, the Bishop and the nuns, young people in country places absorbed the elements of a French-style education from notaries, *curés*, and those of their own mothers who had had some schooling. Thus children were enabled to develop along Canadian lines, drawing unconsciously meanwhile on the boundless resources of their mother country.

Other factors contributed to the intellectual climate. Some Jesuits were more than mere missionaries. Some notable people in the administration were more than civil servants. Some were scholars already well known in Europe. Others were remarkably well versed in literature.

The explorer Lescarbot was also lawyer, poet and playwright. He was in Acadia in 1606, and his passion for the theatre had not deserted him. When he was asked to provide the Governor, Poutrincourt, with some suitable entertainment, he could think of nothing better than to write an allegory; this was set on land and sea and was entitled *Théatre de Neptune*. The Indians were thrilled by the play, and many of them performed in it themselves in their own multi-coloured native dress. In 1640, in order to celebrate the first birthday of the future King Louis XIV, the Governor Montmagny arranged in the Dauphin's honour a performance of a tragi-comedy by extempore players. The author of one of the *Relations* observed that he had never thought to see in Quebec 'such a fine production, so full of good players'. The play had certainly never been published, and was only recently composed. It was probably the work of a Jesuit which would explain its religious undertones and the commendation from the *Relations*. It portrayed the soul of a pagan pursued by demons, who spoke in Algonquin language. The Indians were so terrified that they threw themselves into the arms of the thin and bearded actor representing the Christ; he was the notary, Martial Piraube.

The custom grew whereby plays of native inspiration were written to celebrate an important event. The arrival of the Governor d'Argenson in 1648 was acclaimed by the staging of a play in French, Huron and Algonquin. The spirit of civilized France and the spirit of the forests were made to confront each other in naïve and grandiloquent dialogues. Nobody understood the passages in Indian dialect, but the actors were applauded, and the local colour very much enjoyed. In 1646 the first copies of *Le Cid* reached the Jesuit college, and the actors set about performing it. In 1651 there was a performance of *Heraclitus* only four years after the play had been produced in Paris. The banning of Molière's *Tartuffe* had its repercussions in Canada, and created a schism between the Bishop and the Governor. Its producer Mareuil was threatened with excommunication, debarred from communion, and imprisoned for having attempted to ignore the embargo. This incident did not, however, prevent other works of playwrights from the 'Grand Siècle' from being performed, as and when they were composed.

Scientific observations contained in the descriptions of Jacques Cartier's and Champlain's voyages had already aroused the curiosity of scientists in Europe. In 1632 Galileo was trying to convince his contemporaries that the earth revolves on its own axis. This advanced theory was not, of course, to the taste of the official scientists of the era. In order to ensure for himself that eternal repose from whence he could once and for all silence his enemies, Galileo made a formal recantation of his views at the same time murmuring to himself: 'Nevertheless it does turn!' Later he was admitted to be right. But at the very time when Galileo was experiencing his difficulties, a poor and humble missionary, lost in the countryside of New France, unconsciously and ingenuously supported his theory. The Jesuit, Paul Le Jeune, who was in quarters in Quebec, dreamed of Galileo's theory while he contemplated the heavens; and he noted in one of the pages of his journal, entitled 'Brième Relation', which he was preparing for his directors in France: 'the other day I was calculating how much earlier the sun on your horizon rises than it does here, and I found that daylight visits you rather more than six hours earlier than it comes to us'. The following year an eclipse of the moon finally put an end to his doubts: 'The almanac said that this eclipse would arrive in France at midnight, and we saw it at six o'clock in the evening.'

An insignificant sentence in a *Relation* written in 1642 and dealing with the Huron country tells us that European scientists requested the missionaries to report on their observations. To fulfil this request the Jesuits themselves had to know something of scientific problems. One of them wrote that 'for the information of various people who have asked us for notes upon any eclipses we might observe in this country, we could mention the most extraordinary lunar eclipse which we witnessed on the evening of April 14th of this year, 1642'.

In the heart of Indian country far from any civilization, some French Jesuits, accompanied by explorers from their own country and surrounded by curious Indians who watched dumbfounded, stood upon the top of a hill from whence they could look down on the five Great Lakes which make up a complete inland sea, and observed the heavenly bodies by means of the makeshift instruments which they had been able to salvage from numerous shipwrecks. Not content with the new world they had discovered, they sought and found others in the vastness of the firmament. Two comets appeared and were seen momentarily. Now new doubts arose in their minds. A few days afterwards, one of them conscientiously observed in his notes: 'We are purposely leaving out the observations we made on the second, seventh, eleventh, thirteenth, fourteenth of the same month of January, for the wind and excessive cold have upset our instruments, and we have not been able to put them together with the accuracy required for such investigations.' The great earthquake of 1663 was the subject of numerous discussions in scientific circles of the time, and the authors of the *Relations* devoted to it several pages of wide-ranging scientific explanation. When later a parhelion or mock sun appeared over the region around Lake Superior during the winter of 1670–1671 it was described with extraordinary clarity and scrupulous accuracy.

Canada soon excited the curiosity of botanists. Jacques Cartier mentions here and there in his accounts certain species of flowers unknown in Europe. He brought back to France specimens which the amateur botanists in his expedition had identified as being indigenous. He was particularly impressed during the epidemic of scurvy in the hard winter of 1535 to 1536 by the extraordinary medicinal value of a certain tree the 'anedda', which a Canadian scientist, Jacques Rousseau, identified as the white cedar. Descriptions of trees and flowers in the New World take up more space in the book than the account of Champlain's voyages, and the chronicles of those early explorers Lescarbot and Sagard. Less than thirty years after the foundation of Quebec, the Parisian botanist, Carrenti, published the *Canadensium Plantarum Historia,* an anthology describing a hundred species; Rousseau identified forty-three of these, thirty-eight of which are illustrated and today still retain their place in the *flora* of Canada. Pierre Boucher in his work of propaganda, written to encourage colonization in Canada, and published in 1664, had a high opinion of the species of forest trees in the country he described so carefully. A woman of Canadian birth, born in Quebec in 1664, and the daughter of the explorer Noel Jérémie, sent her notes upon the secrets of Indian medicine to scientists in Paris, and obtained shrubs and roots which she sent to the Directors of the Jardin des Plantes in Paris. Charlevoix and Lafittau several times mention the plants of Canada, and some of their original notes are still read with interest by European scientists.

Two doctors, Michel Sarrazin and Jean François Gaultier, together with a Governor, La Galissonnière, were attracted to the botany of the New World as a scientific study. Michel Sarrazin, gifted with an enquiring mind, discovered a completely new world during his first stay in New France. He returned there as one of the King's doctors in 1697; but botany interested him more than medicine—a preference which seriously upset the *Conseil Supérieur,* who ordered the clerk to record: 'Since his return to Canada, the Sieur de Sarrazin has acquired other interests besides the treatment of the sick, and has been spending a great deal of time dissecting the rare animals in this country or in search of unknown plants; there is every reason to believe and to fear that when this work is completed to his complete satisfaction, he will return to France.' Scorning this lack of imagination and the objections of the *Conseil Supérieur* Sarrazin went on with his research. He was soon appointed a representative member of the Academy of Science, where Réamur was appointed to give readings of his reports. Despite the fears of the Council, this able scientist did not return to France. He died in Quebec in 1734, unnoticed and in poverty. 'The most advanced researches of Michel Sarrazin', wrote Rousseau, 'are concerned with the properties of maple-trees and with an extraordinary bog-plant, whose strange bottle-shaped leaves entrap insects, and which Tournefort named *Sarracenia.*'

The relatively large number of private libraries also shows the range of intellectual curiosity of this élite. All religious bodies, priests, and high officials possessed a selection of personal books, which they allowed their friends to read. The library in the Jesuit college in Quebec, well-stocked with all manner of books, was also used as a public reading room and reference library. In 1645 Abbé Nicolet sailed to the Ile aux Oies on a mission, taking with him in his baggage, two books borrowed from the Jesuits. In 1706 Father Raffeix asked for the return of four books from the estate of the King's hydrographer, Jean Deshaies, which had been lent to the latter. Deshaies himself possessed a fairly large library for those days. The presbytery of Saint-Joseph, at the Pointe-de-Lévis, was a sort of temporary lodging for missionaries coming from the south bank of the St Lawrence, on their way to the capital. Each visitor borrowed his favourite author or some new book. The colonists themselves made use of the services afforded by this library, for in 1740 the Vicar-General, deploring the disappearance of many works from it, urged the churchwardens of each parish to try to recover them. All those who could read, even those in the country districts, gained in prestige if they owned books on religion or history. Many valuable books of this sort belonged at that time to Antoine Desrosiers and Jacques Turcot, both of whom had become seigneurial judges, having educated themselves some-how or other despite the daily grind which faced them as colonists. Desrosiers 'made his cross' on his marriage contract in 1647 at the end of the document. He seems then to have been illiterate or at least scarcely educated. Yet one can see perfectly legible signatures made by him a few years later on numerous legal documents, and at his death, among his belongings he bequeathed to his son-in-law, Turcot, works of law and history; among other works were *La Coûtume de Paris* in two volumes, *l'Ordonnance Civile* and 'six small volumes by various authors'. The library of a modest country notary who was also a farmer, François Bigot, contained in 1710 a bound volume entitled *Le Parfait Notaire,* a normal item of any scrivener's property, but the inventory also listed works of general history 'all very worn'. The father as well as the mother of this notary was illiterate. But as his father had farmed for Pierre Boucher, perhaps young Bigot shared the studies which Boucher arranged for his own children, and maybe his taste for study and his own ambition later led him to become Royal notary. Finally we read that in the inventory of the effects of Jean Terme, a settler in the Ile de Orléans who had been murdered by a jealous neighbour, 'eight books of various kinds, very worn', are listed.

In 1748 Peter Kalm observed that the Canadian peasant's level of education compared favourably with that of the peasant in France. This was because priests and important people in the countryside expected, as did the city dwellers, to be informed of any new ideas which were of interest in France and in Europe. In Montreal traces have even been found of two tradesmen who called themselves booksellers, and indeed lived on the sales of books: Sanschagrin in 1741, and Baregeas in 1754. In 1753 Mgr de Pontbriand obtained 1,900 books from the Court, most of them pious works and biographies which he distributed in the countryside 'to people who are able to benefit from them'. In the last years of French rule two particularly excellent private libraries were in existence, and these contained classics, both ancient and modern, biographies, and works on the history of nations. There were more than 3,000 volumes in the library of François Cugnet. Louis-Guillaume Verrier possessed 4,000.

There is much evidence of the purity of language used by the Canadians under French rule. This evidence is taken from contemporary observers who were generally impartial, and who are accepted as authorities in other fields. 'In no other place is our language spoken more purely, one can detect no accent,' remarked Charlevoix. Bacqueville de la Potherie, the historian, commented on one peculiar fact: 'Although there is a mixture from almost every province in France, one can detect nothing of this in the speech used by Canadians.' He added that they spoke perfectly well 'with no accent'. D'Aleyrac was even more explicit: 'There is no dialect in this country ... All Canadians use a speech resembling our own. In everyday speech they borrow expressions from naval language: they say "to moor", instead of "to fasten", "to haul", instead of "to pull", referring not only to a ship but any other object. They have coined various words, like "toque" or "fourole", to mean a bonnet of red wool. They say a "pocket", instead of a "bag", "mantlet", instead of a "short straight dress", and a "squall" when they mean a lot of wind or rain or snow; they say "annoyed", instead of "bored", and they say "to lack something", instead of "not having everything one requires"; they call the afternoon the "relevée", "luck", instead of "happiness", "bit" for "moment", "ready", instead of "prepared for". The most current expression is "worthless", which means that a thing is hard to do or is too troublesome. They borrowed this expression from the savages.'

D'Aleyrac was wrong here, for old dictionaries mention this term as current in the excellent French of the sixteenth and seventeenth centuries.

There is no doubt that the colonists who came from different provinces in France did contribute some peculiarities of language from their own regional speech. But, from the accounts we have quoted, obviously everyone both spoke and understood the ordinary language of France, such as writers of Rabelais', Montaigne's and Molière's time put into the mouths of their characters. This use of a universally popular speech is confirmed by the depositions of witnesses in the courts, depositions preserved in the archives of clerks and notaries of this period. A tailor, Nicolas Gaillou was questioned as to whether one of his companions had dispensed alcohol to the Indians, first confessed to illiteracy, and then continued: 'having heard through common gossip that Martin Foisy, a farmer of the Sieur de Bourjoly, has traded drink with the savages, I know nothing of it. If anyone has done so it was all unknowingly.' The notary of la Tousche drew up a contract in 1667, beginning in the following manner: *'Concession atentée par Jean Le Moyne à François Frigon.'* The word 'arenter' does not occur in Littre's dictionary, or even in Trévoux's. Yet the poet Villon used it: *Le jardin que maistre Pierre Bobignon m'arenta.* These are only a few examples of pleasing archaisms which came naturally to the lips of the colonists, who remembered the speech of their native provinces.

The written language also provides some amazing examples of style. Marie-Angélique Hamel was born in the parish of the seigneurie of Deschambault in 1700. Her education was rudimentary. Nevertheless when she was fifty years old, she still remembered enough of her studies to be able to compose the following letter, the original of which is preserved in the archives in the province of Quebec: 'Monsieur and Madame, since my son wishes to marry Mademoiselle your daughter, and he tells me you have given your consent, and since I know that Mademoiselle is a virtuous girl of good family, I wish to add my own consent to that of my husband. We are both pleased with the choice our son has made, and my husband and I join in sending you our sincere compliments and likewise to Mademoiselle your daughter, and I remain your very humble servant.'

This then was the cultural level reached by the nation after over half a century of existence. It was retained until the end of French rule, after which books for study became very rare. Teachers were obliged to copy out by hand pages of the works from which they quoted. At the Ursuline convent in Three Rivers there remained only one French grammar. This was placed upon a desk in the centre of the classroom. The page was held open by a slip of polished wood. Each pupil walked up in turn to learn his lesson for the day, and only the mistress was allowed to turn the pages of the book which was respected as though it were a holy relic.

Teaching, especially in the countryside, was elementary or even fragmentary. Nevertheless it was sufficient to guard against the danger, always anticipated by the Intendants, of Canadian youth becoming Indianized. It was even comparable in quality with the education given in France at the height of that country's intellectual enlightenment. According to Taine, France, on the eve of the Revolution, had about one school in every two parishes. The same proportion could be found in Canada at the end of French rule, and these figures do not include the unpaid lessons given by educated mothers, or notaries, to the children in the villages. From 1693 to 1703, when the population in Quebec stood at barely 1,500 people, 130 pupils were registered at the little seminary. On starting school, twenty-three of these already possessed a knowledge of Latin, sixty-eight of them could read and write, and only eight of the children were completely untutored.

The rapid and complete adjustment which these people made to a way of life they adopted as their own was reflected in their craftsmanship and in articles made by hand. These expressed an astonishing sense of balance, good taste, and a love of beauty. The source of this discerning taste was the school known as 'Ecole de Saint-Joachim', which was founded through the offices of Mgr de Laval. It was a small institute of arts and trades, but every subject was taught there; painting, sculpture, gilding, drawing, woodwork, cobbling, theology, mathematics, Greek and Latin. In short it was a small university, where was recreated the atmosphere of the Grand Siècle of French classicism, a feeling which the pupils adapted with ease to their needs in this country. Teachers of a high calibre could be found there. Father Luc, a Recollect, and a pupil of Simon Vouet in Paris, and his class-mates included Michard, Le Brun, Le Sueur, Le Nôtre. When he retired from the world to attire himself in the rough serge of the Franciscans

Father Luc, despite his vow of poverty, managed to preserve his love and knowledge of the arts. The school of Saint-Joachim enjoyed a period of brilliance. Its pedagogy, according to the opinion of one specialist in the matter, Gerard Morisset, was 'brimming with social and practical sense, broad and flexible in its ideas, and by allowing talent to blossom it excluded individual conceit, and suppressed the sterile hierarchy of the arts, thereby ensuring the professional standing of its pupils'. Further on, Morisset examines the results: 'As wise and thoughtful men, these people did not attempt to instruct in great matters nor to imitate the learning of others, they were conscious of their own talent, of their own strength and of the material in their hands, as well as of the economic conditions under which they lived, and so with the logic of country people they were content to do small things well.'

A great proportion of the purest strength of the soil of France was rooted here in this newly established nation. Here too was mingled a deep religious feeling which helped to straiten its growth. The mysticism felt by the first founders was added to the constant feeling of danger during the years of terror, and it wrought a spirit which was both practical and elevated. Most of the Governors and Intendants were to endorse Hocquart's observation: 'Religion means much to them all.' The traveller Kalm observed that the colonists of New France devoted much more time to their prayers and outside devotions than did the English and Dutch in the British colonies. He was struck by the way in which the soldiers at Fort Saint-Frédéric met together for morning and evening prayers.

And so native instincts purified by spiritual and religious feeling found their way into the minds of this nation, which gradually discarded its racial origins. In 1700, when the first generation born in Canada was at the height of its powers, observers were already attempting to analyse the stages of its extraordinary and rapid development. This physiological phenomenon intrigued Bacqueville de la Potherie, Lebeau, d'Aleyrac, and more especially Charlevoix who lingered over his description in which he examined it in great depth. Apart from the language—in which these people retained a classic purity—Charlevoix observed other signs; the carefree spirit, the 'gentle and polite manners which everyone seems to possess. Boorish behaviour in speech as well as in manners is never contemplated, even in the most distant parts of the country-side'. His comparison with the Saxons who had colonized the coast in the South by no means unfavourable: 'Anyone who attempted to judge these two colonies by their mode of life, or by their behaviour and the speech of their people would not hesitate in concluding that the balance is in our favour: ours is the most flourishing.' The writer goes on to delineate the essential features: the air one breathed in this enormous continent never ceased to strengthen a spirit of independence and an aversion to routine hard work, which was accentuated by the example of and by contact with those native inhabitants, the Indians, 'who are happy in free-dom and independence', and this was more than enough to mould and crystallize this characteristic. Every other serious observer over the years, Kalm, for instance, La Hontan, and Bougainville, summed up the people of Canada, using the same sort of words as Charlevoix and reaching very much the same conclusions. Bougain-ville, a witty cultivated man, who was a member of many scientific bodies, and who was so harsh in his judgment of Canadian officers, yet had nothing but praise for the people themselves. He wrote half a century after La Hontan: 'They are undoubtedly of better material, they have more spirit and a better education than the people of France.' As to the explanation of this: 'Their spirit of independence derives from the fact that they pay no taxes, and that they are able to hunt and fish.'

All these features contributed to the fashioning of a nation, which, but for the events of 1760, was preparing to present France with a whole new continent.

CONCLUSION

In the course of this book we have tried to summarize the development and, so to speak, the transformation of a nation of pure French origin, which took root in a strange land 2,500 miles from the mother country. By virtue of the prevailing conditions, above all the climate, the immensity of the area, and the proximity of the Indians who surrounded them, this population evolved a new culture. But in two essential ways it remained French: in its language and religion. And now suddenly the chance of a war's ending placed them under the protection of a country which was alien in both.

It is only logical to wonder what were the reactions of France, of England, and of the conquered people in the face of these events: the capitulation of Quebec in 1759 and the Treaty of Paris in 1763.

The reaction of France, it must, alas, be admitted, was somewhat graceless and irresponsible. She was tired of the war and she abandoned half of North America with a certain relief. Economically and morally she was worn out. Even as early as the Seven Years' War, New France had proved too great a burden for her to carry, and she hastened to lay it down. The Minister Berryer's famous remark, evoked by Bougainville's urgent pleas for aid in Canada, 'When the house is on fire there is no point in trying to save the stables', could be mistaken for cynicism, but was in fact simply a poignant cry of despair.

The French élite of the time set the feeling of disinterest in the future of Canada. As Pierre Gaxotte justly observed: 'Not only did the *encyclopédistes* misinterpret the great colonizing thrust, which was the dominant feature of their century, and not only did they fail to understand either the motive for it or its power, but they put every obstacle they could in the way of French expansion. They never ceased to depreciate the colonies, to slander the colonists, to ridicule their efforts and to travesty their achievements.' On October 3, 1760, Voltaire wrote to Choiseul and besought him to act: 'If I only dared, I would implore you on my knees to rid France

217

for ever from the administration of Canada. By losing Canada, you lose nothing; if you want her restored to you, you restore a perpetual source of war and humiliation—no more.' Two years later, on September 6th, he returned to the attack: 'Like the public, I greatly prefer peace to Canada, and I believe France could be happy without Quebec.' Choiseul himself at one time declared that 'Corsica is of much greater interest than Canada'.

It was in this atmosphere that the Treaty of Paris was signed on February 10, 1763. This ceded to England the two poles of the future world: India and Canada, in return for the 'blessings of peace' which Voltaire demanded and which were specifically referred to in the Treaty itself: 'It has pleased the Almighty to bestow the spirit of union and concord upon the Princes whose lack of concord has brought disaster to four corners of the world, and to inspire in them the determination to allow the blessings of peace to succeed the disasters of a long and bloody war.' The clauses in the Treaty were accepted despite the vehement protests of the Chambers of Commerce in great provincial towns such as Bordeaux, Marseilles, La Rochelle, Nantes, and Dieppe. To close for ever this page in history, Louis XV agreed to celebrate the signing of the Treaty by minting a commemorative medal.

In spite of this spirit which really sounded a note of deliverance, Choiseul, with his diplomat's mind, always believed that Canada would be returned to France: 'The English will never keep Canada,' he wrote in his turn to Voltaire. 'I should be grateful if you would defer judgment of this matter until you have seen the dénouement—we may be only at the third act.' What is more French officers returning to their own country received orders to remain in Touraine in case of recall to the colony.

But hopes like these were never realized. Once again England put into practice her famous doctrine of 'What we have, we hold'.

Yet a small group, which included General Murray, shared Choiseul's views. They thought Canada might be returned to France: 'If we are wise', he confided one day to Comte de Malartic, 'we shall not keep this country. We must give New England the bit to champ, and it is Canada which will occupy her when we give it up.' But most people held an opposite view, and prepared to treat the settlers as subjects, finally conquered, Papists at that. Besides, the Prime Minister, William Pitt, put an end to any idea of retrocession by declaring in the House of Commons that, since the Treaty of Paris, England had become the greatest power and that she would be still greater now that she had dethroned her main adversary. Therefore England was to keep Canada.

A superficial politeness hid the real intention, which was to dominate, and in the end to stifle, Canada. In Quebec, Canon Briand, who administered the diocese during the absence of the Bishop (Mgr de Pontbriand died in 1759) received orders to pray during the Sunday service henceforth, 'for the King George III, the Queen and for all the Royal family, according to the usual form of prayer, and declaring each one by name'. This order was accompanied by another obliging all settlers save the Captains of militia, to surrender their arms to the General in charge of the administration of their Government, and to swear the oath of allegiance.

The broader understanding shown by certain Swiss attached to the Army of occupation, such as Haldimand and the secretary Bruyère, who were Protestants, yet French-speakers, did much to soften the blows which fell during this period of transition.

A Frenchman by birth, Canon Briand obeyed official orders because he had experienced so much of the changes and chances of war and of the vagaries of treaties. But when these proud and independent settlers heard from the pulpit the foreign names of those for whom they were supposed to beg Divine protection, they scowled, shrugged their shoulders, and shut their eyes in silent protest. When they were safely out of Church, they cursed their predicament: 'Nobody is going to stop me speaking French to my horse when I am in the fields,' one obstinate settler was heard to remark. Here were the seeds of passive resistance sown to last for a very long time, and to prove obstinate and invincible.

With rage in their hearts, the Canadians laid down their arms and took the oath of allegiance to a country they had fought against for as long as they could remember. They no longer possessed anything: no animals, no harvests, no hope. Almost everywhere throughout the countryside their farm buildings had been burnt down. Sons from almost every family had been killed in the war. The authorities who had been in the colony had returned to France with the able-bodied forces of the Army. The settlers were alone, finally, alone, with the priests who were part of their ranks; these had not forsaken them.

After the first shock of bewilderment had passed by, they set themselves once more to work. And here the whole strength of the seigneurial system, set up throughout the country, came into its own. These people who had lost everything, at least still possessed their own land, and which was wholly theirs. Like the first colonists, their ancestors, they took heart once more after years of trial, and swore to survive and to group themselves within the seigneuries of their three Governments. These 60,000 settlers of French descent dug themselves into this little corner of the American continent which already contained more than a million English. Nobody would be able to dislodge them.

This nation, as it had under French rule, wished to preserve its freedom and the way of life it had created for itself.

INDEX